Chaplin at Essanay

Chaplin at Essanay

A Film Artist in Transition, 1915–1916

JAMES L. NEIBAUR

McFarland & Company, Inc., Publishers
Jefferson, North Carolina, and London

ALSO BY JAMES L. NEIBAUR
AND FROM MCFARLAND

*Arbuckle and Keaton:
Their 14 Film Collaborations* (2007)

*The RKO Features: A Complete Filmography
of the Feature Films Released or Produced
by RKO Radio Pictures, 1929–1960* (1994; paper 2005)

The Bob Hope Films (2005)

*The Jerry Lewis Films: An Analytical
Filmography of the Innovative Comic* (1994)

Tough Guy: The American Movie Macho (1989)

Movie Comedians: The Complete Guide (1986)

Frontispiece: Charles Spencer Chaplin, circa 1916.

LIBRARY OF CONGRESS CATALOGUING-IN-PUBLICATION DATA

Neibaur, James L., 1958–
  Chaplin at Essanay : a film artist in transition, 1915–1916 /
James L. Neibaur.
    p.   cm.
  Includes bibliographical references and index.

  ISBN 978-0-7864-3512-8
  softcover : 50# alkaline paper

  1. Chaplin, Charlie, 1889–1977 — Criticism and interpretation.
2. Essanay Film Manufacturing Co.   I. Title.
PN2287.C5N45   2008
791.4302'8092 — dc22   2008029414

British Library cataloguing data are available

©2008 James L. Neibaur. All rights reserved

*No part of this book may be reproduced or transmitted in any form
or by any means, electronic or mechanical, including photocopying
or recording, or by any information storage and retrieval system,
without permission in writing from the publisher.*

Cover images ©2007 Shutterstock

Manufactured in the United States of America

*McFarland & Company, Inc., Publishers
  Box 611, Jefferson, North Carolina 28640
    www.mcfarlandpub.com*

For Peter Jackel,
a longtime friend and fellow Chaplin fan

Acknowledgments

Many thanks to the following for helping to make this book possible: Phil Posner, David Shepard, Rob Farr, Joe Moore, Don Kapla, Ted Okuda, Dave Maska, David Kiehn, Steve Massa, Doug Sulpy, Brent Walker, David A. Gerstein, and the late John McCabe.

Table of Contents

Acknowledgments — vi
Introduction — 1

1. Chaplin at Keystone: The Artist as Apprentice — 11
2. The Essanay Studios — 25
3. The Essanay Films — 32
   - *His New Job* — 33
   - *A Night Out* — 46
   - *The Champion* — 57
   - *In the Park* — 68
   - *A Jitney Elopement* — 76
   - *The Tramp* — 84
   - *By the Sea* — 94
   - *Work* — 99
   - *A Woman* — 107
   - *The Bank* — 113
   - *Shanghaied* — 121
   - *A Night in the Show* — 126
4. Chaplin Signs with Mutual — 133
   - *Police* — 135
   - *Burlesque on Carmen* — 144
   - *Triple Trouble* — 158
5. Mutual and After — 169

Appendix A: His Regeneration — 179
Appendix B: Edna Purviance — 182
Appendix C: Chaplin's Post-Essanay Film List — 188

Table of Contents

Appendix D: Supporting Players — 191

Appendix E: Compilation Films and Anthologies Featuring Chaplin Essanay Footage — 200

Appendix F: Chaplin Cartoons — 203

Bibliography — 205

Index — 209

Introduction

Charles Spencer Chaplin is perhaps the single most important figure in the history of motion pictures. To make such a lofty claim about any filmmaker may seem like hyperbole to those who immediately think of such significant pioneers as D.W. Griffith, Georges Méliès, and Edwin S. Porter. But while other filmmakers gave cinema its narrative syntax, pioneered the moving picture's technological capabilities for maximum effect (close-ups, editing), and captured the first acting for the cinema, it is Chaplin who fleshed out an enduring character, understood the dramatic element in humor, and ultimately created a consistently brilliant series of remarkable motion pictures that have maintained their impact over generations. His rapid development, his timeless artistry, and his enduring legacy qualify him as perhaps the finest motion picture artist in the medium's history.

Initially it might seem to some film enthusiasts that yet another book on Charlie Chaplin is completely unnecessary. His importance to cinema has been well documented by a variety of fine biographies and broad filmographic studies. However, it is to this writer's thinking that a broad overview of Chaplin's entire filmography will no longer suffice. Each area of his work is so complex, so brilliant, and of such historical and aesthetic significance that it demands more intimate attention than a full filmographic overview can provide. There are simply too many details attached to each portion of his filmography. And, due to strides made in film restoration and the availability of the Chaplin films from each period in his career, now is the perfect time to study these movies within their cultural and historical context. Each period in Chaplin's career is, in and of itself, a time of artistic growth offering important landmark films. It would seem essential to examine each area of his work with the careful scrutiny nec-

Introduction

essary for a true appreciation of every separate production's significance. Thus, a broad overview of his entire filmography would only scratch the surface.

Just as a writer can offer an entire book specifically studying the Shakespearean sonnets, we can do likewise with just a portion of a great filmmaker's work. In the case of this study, Chaplin's Essanay period shows his cinematic art in transition, presents amazing growth in the course of only one year, and is filled with iconic images.

It is unfortunate that the availability of Chaplin's feature films — from such deep and fulfilling works as *The Kid* (1921) and *The Gold Rush* (1925), through the flawed, indulgent, yet interesting talking features like *The Great Dictator* (1940) and *A King in New York* (1957) — has caused many enthusiasts to shortcut through the first years of his career, foolishly dismissing the earlier material as being of only marginal significance. In fact, Chaplin's career began very strongly at Keystone, showed a discernible improvement at Essanay, and peaked at Mutual in 1916–1917, where he made perhaps his finest films. Much of what he did from that point onward maintained this lofty level, but could not surpass it. He had reached a level of perfection that was, and remains, insurmountable.

This book on Chaplin's Essanay period carefully examines the sixteen Chaplin comedies produced by that studio, showing Chaplin as an artist in transition from the knockabout Keystone farces to the refined, brilliant Mutual productions.

Chaplin worked at G.M. Anderson and George K. Spoor's Essanay studios for one year, making fifteen films (*Triple Trouble*, which was assembled by others after Chaplin left the studio, used outtakes, discarded scenes, and snippets from other films). He had just finished a stint at Mack Sennett's Keystone studios where he emerged as a director of cinema, learned how to perform for the intimate motion picture camera, and started exploring comedy ideas that could be effectively staged through film.

It was at Keystone that Chaplin created the Tramp character, directed his first films, and learned the basics in regard to performing for the camera. Although limited by the fast pace insisted upon by Sennett, Chaplin immediately showed nuances of character that went beyond the broad gestures of other Keystone funnymen. Once Chaplin began directing his own films at Keystone, he tried to inject more substance into his character, and

Introduction

greater depth into the stories, while still maintaining the necessary brisk rhythm dictated by.

Through all of this, Chaplin was searching for his own style and rhythm, and soon realized that his character and ideas worked more effectively at a leisurely pace. He wanted to develop situations, experiment with new ideas, and allow his character more substance. He got a few chances, especially when the popularity of his films gave him a certain artistic leverage. However, the budget-minded Sennett still did not allow time for much experimentation, and thus, after 35 successful films throughout 1914 (including an offbeat costarring role as a wily city slicker in the Sennett-directed landmark feature-length comedy *Tillie's Punctured Romance*), Chaplin searched for another outlet for his creative ideas.

Sennett did not want to lose Chaplin, and offered him a jump in pay and greater creative control. But he could not match the offer from Essanay, which, in line with Chaplin's incredible popularity, made Chaplin the highest paid motion picture artist in the world. At Essanay he further developed his onscreen characterization, and added a more subtle nuance to his slapstick presentation. This was honed a year later in the twelve films Chaplin made at the Mutual studios.

Boldly placing Chaplin in the firm and lofty position above all other comedians is not in any way an attempt to undermine the fine work of his contemporaries, like Buster Keaton, Harold Lloyd, or Roscoe Arbuckle. Chaplin, however, has always stood at the forefront. He is the true innovator of everything we know as screen comedy, and of comedy characterization. Even as each of these other fine comic craftsmen were enjoying their initial popularity with moviegoers, Chaplin remained at his own level, both artistically and commercially.

Chaplin's work was discovered and embraced by the masses almost immediately upon his entering films with Keystone in 1914. His popularity increased to gargantuan levels, and by the time Chaplin was well into his Essanay contract, his name and image had become a veritable cottage industry, with dolls, songs, and other such items bearing his moniker and likeness.

At Essanay Chaplin was able to step back and take the time to explore and reinvent what he had learned at Keystone. He was able to take more time to create each film, and he started shooting multiple takes, much to the chagrin of his actors.

Introduction

As with many creative individuals, Chaplin's first ideas were not always his best. He needed the time and the freedom to try out different concepts until he arrived upon what worked most effectively. Chaplin was a notorious perfectionist, and as he got older and his projects more ambitious, some argue that there was an obsessive quality about his work. But even as early as his first films, Chaplin had a particular vision that caused him to clash with his directors. Gaining control of his work early on was imperative.

Chaplin's exploration at Essanay was generally about character and gags. The Essanay period, when examined film by film, shows a careful, effective evolution in these areas. There was greater depth to Charlie the Tramp, the humor was better paced and more elaborate, and the situations offered a bit more subtlety.

The first few Essanays are refined examples of Keystone efforts. The very first Essanay, appropriately titled *His New Job* (1915), is a reworking of ideas Chaplin used in his Keystone one-reeler *The Property Man* (1914). *A Night Out* (1915) is an expanded two-reel version of the one-reel Keystone production *The Rounders* (1914), with cross-eyed Ben Turpin replacing Roscoe Arbuckle from the earlier film. And while *The Rounders* is one of Chaplin's better Keystones, *A Night Out* surpasses it, and is still not among his best from the Essanay period. It is, however, perhaps his best constructed film to that point, and it shows a real progression from the Keystone output.

In praising the transitional Essanay films, the author does not want to promote the idea that the Keystone period is too primitive and, therefore, contains Chaplin's weakest or least interesting material (one could perhaps make a better case for describing the later talkies this way). The chapter on Chaplin's Keystone period will give some attention to his best work at that studio, including such important efforts as *Kid Auto Races*, *Mabel's Married Life*, *His Trysting Place*, and *Dough and Dynamite*. But as wildly hilarious as the best Keystones can be, at Essanay Chaplin realized other ways of developing stories and characters on film. His technique did not advance as much cinematically or technologically as did the films of, say, Buster Keaton, but his narrative structure, action within the frame, performance, and gags all evolved from film to film, and showed discernible improvement. Some real innovations were made.

Introduction

For years the transitional Essanays were overlooked, even by the most passionate Chaplin enthusiasts. The chief problem was the condition of the films. There was a practice of constantly rereleasing older Chaplin product once he left a studio, which went on to increase his massive popularity. Thus, the films he made at Keystone and Essanay were frequently rereleased, often retitled and pawned off as new films, and their condition worsened through overuse. In fact, at the time of this writing, the Keystone films are undergoing a massive and necessary restoration by the British Film Institute.

For many decades the Essanay comedies were represented by shoddy prints that had been duped endlessly and not been cared for since their initial release. Even the better home movie distributors such as Blackhawk Films, which used the best existing preprint elements, offered prints that were watchable — but not to the point where real study was possible. A good print is necessary when looking for subtleties that help make a film effective. So, although Chaplin's Essanay series has been accessible rather steadily since the days of 8mm duping allowed condensed versions to be easily accessed for the toy movie projector market, such distributors never offered the Essanay series in particularly good prints. The preprint material itself was so lacking in quality that obtaining good 8mm or 16mm prints was virtually impossible. The second- or third-rate images by which the Chaplin Essanay series was represented caused most silent film enthusiasts to casually overlook Chaplin's entire output from this period. Hence, over time, the Essanay period is certainly the least discussed and most misunderstood of Chaplin's entire cinematic oeuvre.

At the end of the 20th Century, film historian and archivist David Shepard carefully managed a full restoration of the Essanay films after seeking out the very best existing material on each. They were made accessible on VHS and DVD by Kino and Image Entertainment. For the first time since their initial release, the Essanay films are represented by clean, complete prints and new music scores.

Consequently, it is now time to single out the Essanay films and offer the long-deserved thorough examination of this essential period in Chaplin's career. This study is an attempt to understand how each film during the Essanay period is significant in Chaplin's development as a comedian and filmmaker. Some films, such as *The Tramp, A Jitney Elopement, The*

Introduction

Bank (all 1915), *Burlesque on Carmen*, and *Police* (both 1916), are among the most important productions of his career. Others, such as *Work* and *The Champion* (both 1915), are interesting uses of pure comedy with identifiably greater nuance and refinement than the knockabout Keystones. Finally, a film like *Triple Trouble* (1918), which was concocted by Essanay out of discarded footage two years after Chaplin left the company, says a great deal about studio practices and how, even during the motion picture's relative infancy, the industry willingly devoured its own.

Along the way we also look at Chaplin's massive popularity, which was firmly established during his Keystone tenure but reached mythical proportions at Essanay. This is long before such brilliant artists as Keaton, Lloyd, and Langdon had achieved the heights of their respective careers (Arbuckle enjoyed a similar level of popularity concurrently with Chaplin, but his career was cut short by scandal in 1921). By his second year in movies, Chaplin's work already surpassed any other film star, as it entered the pop culture lexicon, having spawned contests, imitations, and comic strips.

One of the truly amazing things about Chaplin's work is how rapidly it developed. The Keystones were shot in a matter of days, and released as frequently as one per week. Through this period he developed ideas as a comedian and filmmaker with the limited possibilities afforded by his position, and still managed to turn out some truly remarkable comedies. He made fifteen films over a year's time at Essanay and another twelve at Mutual during the next year. So from his movie debut in 1914 to the completion of his Mutual contract in 1917, Chaplin had made extraordinary artistic progress in a mere handful of years. When one compares his frenetic first Keystone, *Making a Living* (1914), to his brilliant final Mutual, *The Adventurer* (1917), the level of Chaplin's artistic development in a mere three year period becomes staggering.

Retrospect often causes some to look only at the most heavily discussed pictures, the greatest hits packages, of past film performers. Some may even limit themselves to Chaplin's silent features, as if screening *The Kid*, *The Gold Rush*, *The Circus* (1928), *City Lights* (1931) and *Modern Times* (1936) could possibly give anyone a comprehensive understanding of one of cinema's most important artists. Certainly Chaplin's work cannot be appreciated without fully acquainting oneself with the extraordinary

Introduction

Mutual period. It could be argued that the films Chaplin made at Essanay are just as important, despite the fact that the Essanay period may have been the least discussed of Chaplin's career.

For instance, Chaplin's talkies, which are certainly interesting but still arguably the weakest films of his career, have enjoyed more study than the Essanays. The idea that an effort as flawed as, say, *Monsieur Verdoux* (1947) has garnered more attention than the far superior Essanay production *Burlesque on Carmen* is preposterous.

At Essanay, Chaplin learned so much about the camera, editing, story construction, and performance that it is clearly evident with each film from this period that a real transition was taking place. Comparing his earlier Essanay efforts to his final ones will truly display just how much the comedian and filmmaker had learned over the year's time that he worked for the company. It is a most fascinating creative evolution to observe. That his best work was at Mutual, just after the Essanay period, means that we can see Chaplin's real development from the beginnings of his film career to when he had perfected his craft. The artist in transition is, indeed, an inspiring thing to behold.

There isn't as much of an overall feeling of transitional development when looking broadly at the Essanay output. Each separate film has a great deal of significance for its presentation, its importance to the Chaplin filmography, and how it allows the evolution of the artist to shine through. At first the films appear to be more refined workings of Keystone ideas that Chaplin had not been previously allowed to fully explore. By the time he made *The Champion* (1915) Chaplin realized the importance of the character gaining sympathy from the audience. The subtlety of situation in *A Jitney Elopement* was clearly innovative, leading to *The Tramp*, which is a true milestone in cinema in that it is the first film where Chaplin blended comic and dramatic elements that ranged from wild slapstick to heavy pathos. Later Essanay films *The Bank* and *Police* capitalize on these methods, showing the even greater refinement that would establish itself much more completely at Mutual.

Since each Essanay effort displays another step in the development of Chaplin's screen work, it is important to point out just how much impact each film had during this aspect of his career. In order to truly appreciate the evolutionary process of the Essanay series, it is important

Introduction

to know a bit about Chaplin's Keystone apprenticeship and how he grew at that studio. He had come from the English music halls, with a wealth of comic ideas that could translate to the new medium of film. His lack of cinematic knowledge and understanding was overshadowed by his genius at performance. He quickly learned the basics of filming, and was eager to assume full creative control over his work. From his first directors, such as Henry Lehrman, George Nichols, and Mabel Normand, he learned what to do (and, often, what not to do), and he injected his own ideas about how to make his films funny (as he had with his Karno stage act, but now enhanced by cinema's technological possibilities).

Along with some initial understanding of the Keystone (and Karno) period, it is also essential to know something about Essanay's history and how it differed from the atmosphere that was provided at Keystone. Essanay, as a studio, specialized in comedies and westerns, churning out a series of popular-yet-unremarkable subjects that nevertheless are of great historical significance. Once the studio acquired Chaplin's services, and his stardom shot beyond any performer in film's short history up to that time, Essanay found itself needing to provide a higher print run for theater owners who clamored for more product. But up to that point, Essanay was enjoying some good, consistent success with its Broncho Billy westerns and its Snakeville comedies (sadly, few of these important films exist today, allowing us less of a look at Essanay's product than we would like, but enough survives to understand the durability of its output).

After introductory chapters establish the setting and bring the reader up to date on Chaplin's career at this point, the text then carefully examines each of the Chaplin Essanays films in the context of the comedian and filmmaker's professional and artistic life. The discussion of each film clarifies why these transitional masterpieces warrant the status of being among Chaplin's most significant work. The text cannot take the place of actually screening the films, but does offer a thorough assessment of each title in order to point out the many areas of performance, narrative structure, and refined physical comedy that made Chaplin the world's most popular entertainer of this period, and to demonstrate the importance of his Essanay pictures.

The Essanays are filled with iconic images that have lived on to become some of the most notable still photos from Chaplin's career. The

Introduction

famous shot of a forlorn Charlie and his bulldog is from *The Champion*. The equally notable shot of the Little Tramp walking down a beaten path, away from the camera, is from *The Tramp*. The well-known shot of a battered Charlie emerging from debris, his head through an oven, is from *Work*.

Chaplin has been accused of taking an old-fashioned approach to filmmaking, chiefly because his talkies are often comparatively amateurish in their cinematic presentation, while Chaplin's dialog sequences are discursive. But much earlier, during the medium's relative infancy, Chaplin did experiment a bit with using the cinematic process to enhance gags, most notably in the Essanay short *Shanghaied*, which simulates the rocking of a boat while the actors respond in kind (something that would be revisited in the Mutual film *The Immigrant*). Chaplin uses the camera to simulate movement, creates a technological device to present the rocking action, and directs his actors against these elements so that an effective presentation can be made. This is not for the story or a central gag, but simply to establish a setting and situation upon which Chaplin could build more comedy. It is only a marginal thing, but, during this early period of the motion picture, it was an innovative technical marvel just the same. The importance of such Chaplin Essanay movies as *A Jitney Elopement*, *The Tramp*, *Work*, *The Bank*, *Police*, and *Burlesque on Carmen* lies chiefly in their construction and presentation as the transition between Chaplin the comedian and Chaplin the filmmaker.

Chaplin at Keystone: The Artist as Apprentice

In order to understand and truly appreciate each development in Chaplin's film career, some background information is necessary.

Charles Spencer Chaplin was born April 16, 1889, in London, England. His family was very poor, his father was an alcoholic, and his mother was mentally ill. Chaplin had to fend for himself at a very early age. He found his way into show business while still a youngster, struggling in vaudeville as a boy. By the age of 20 he was with Fred Karno's theatrical troupe. It is with this troupe that Chaplin created a variety of character traits and amusing gags, many of which he would later use in his films.

In a three-part story on Chaplin that was published in the July, August, and September 1915 issues of *Photoplay*, the stage work that brought Chaplin to the United States was recalled:

> About 1910, Fred Karno put on a variety act called, "A Night in a London Music Hall." It concerned the adventures of a very badly splificated young swell in a box at the music hall. The stage was set for a miniature music hall with the boxes at one side of the stage. The tipsy young swell sat in one of the boxes. He tried "queen" all the beautiful ladies on the music hall vaudeville bill. Several times he climbed over the edge of the box onto the miniature stage. Most of the time he was either falling into or out of the box. The swell had to do about a million comic falls during the progress of the sketch. It was very funny and ended in a riot of boisterous mirth. In England, the part of the tipsy young person was taken by Billie Reeves, a well known comedian who is now with Universal. The sketch made such a hit that Karno finally

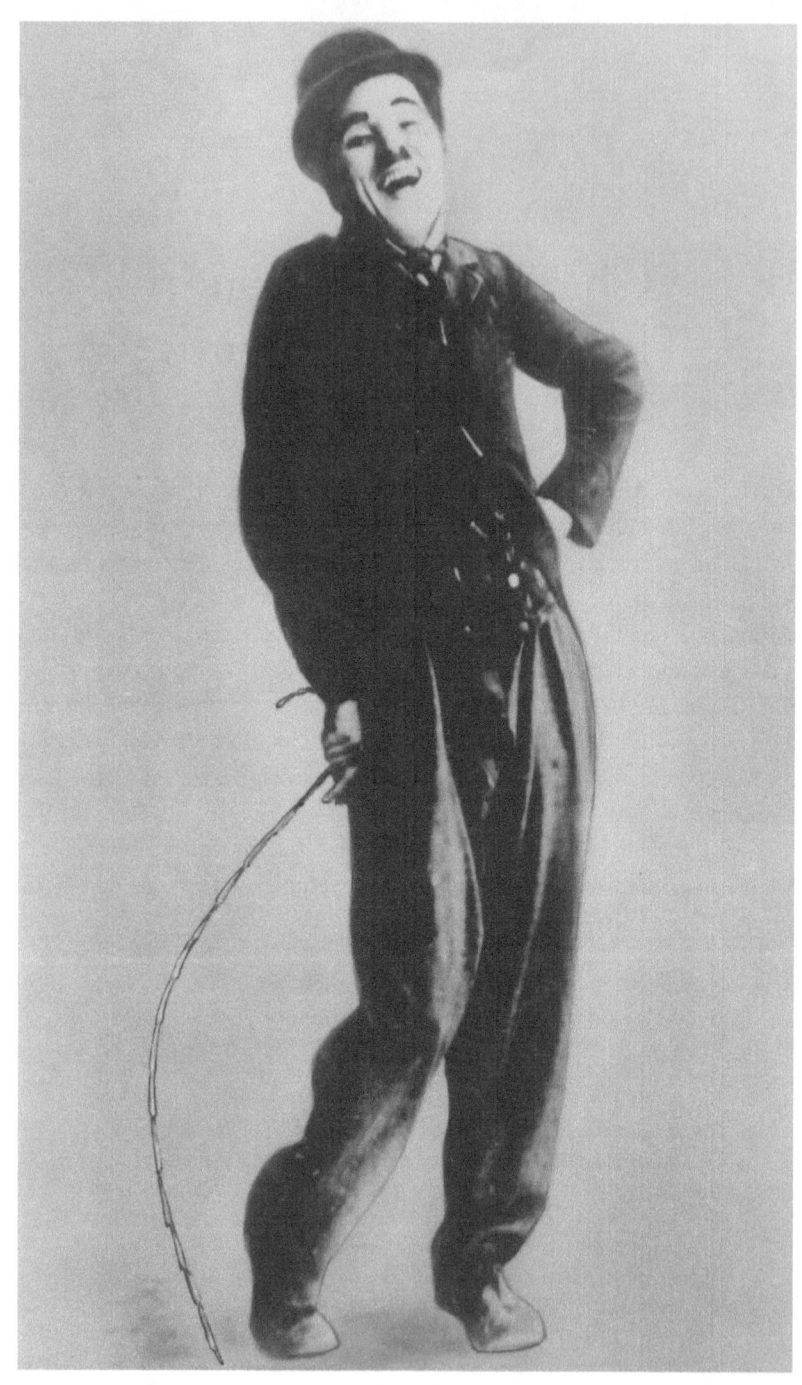

decided to send it over to the United States. Reeves proved to be a riot here, and Karno organized and sent over a number two company to tour the western states. Charlie Chaplin was employed to head the number two company. His salary was $50 per week....

Chaplin's western tour was a huge success. During his third year someone conceived of the idea of getting Chaplin to come into moving pictures. Mack Sennett, who heads the Keystone Comedy Company, was consulted and approved of the idea. He was delegated to sign up Chaplin. Chaplin was then getting $75 per week. Sennett offered him $175 per week.

Mack Sennett, circa 1915.

Mack Sennett was born in Canada on January 17, 1880, coming to the States at the end of the 19th century. By 1908 he was acting in Vitagraph films, some of which were directed by D.W. Griffith. Two years later Sennett started directing. In another two years he formed the Keystone production company, quickly assembling a stock company of movie comedians that included Fred Mace, Mabel Normand, Roscoe "Fatty" Arbuckle, Chester Conklin, Ford Sterling, Charley Murray, Al St. John, Minta Durfee, Alice Davenport, Mack Swain, Edgar Kennedy, and Slim Summerville. The comedies produced were largely improvisational slapstick affairs with little subtlety. The gags and stunts were amazing, and the sequences outrageously funny, so they very quickly became in demand at theaters. Sennett formulated a group of wacky policemen known as the Keystone Cops to poke fun at author-

Opposite: Charlie in his famous Tramp costume, circa 1916.

Chaplin at Essanay

ity. He also created the Mack Sennett Bathing Beauties, a group of attractive young women from whose ranks many a star was born.

Chaplin arrived on the Keystone lot in December of 1913. In a story for the *Washington Post* on October 3, 1915, Chaplin recalled:

> I received a very liberal offer to go into the moving pictures, which I accepted at once. It is in my work on the screen that I have come to find that the real development of comedy is a very fascinating study. The longer I stay at it, the harder I work, for it takes every bit of a man's time, thought, and energy.

Chaplin's first film, *Making a Living*, was a slapstick one-reeler typical of the Keystone studio. Clad in top hat and coat, Chaplin resembled the villain in an old-time melodrama. While his pantomimic skills were noticeable from the outset, this typical Keystone was an atypical Chaplin film, and its significance rests solely on its being his first.

The noted Tramp costume was in place for Chaplin's second release, *Kid Auto Races at Venice*. This is the film that endeared Chaplin to movie audiences. It is essentially footage of an actual auto race that is being filmed for newsreels. Chaplin the Tramp keeps purposely wandering in front of the newsreel cameras in an attempt to be noticed, much to the chagrin of the cameramen. It is a one-joke idea, but Chaplin's variations on his interruptions make it funny throughout.

Most American film comedians of the early 1910s were superficial talents in funny costumes. There were a few exceptions, many of them active at Keystone, but Chaplin's vision was more character driven than relying completely on gags. Thus, rather than not fit in at Keystone, Chaplin was able to stand out as superior. In *Kid Auto Races at Venice*, which was directed by Henry Lehrman, the Tramp is repeatedly shoved out of the way by directors and cameramen. Much of the moviegoing public in 1914 consisted of immigrants, new people in a new land, many of whom felt out of place in this country. They identified with Chaplin's Tramp character as a fellow outsider who perseveres despite being knocked down and pushed aside by those in authority. Audiences immediately had a rooting interest in Charlie. Period reviews indicate that audiences roared with laughter at this film, and each subsequent Chaplin production for Keystone was hailed by period critics as funnier than the previous one.

1. Chaplin at Keystone

Charlie in a posed shot from *Kid Auto Races at Venice* (1914). Frank D. Williams plays the cameraman and Henry Lehrman the harried director.

Chaplin locked creative horns with his first director, Henry Lehman, who complained to Sennett that he could do nothing with this English newcomer. Chaplin was then handed over to George Nichols, a real old-timer with many credits. Things started to go smoothly at first, but soon Chaplin went from making suggestions to challenging the director's authority on nearly every sequence. Finally, Mabel Normand was at the helm. Normand was truly beloved on the Sennett lot, and was one of the finest and most fearless slapstick performers of her time. In his autobiography, *King of Comedy*, Sennett stated:

> Mabel Normand and Charlie Chaplin had much in common. She was as deft at pantomime as he. She worked in slapstick, but her stage business and her gestures were subtle, not broad. Mabel Normand could do anything that Chaplin could do. To me she was the greatest comedienne that ever lived.

Chaplin at Essanay

Chaplin liked Mabel, as did everyone, and she was known for fixing problems with performers and getting the best out of those whose rough edges needed to be honed. When Sennett was ready to fire the stage-trained Roscoe Arbuckle after one day, Mabel stepped in and worked with Arbuckle, resulting in their films together quickly becoming among the most profitable for the company.

However, when it came to his work, Chaplin forgot about friendships. He was already a perfectionist with a real vision as to how he wanted his films shot. He and Mabel fought constantly, and she would often end up in tears. Some of the less tolerant actors on the Keystone lot were ready to confront Chaplin physically, but Mabel would not allow that to happen. As an artist, she realized Chaplin needed greater input. They received co-directing credit on the Keystone two-reeler *Caught in a Cabaret* (1914), which turned out to be the best film either had made up to that time. Legend has stated that Mabel directed her own performance, Charlie directed his, and they shared on the general structure of the film. However, comedy film historian and Keystone authority Brent Walker has indicated that Normand is credited alone as director in the studio's negative record. Chaplin, however, claims it as "my own" in a 1914 letter to half-brother Sydney, as indicated in biographical sources, including Chaplin's own autobiography.

Chaplin was indeed eventually allowed to direct his own films, but there is some confusion as to exactly what his first solo directorial effort at Keystone was. Brent Walker, for instance, has some misgivings with the idea that it is *Twenty Minutes of Love*, as reported in nearly all Chaplin sources, indicating that both the negative record and the official listing of Keystone releases signify Joseph Maddern as the sole director. Walker believes Chaplin may have had some business he was able to work into the film, but was not the director in the sense that he soon would be. Brent Walker told this writer:

> I think many historians have gotten caught up in the "genius theory." ... i.e. the person who became the greatest later on *must* have been responsible for everything earlier, and for that reason Chaplin's name was added as director on several early Keystones. Remember, at the point these films were made Chaplin was still a few months into his Keystone stint, and Sennett did not give the

directorial reins that easily. At that point he tended to prefer hiring directors with a track record of experience as directors, i.e. George Nichols, Wilfred Lucas, Robert Thornby and Joseph Maddern. Keystone hadn't yet become the "director factory" it would soon become, with people promoted from within.

It wasn't until early 1914 that he allowed the two stars who had been with him from the beginning — Ford Sterling and Mabel Normand — to start directing themselves. And after the reported complaints from men about working for Mabel, Sennett stepped in and co-directed a couple of films, then took over direction of the "Mabel" films by himself. Remember that even though Chaplin was starting to gain in popularity, Sennett would have been strongly biased in favor of Mabel over Chaplin at this point. Indications are that Chaplin did not direct Mabel Normand in a film until (excluding the Mabel cameo in *The Masquerader*) *Gentlemen of Nerve*. At that point, later in the year Chaplin had firmly established himself.

Roscoe Arbuckle was also very popular, but he was at Keystone for a year before Sennett allowed him to direct himself (just a month before Chaplin was allowed to do so). All indications from the primary records are that Sennett allowed Chaplin to direct for the first time with the one-reel *Caught in the Rain*, but this was a film that did not include Mabel Normand (otherwise, he probably would not have been allowed to direct that either). Sennett is credited alone for *A Busy Day* (he is seen in the film) and *The Fatal Mallet*.

The only two official primary records are blank for the period of 1914 after that, so there is no actual official documentation that Chaplin directed himself in the films. However, it is very likely that he next directed *Laughing Gas*, and virtually every other of his shorts after that.

The one exception is *The Rounders*, where it makes much more sense to speculate that Roscoe Arbuckle and Chaplin jointly directed rather than Chaplin by himself.... At that point Arbuckle was the senior of the two at Keystone, and was also immensely popular. No doubt, Sennett allowed Charlie Chaplin to insert his ideas and business into these earlier films, and maybe even take the lead in directing a scene or two.

I've found in Motion Picture News Studio Directory bios and the like it was common for people to take credit for directing things they did not actually direct. Henry Lehrman, after leaving Keystone, took out trade ads in which he claimed credit for the ideas on virtually every big Keystone film made up to that point. Therefore, I take words like "my own" with a grain of salt as to what they actually mean, even if the person writing it went on to make *The Gold Rush* and *Modern Times*.

One thing Sennett could not argue with was Chaplin's success. By his seventh film, theater owners were asking for more Charlie Chaplin product.

In a lengthy profile on Chaplin that appeared in the July 1915 issue of *Photoplay*, writer Harry C. Carr stated:

> As a director, Chaplin introduced a new note into moving pictures. Heretofore most of the comedy effects had been riotous boisterousness. Chaplin, like many foreign pantomimists, got his effects in a more subtle way and with less action. Also he worked alone to a greater extent than any other picture comedian. By making the most of the little subtle effects, Chaplin enlarged the field of all motion picture comedies. It goes without saying that the simpler effects a man needs for his fun making the more effects he has to draw on. Also in his role as a director, Chaplin has had the reputation of being the most generous star in the movie business. Every comedian was allowed to grab all the laughs he could get. Chaplin always insisted on having them do the comedy stuff in his way, but he always built up their parts for them without regard for the fact that his own might suffer.

Chaplin was all about the finished product.

Now, with 20–20 hindsight, we can see that the Keystone films Chaplin made, even after he started directing them, were forming the basis for what he was to become at Essanay. There are several important landmarks. *The New Janitor* (1914), for instance, presents Charlie as a put-upon working class sort who becomes a hero. This could be considered something of a portent to the more in-depth work he would do at Essanay, especially his milestone *The Tramp* (1915), which has a similar structure and is also filled with extraordinary comic invention; and another Essanay, *The Bank* (1915), which gives him a janitorial occupation and blends comedy and pathos with perfect cohesion.

In *Mabel's Married Life* (1914) there is a fascinating bit of pantomime where a drunken Charlie plays against a dress dummy, believing it to be an intruder. The cleverness of this sequence was another portent to Essanay, where he would further refine his comic presentation by adding more character-driven comedy to the slapstick gags. His second Essanay film, *A Night Out* (1915), had him revisit the drunk act and again respond to inanimate objects with as much confusion as vigilance. This idea culminated in the Mutual classic *One A.M.* (1916), in which Chaplin takes a drunken reaction to inanimate objects to an even greater level of brilliance.

In lauding the Essanay period that follows, the author is not trying to indicate that Chaplin's Keystone films were dismissible knockabout farces that are of mild historical interest but are not particularly good films. While flawed (as are his much later talkies, but for different reasons), the Keystones show a distinct evolution in Chaplin's gag structure, especially after he started directing himself. Some of the best films from this period are worth discussing.

His Trysting Place is a good example of the marital comedies Chaplin made with Sennett darling Mabel Normand. The basic setup of Mabel being the put-upon wife and Charlie the neglectful husband is used for some of the funniest gags in all of Chaplin's films. One of the highlights is the dinner sequence with comic heavy Mack Swain (who appeared in many Keystones, including his own starring series, as well as several with Chaplin). Mack is a large, imposing man who Chaplin the director offsets with diminutive Charlie the character as the two share a crowded frame while Mack sloppily eats and annoys. It results in a food fight that does not jump immediately into chaos, but builds artfully. Mabel, as the put-upon wife, is allowed by her director to command her scenes in such a manner that there was no friction between them when Chaplin is at the helm.

Keystone comedies usually took a standard setup that looked like a good setting for some delightfully messy comedy. Chaplin did this with *Dough and Dynamite*, where a bakery provides ample opportunity for wild Keystonesque slapstick. But under Chaplin's direction, and with his character, the creative gags are performed that much more effectively.

While certainly the apprenticeship period in Chaplin's cinematic career, the Keystone period is actually quite brilliant, as is the studio's entire history and immense importance to screen comedy. Chaplin's one-year tenure there was neatly capped by an ambitious six-reel feature, the first comedy feature ever made in America.

Tillie's Punctured Romance (1914) was directed by Mack Sennett. It

Marie Dressler and Chaplin in *Tillie's Punctured Romance* (1914).

casts Chaplin as a wily city slicker who woos a wealthy farm girl (Marie Dressler) to the big city. *Tillie's Punctured Romance* is characteristically uneven. The film alternates between boorish slapstick and subtle nuance, from narrative plot to knockabout gags; and, as with any first time venture, it is far from flawless. But bombastic Tillie's attempt to survive in the big city, Chaplin playing against type as a devilish con, and a cast of Keystone favorites (virtually every actor on the lot sans the conspicuously absent Roscoe Arbuckle) make it fascinating viewing today. The Keystone Cop climax and final shot of the duped Tillie and the ashamed Mabel

1. Chaplin at Keystone

making up with an embrace cleverly and effectively wrap up this extraordinary movie milestone.

In the course of a year, Chaplin completed 35 films at Keystone, including one- and two-reel subjects as well as the feature-length *Tillie's Punctured Romance*. An analysis of his best work at Keystone would show Chaplin's ability refining the slapstick of that studio's style, with an eye toward greater depth of character. Roscoe Arbuckle made similar strides, and his career parallels Chaplin's (he would leave Keystone for a triumphant series of short comedies at Famous Players–Lasky two years later, but would be ruined by scandal in another five).

Chaplin's popularity was, by this time, enormous. He was just on the cusp of becoming bigger than the picture business, his character entering other areas of popular culture, including advertising and popular songs.

Oddly, the Keystone comedies did not advertise its actors by name. People knew Normand and Arbuckle as "Mabel and Fatty" because they were billed that way in the titles of their comedies (e.g. *Fatty and Mabel Adrift*, *Mabel's Busy Day*, *Fatty's Tintype Tangle*, et. al.). Chaplin was referred to in the inter titles as Charlie, but his full name was never a part of the titles on his Keystone productions. Period reviews would often not know how to refer to the actor. And yet the films were so popular, so sought after by theatergoers, that word-of-mouth would sustain their massive success. When Chaplin went to Essanay, and his name was in the advertisements and subsequently became known, Keystone would use his name in rereleases. There is evidence of films like *Laughing Gas* and *Mabel's Married Life* showing Chaplin as the star in newspaper ads when they played in theaters just after Chaplin's first Essanay release.

Despite not having his name in ad copy, the Chaplin films stood out for audiences and producers alike. His ideas were frequently imitated, but with little success. Chaplin was obviously an especially talented comedian, and his films were definitely superior to most of what was being offered to moviegoers during this early period of the motion picture. After a year with Sennett, Chaplin completed 35 one- and two-reel films, most of which he directed himself. His popularity and prestige rose very quickly.

The immense popularity of Chaplin's films was not lost on Sennett's rivals, and as the comedian's contract headed towards its annual renewal, Sennett was prepared to offer him $450 per week, which is far more than

1. Chaplin at Keystone

he had been making. Other offers had some significance, but suddenly a rumor circulated that Chaplin was also looking for a $10,000 signing bonus, as well as a hefty weekly salary. He did not start the rumor, but when Essanay representatives agreed to such terms, Chaplin readily accepted. Sennett could not match such an offer. He stated that it was more than he himself was making. Chaplin finished up his contractual obligation to Keystone and was on his way to film for Essanay.

A story in the December 23, 1914, issue of *The New York Dramatic Mirror* stated that "Charlie Chaplin, the comedian who has created such a following since his advent into pictures a comparatively short time since, announces that he will leave the Keystone studio. Rumor sends him to various studios, the Essanay being the latest whisper."

Only three days later, on December 26, 1914, *Moving Picture World* reported:

> The announcement was made in New York on Monday evening December 14 by George K. Spoor, president of Essanay Film Manufacturing, that Charles Chaplin, famous screen comedian, had signed with his company. The information was contained in a telegram from G.M. Anderson from Niles Calif. Mr. Chaplin in a remarkably short time has created for himself a unique position in the film world. He is a man who seldom gives one an opportunity to laugh with him; at the same time he gives occasion aplenty to laugh at him. The name of the director under whom he will work has not been announced, but it is assumed that he will be under the general direction of Mr. Anderson at the Niles studio situated near San Francisco.

Sennett did not have too much of a problem losing Chaplin. He'd recently survived losing both Fred Mace and Ford Sterling, both of whom had been top Keystone stars, and he would soon lose Roscoe Arbuckle and Al St. John when Arbuckle accepted a lucrative offer from Joseph Schenck and took nephew St. John with him. Sennett believed no star was bigger than the picture business, and would later acquire such top-notch comedians as Ben Turpin and Harry Langdon. Even Charley Chase and Harold Lloyd had some Keystone experience before embarking on more success-

Opposite: Chaplin put together the Tramp costume at Keystone.

ful careers elsewhere. Buster Keaton is the only giant of silent screen comedy never to have worked at the Mack Sennett studios (Keaton, in fact, began his career with Roscoe Arbuckle after Arbuckle left Sennett for Schenck).

For Chaplin it was a new adventure in his show business career, and he was eager to enjoy not only the enormous salary and bonus, but more time to work out his many ideas, to secure and even greater creative control over his work than Sennett could allow. His vision was vast, down to every aspect of the production, including each character (some actors were chagrined at being directed in so exacting a fashion). Complete control, as promised by Essanay, was Chaplin's opportunity to match his imagination completely.

Essanay afforded Chaplin the ultimate creative challenge necessary for this aspect of his film career. It allowed him to grow and prosper as an actor and filmmaker. From the perspective of having just established himself at Keystone with a series of very popular comedies, it was exactly the creative challenge Chaplin needed. Had he stayed with Sennett, who would most assuredly have been so stubborn as to refuse to extend Chaplin any more creative control than he was currently enjoying, he may have felt that he was merely stagnating in films, and gone back to the stage and touring. It would have been an unfathomable loss to the development of the motion picture.

Essanay was not quite prepared for the level of filmmaking genius that Chaplin was wanting to bring them. While noted for consistent, durable film product, especially in the western and comedy genres, Essanay could hardly be ready for ideas that would expand the mind of cinema itself. With film being an infant medium in late 1914 when Chaplin signed his Essanay contract, it could not be realized that this popular, highly paid new comedian would have ideas that would change popular culture by transforming the movies into a veritable art form. This was accomplished during Charlie Chaplin's tenure at the Essanay studios.

2

The Essanay Studios

The Essanay company began in 1907, the name formed from the first initials (S and A) of its founders' last names — George Spoor and Gilbert Anderson.

Anderson was born Max Aronson in Little Rock, Arkansas, on March 21, 1880. His interest in theater as a youngster began after the family moved to St. Louis, Missouri. This passion manifested itself by the time Anderson was in his early twenties, when he began appearing in a variety of local theater productions. He eventually found his way into a few early Edison movies, most notably *The Great Train Robbery* (1903), which was directed by Edwin S. Porter and has gone down in history as being among the first films to tell a narrative story using editing. It was not the first narrative film, but it was the first to establish a clear structure of the western action drama by using crosscut editing to increase suspense. The reaction of the film's first audiences was so enormous that the impact has been felt throughout the history of cinema. It didn't make Anderson a star, but it certainly solidified his choice to remain in the moving picture business.

Anderson, however, expected more narrative films like *The Great Train Robbery* to be made, but both Edison and Porter simply returned to the routine moving pictures that were far less creative or expansive. When a touring company of the play *Raffles* came through St. Louis, Anderson got the idea to make it into a film, and contacted Edison's rival, the Vitagraph Company. He managed to convince the three partners that ran Vitagraph — Albert E. Smith, William T. Rock, and J. Stuart Blackton — to allow him to produce and direct *Raffles* as a seventeen minute full-reel film. It was released on September 23, 1905, and was a smash hit. Anderson remained with Vitagraph for the next year, directing several comedies and dramas for the studio.

By the next year, Anderson was directing his first westerns, this time for the Selig Polyscope Company in Chicago, with some of the westerns shot on location in Denver. His westerns *The Girl from Montana* and *The Bandit King* (both 1906) were especially successful.

Anderson met George K. Spoor in early 1907. Spoor was born December 18, 1871, in Highland Park, Illinois. He was already managing an opera house in Waukegan, Illinois, by the time he was 22. Spoor was fascinated when he saw his first moving picture in the late 1890s, and soon partnered with inventor Edward Amet, who made projectors and films to show, while Spoor found vaudeville houses at which these movies could be presented (a projectionist was provided).

Spoor was impressed with Anderson's track record at making successful films, and the two formed a partnership where Spoor provided the necessary funds for Anderson's productions. The first film under this agree-

The entrance to Essanay's Chicago studios as it looks today.

2. The Essanay Studios

ment, *An Awful Skate* (1907), was a smash success. The S & A, or Essanay, company was born.

Essanay slowly developed a steady stream of popular productions during its first ten years of existence. Anderson had a flair for directing comedies, but soon developed even stronger skills with the western film.

Bad weather in Chicago during the winter months forced the company to set up productions further west. In January of 1907, Anderson filmed four westerns in the Golden, Colorado, area. One of these, *The Road Agents*, was released in March of that year. According to the March 27, 1909, issue of the *New York Dramatic Mirror*:

> This is one of the best pictures of any description we have seen from the Essanay Company in a long time. It is thrilling without being unreasonable, and it is acted with an appearance of reality that gives us the impression of looking at actual events.
>
> No attempt is made to incorporate a complicated love story in the holdup and the capture of the road agents, and there is no maudlin sentiment introduced to create sympathy for the criminals.... If other Essanay western thrillers are anything like as good as this one we predict a wide demand for them.

Anderson continued making his own westerns with his new company, including the 1910 short *Broncho Billy's Redemption*. This film was significant in that it showed the western lead sacrificing his own freedom to take care of a sick rancher and his daughter. By adding another dimension to the western character, the movie cowboy hero was born. Audiences responded very favorably, and Anderson became known as Broncho Billy throughout a series of western shorts from 1910 to 1915 in which he starred, produced, and directed. As the first cowboy hero, he established character traits that were later used by such western movie stars as Tom Mix, William S. Hart, John Wayne, and Clint Eastwood (who actually titled his 1981 feature film *Broncho Billy* as a tribute to Anderson, although it had nothing to do with him or his story). By the beginning of 1914, just as Chaplin was starting his tenure with Mack Sennett's Keystone studios, G.M. Anderson was proclaimed by the *San Francisco Chronicle* as "The King of the Movies."

By this time Essanay had made hundreds of films and established a stock company of noted picture players. Augustus Carney was among the first comedians to star in a regular series. Cast as Alkali Ike, Carney was very popular with rural audiences during the first part of the 20th Century. Anderson continued his popular Broncho Billy series, and also directed the Alkali Ike films. Future MGM star Wallace Beery appeared in drag as the female character Sweedie in a series of comedies. Cross-eyed Ben Turpin got his start in the studio's Snakeville comedy series. Legitimate stage actor Francis X. Bushman became the studio's biggest star, playing in more prestigious dramatic productions.

Chaplin's Keystone comedies had been making a real impact with audiences, and therefore were sought after by theater owners throughout the nation. Standing out as special among many nondescript mirthmakers, Chaplin realized the popularity of his films, and word got out that he was interested in renegotiating for more money once his Keystone contract ran out.

Chaplin's contract with Keystone was days away from ending when he attended a Motion Picture Industry Ball in November of 1914. The event was sponsored by the Screen Club of San Francisco at the Coliseum on Baker Street. He has just finished his final Keystone production on his contract and was interested in expanding his opportunities. Sennett offered him $450 per week, but Chaplin believed he could get as much as $1000 per week as offers from other studios became known.

Essanay representative Jess Robbins, along with Anderson, met in December of 1914 with Chaplin and his brother Sydney, a fellow actor-comedian who also acted as Charlie's business manager. After some negotiating, a deal was reached at $1250 per week and a signing bonus of $10,000.

The Washington Press on December 19, 1914, stated: "Members of the Essanay Film Company at Niles are jubilant over the addition to their staff of Charles Chaplin, comedian. Chaplin was with the Keystone company for some time, and is by far one of the most popular comedy artists in the motion picture industry." A $10,000 signing bonus and a salary of $1250 per week were astronomical sums in late 1914. Spoor balked at the amount Chaplin was promised by Anderson and Robbins, but colleagues indicated he would make that much back very quickly with a star like Chaplin (Spoor later would make the rather far-fetched claim that he'd never heard of Charlie Chaplin until the comedian was signed).

2. The Essanay Studios

Essanay star actor Francis X. Bushman (left) and G.M Anderson (right) flank an arriving Charles Chaplin in late 1914.

At this time Essanay had studios in Chicago and in Niles, California. Chaplin went to the Niles branch and was taken aback by the surroundings. He didn't like the drab studio or its location. He was invited to instead film at the Chicago facilities.

In the January 16, 1915, issue of *Motography*, writer Clarence J. Caine profiled Chaplin's arrival at Essanay:

> He arrived in Chicago the latter part of last week, in company with Broncho Billy Anderson, and will remain at the Essanay studios in that city indefinitely, producing his inimitable farce come-

dies which have proved such a drawing card for exhibitors in all parts of the world. He seldom moved as fast while on the screen as he did during the first few days of his stay in the Windy City. Charlie was wanted here and Charlie was wanted there, from the time he arrived in the morning until he left at night. Therefore it was a rather difficult task to catch him, but I finally managed to corner him in the advertising department of the big studio on Argyle street for an interview.

During the interview with Caine, Chaplin explained his understanding of the type of comedy he had been doing for the screen:

> I have a distinct theory regarding farces, and one which, to my mind, meets with public favor. I believe that a plot which could easily become a dramatic subject, but which is treated in an amusing manner and which burlesques events of daily life, with which the average person is familiar, depending principally upon its humorous action for laughs, is the one to make a successful farce comedy. There are many things in farces which I do not favor. I believe I have been ridiculed for some of my actions, but whatever I have done has been unintentional, I am sure. My one object in life now is to amuse, and to do it in a clean way. Many persons see a subject on the screen and say that such-and-such a thing should be done this way or that. They do not realize that we do things on the spur of the moment and that our minds are under a constant strain, for we must concentrate on our work from morning till night.

Chaplin paused, and then was asked if there was anything he would like to tell the readers in conclusion.

> Just say that I am doing my best to please them and that I hope my releases under the Essanay banner will be as agreeable to them as my past work. And say! Tell them I'm just a fellow, a human being like they are and that I enjoy almost everything that is enjoyable.

According to Roger Manvell, in his book *Chaplin*, the comedian's Essanay tenure resulted in a variety of character touches:

> In these films, Charlie's face becomes more sympathetically expressive. His nose twitches, as if his mustache were tickling, and

2. The Essanay Studios

his fastidious grimaces express a world of doubt and misgiving. The changes in his expression reveal comic dumbfoundedness, tongue-in-cheek triumph at getting away with murder, affected innocence twisting into a fatuous grin, a coy smirk at a nude statue, sudden laughter in moments of success, scowls of outrage when faced with evil opponents, or deadpan nonchalance when playing the drunk doing outrageous things.

David Robinson, in his book *Chaplin — His Life and Art*, pointed out that Chaplin respected the production line methods of Keystone while employed at that studio, but at Essanay he declared his independence by taking much longer over his films.

With a host of new ideas he was excited about trying, and a studio that was content to let him explore his creativity without incident, Chaplin was anticipating a wonderful working relationship at Essanay. He wanted to start work immediately. So he arranged for sets to be constructed, assembled a cast and crew, and then embarked on his first Essanay subject, appropriately titled *His New Job*.

3

The Essanay Films

In assessing the films Chaplin made for Essanay, one is confronted by a few problems that should be addressed at the outset. Because the films are in the public domain, they are readily available to many low-level distributors of VHS tapes and DVD discs, while the accessibility of the same movies on 8mm or 16mm film allows for another aspect of projection. It is important to seek out the best available sources for projection, and to investigate how these sources are assessed by film experts.

When this writer has spoken to various Chaplin scholars they have indicated some problems with the currently accessible Essanay films. The restored versions utilized by this study are said by some scholars to be incomplete on some titles; but usually this means that only a few frames — literally a few seconds — might be missing from a shot. There is also some complaint as to the speed presented on more modern restorations of these films. Comedy film scholars claim that the faster speed with which we became familiar is, in fact, the proper speed for projecting these comedies. The restorations that slow down the speed to a normal pace may meet the expectations of modern day sensibilities, but, according to historians, it takes away a bit of the authenticity (in that we are not seeing the films as they were presented at the time of their initial release).

Of course, some may look at these points as nitpicking. But we should have some concern for authenticity regarding our cinematic heritage to the same as we would for literature, music, or any of the fine arts.

This writer, then, has assessed the Essanay films based on the best prints currently available on DVD, and, whenever possible, has also watched a 16mm or 8mm film print that professed to be complete. There were no discernible differences between the prints examined on film and the same ones seen on DVD; the speed on the film prints was, however

3. The Essanay Films

able to be adjusted to make them closer to the projection speed that audiences of 1915 and 1916 would have seen. Comedy film historian Richard Roberts told this writer of a friend who did not care for Chaplin based on the restored films at slower speed, but who changed her mind after viewing some of his films at what is believed to be the proper pace. Roberts added that silent comedies are supposed to move. Finally, there has been some discussion as to how appropriate the music is on currently available Chaplin prints.

So, then, the following assessments of the Chaplin films at Essanay are based on screenings that attempted to investigate different sources for projection, utilized different speeds, and compared them with and without musical accompaniment. It has to be realized that these films were meant to be shown clearly, at a proper speed, with live musical accompaniment and a large, enthusiastic audience. We cannot capture all of these elements, just as we cannot force ourselves into the same mindset as the 1915 audiences who were unaware of future cinematic developments that we, in the 21st Century, would find commonplace. This assessment of Chaplin's pivotal Essanay comedies, then, will be based on the most complete prints on DVD that are currently available — David Shepard's restorations released by Kino and Image Entertainment — and backup prints in 8mm and 16mm released by Blackhawk Films during the early 1970s (at the time when Mr. Shepard was among those working on their restoration).

His New Job

Cast

Charles Chaplin	Film Extra
Ben Turpin	Film Extra
Leo White	Actor, Receptionist
Robert Bolder	Studio President
Charlotte Mineau	Film Star
Charles Stine	Director
Arthur Bates	Carpenter
Jess Robbins	Cameraman
Charles Hitchcock	Leading Man
Gloria Swanson	Extra, Stenographer
Agnes Ayres	Extra, Secretary

Credits

Charles Chaplin .... Screenwriter, Director
Jess Robbins .... Producer
Jackson Rose .... Camera

Shot at the Essanay Studios in Chicago, Illinois. Released February 1, 1915. Two Reels.

Charles Chaplin had enjoyed some creative freedom at Mack Sennett's Keystone studios, but his sudden and enormous rise to fame was unprecedented. When the Essanay company put more money on the table than Sennett could hope to offer, and promised an ever greater level of creative freedom, Chaplin realized it was time to move on.

In a large ad for the *New York Dramatic Mirror* on December 30, 1914, there was a sizable picture of Chaplin and the following copy:

> Every exhibitor knows the box office value of the funniest comedian in motion pictures. He is Charles Chaplin, now with Essanay. Get your early bookings through the general film co. Film release dates will be announced soon.

Just about a month later, *His New Job,* Chaplin's appropriately titled first Essanay effort, was released.

While Essanay was anxious to see dividends from their substantial investment, Chaplin was allowed to take the time he felt necessary to create an effective comedy. Chaplin balked when he discovered some of the limitations of the Chicago studios, but initially decided it was better than the surroundings he had witnessed at Essanay's other studios in Niles, California. One of the money-saving situations at the studio was to run the negatives during the rushes. Another was to have the doors closed promptly at six each evening, even if a director happened to be in the middle of a scene. Chaplin saw these as hindrances to his creativity and proceeded to correct these as he became more familiar and comfortable with his new surroundings.

But there was one area where Chaplin would not budge. When he was told that Essanay would be providing him with scenarios, he insisted that he would create his own. It is worth noting that Essanay's scenario department was, at the time, run by Louella Parsons, who would soon become a major gossip-monger for the Hearst press.

3. The Essanay Films

His New Job is terribly important to Chaplin's filmography. At this early point in his transition, we can immediately notice the customary sadistic slapstick being crowded by moments of greater subtlety. The modifications in character and style did not happen all at once, but this slow evolution was still discernible at the very outset of his Essanay tenure.

Roger Manvell explained, in his book *Chaplin*:

> Charlie was now, in effect, an independent creator. As long as he delivered the films, his employers did not interfere with what he chose to do. Indeed, there were no rivals as there had been at Keystone, and no critical expert like Mack Sennett to breathe down his neck and insist on the Keystone hallmark in the nature of his work. Producing a film at approximately three-weekly intervals instead of weekly, Charlie had more leisure to invent and improvise on the studio floor....

His New Job opens with Charlie entering a studio personnel office where various jobs are placed within the movie industry. Not interested in becoming an actor, Charlie is looking for some form of hands-on construction work, but the waiting area includes potential actors as well as potential laborers. He takes a seat next to an attractive woman, who acknowledges him with a friendly smile. Noticing this, Chaplin casually lifts his chair and places it closer to the woman.

With this opening sequence we see the first discernible change in Charlie. Rather than approaching the attractive woman in the manner of the boisterous Keystone Tramp, Charlie is now delicately moving closer to the lady while trying to maintain a certain level of dignity and nonchalance. He avoids calling attention to what he is doing in order to avoid a potentially embarrassing situation. Keystone Charlie would likely not have cared. Essanay Charlie does.

The man in charge of the waiting area wants Charlie to remove his hat. He walks up and points to it, but Charlie mistakenly believes he is pointing out the attractive woman, so he offers a knowing smile and a nod of his head. The man takes the hat off and places it in Charlie's lap. Not realizing the ways of polite society, Charlie puts the hat back on his head. The man removes it again. Unlike Keystone Charlie, who would likely have kicked the man in the stomach and kept the hat on, Essanay Charlie finally gets the message, and the hat remains off, at least until the man in charge is once again preoccupied at his desk. By the next sequence, Charlie is again wearing his hat.

Chaplin was not so much a prop comic. While he effectively used props, his main focus was characters and their interaction. Charlie interacts effectively with the man in charge of the waiting area, but what is most interesting in this first Essanay production is how he reacts. The man is giving a command, asking for rules to be followed. The edgy, rebellious Keystone Charlie would have balked without sympathy, while Essanay Charlie, being introduced here, only responds in a most innocent manner. The fact that he does have his hat back on in the following scene shows that rebellion is still a part of his character, but it is exhibited with greater cleverness and subtlety.

A woman comes out from the interview area and back into the waiting room. As she bends over to fix her shoe, Charlie casually rests his elbow on her ample derriere. The woman admonishes him and leaves in a huff.

Again, Essanay Charlie commits this faux pas unwittingly. He does not brashly and purposely lean against the woman, as Keystone Charlie might have done; he does so without realizing she is there. When she reacts, he grins sheepishly. Charlie continues to commit these minor offenses without malice, and is clearly as embarrassed as he is clueless. This approach to his screen character endears him to the audience even more than the previous rebellious nature of the brash Keystone Charlie. At Keystone his behavior could be amusingly taken as comic rebellion against society's structure; here he is very much wanting to be a part of the working class, and is not lashing out at his surroundings, but attempting to cope with them.

Several people arrive at the offices while Charlie is waiting and jauntily walk past him, going directly into the office to be interviewed. Charlie sits in the waiting area and watches these people receive attention, despite his having arrived earlier. When the man in charge of the waiting room again calls, "Next," Charlie leaps from his chair and heads to the office, but another person rises and enters before he is able to do so, and slams the door in Charlie's face. Keystone Charlie would never have stood for such treatment, and an arse-kicking slapstick brawl likely would have ensued. Essanay Charlie returns to his seat and continues to wait.

Now that Charlie is established as the put-upon innocent, in walks

3. The Essanay Films

Ben Turpin as his boorish, loutish counterpart. Turpin had been at Essanay since the early 1900s. His freakishly crossed eyes, a trademark during his later stardom, were yet to be exploited, and thus he was shunted to the background of several of the studio's Snakeville and Sweedie comedies that Essanay ground out during its earliest years. Chaplin recognized something in Turpin which the other filmmakers had failed to see.

Upon entering the waiting area, Ben takes the seat next to Charlie and rests his leg on Charlie's lap. When Charlie accidentally bumps him with his cane, Ben hits Charlie. Finally the little fellow's ire is awakened. He pulls Ben's cigarette out of his mouth, lights a match on Ben's neck, and flicks ashes in his face. The man calls "Next," Ben gets up, and Charlie high-kicks him in the forehead. Ben leapfrogs over Charlie to get ahead, but Charlie trips Ben with his cane and enters the interview room. He now has his turn.

It may be a bit esoteric to view this sequence as Essanay Charlie attempting to obliterate a representation of Keystone Charlie, which Ben

Charlie at odds with rival Ben Turpin in *His New Job*.

Turpin's character could conceivably be, but the slapstick tête-à-tête with Turpin was a portent of what would occur between the two comedians throughout this two-reeler. It is also a bit of a throwback to Chaplin's confrontational slapstick brawls with Chester Conklin in several of his Keystone productions, and, finally, a preview to the next Chaplin Essanay, *A Night Out*, in which Turpin would have an even larger role.

Once in the office with the head man, Charlie relaxes and sits respectfully for his job interview. The man is hard of hearing and raises his large cone-like hearing device to Charlie, who mistakes it for an ashtray. Again, this is not brash Keystone Charlie who would have deliberately flicked ashes into the device, but the more innocent Essanay version who does so unwittingly. When he tries to wash it out, Charlie gets a faceful of ink, becoming the victim of his own attempt at righting his wrong. Despite what would be considered an unsatisfactory first impression, Charlie is hired as a laborer. He is to work construction near the shooting of a costume drama featuring a gaggle of pretentious movie actors.

The setup is now complete. Chaplin has effectively placed Charlie in the context where he can create gags and gag situations. It is also where we can most effectively make our clearest determination as to the initial evolution of Chaplin's character-driven comedy. How Charlie responds is key to the transition taking place. Finally, Chaplin is able to use the moviemaking subplot to engage in some satire on this level of filmmaking.

The potential is explored only to the extent that the remaining footage of a two-reeler would allow, but Chaplin's cleverness in setting up the situation and taking the time to exhibit perhaps more depth to his character than in any of his Keystone efforts is evident within the first reel.

It should be noted that the waiting area scenes offer future superstar Gloria Swanson quietly clickety-clacking away at a typewriter well in the background. She later stated in interviews that she carefully avoided any of the slapstick in the comedies for which she did bits and extra work during her early period at Essanay, wanting instead to pursue her craft with a career in dramatic roles. She did eventually get her wish, but not before a later stint with Mack Sennett, where she appeared in a number of knockabout slapstick comedies much rougher than the Chaplin Essanays. But time has been kind to Gloria Swanson's legacy. Today she is noted as one

3. The Essanay Films

of the top dramatic actresses of the silent era, her career extending well into talking pictures. (While Swanson's most noted performance in talkies may very well be Billy Wilder's *Sunset Boulevard* [1950], this writer admits to a special fondness for her self-parodying cameo on television's *The Beverly Hillbillies* in a 1966 episode. Such is the definition of a guilty pleasure).

Charlie enters the movie set where his employment is to take place, wandering right into the middle of a scene that had been carefully set by a high-strung director. Charlie is hauled off the set and placed with the head carpenter, to act as his assistant. Almost immediately, Charlie fouls things up by stepping on a board that is resting on a sawhorse, causing the wood to spring up and hit his boss. When carrying the board, Charlie turns and hits his boss again, who shoves Charlie and causes him to turn the opposite way and hit the boss once more with the board. The slapstick complications were definitely Keystone-influenced, but the Charlie character remains unwitting within the framework of his sequence, doing none of this deliberately. His hopeless errors not only result in hilarious, brilliantly-timed slapstick bits, they also continue the depiction of Charlie as the Everyman whose plight is complicated by circumstances.

Charlie walks into a prop area and sees a nude statue, reacting in a surprised, appalled manner. Interestingly enough, seeing nude statues would become something of a recurring bit in his films from this period.

The director is shown dressing down an incompetent actor, whom he fires from the film. Desperate, he calls Charlie over and orders him to take the actor's place. Charlie goes to a dressing room to get into costume, but rather than enter the general dressing room, he enters the star's private area and puts on his costume. On his way to the set, Charlie is sidetracked by a dice game with his old boss, the carpenter. Standing too close the curtain where a scene is being shot, Charlie is stabbed in the derriere with a sword, and responds by stabbing the actor, and then the director, through the curtain in like fashion before finally being brought to the set to film his own scenes.

Once on the set, Charlie is put through his paces as an actor in the film being shot. This is an especially interesting scene. We have witnessed the fast-paced, rhythmic slapstick of this comedy, and now we see Charlie acting out a slow, ponderous, overplayed melodrama. In this film-within-a-film situation, Chaplin the director is able to point out the blatant gestures and extreme melodramatics of movie dramas from the period, contrasting them with the bouncy slapstick we have enjoyed. Within this context, Chaplin is able to parody drama with subtler comic nuance. Charlie does not erupt into slapstick boorishness here. He tries to maintain

Charlie takes a turn at acting along with leading lady Charlotte Mineau in *His New Job.*

dramatic dignity during an emotional scene in the film being shot. Blubbering in character, a kneeling Charlie wipes his tearful eyes and runny nose on the train of the leading lady's dress. One of the most interesting things about this sequence is Chaplin the director's artful use of a dolley shot, something that was rare in American films of this period.

With Charlie now an actor, the carpenter needs another assistant. In comes Ben Turpin to take Charlie's place as the new laborer. When he and Charlie see each other, they engage in a threatening stare-down that is interrupted when Charlie is again beckoned to the set.

Meanwhile, the film's star arrives, enters his private dressing room, and wonders what has happened to his costume. Charlie, still filming, does not realize the flimsiness of some movie props. He leans against a prop post, which is very light, and nearly brings the entire set down around him. When this cumbersome prop lands on Charlie, Turpin is called in to help the director remove it. Turpin is hardly helpful, as he sits on the post that is pinning his nemesis to the floor.

The lead actor enters the set, sees Charlie in his costume, and starts a fight. Charlie ducks his punches and lands some of his own, while errant blows manage to hit the director and the hapless Ben Turpin, who simply gets in the way. In the end, and with the help of a wooden mallet, Charlie exits, the victor.

During the making of *His New Job*, Essanay regulars had to adapt to Chaplin's working methods, which concentrated so completely on the job at hand. Chaplin had to be reminded to stop for breaks and for lunch. His method of performance was fascinating to everyone on the lot, from his fellow actors to the stagehands. Many would stop by the set and watch him work, causing delays in production on other films being shot simultaneously.

This is understandable in that Chaplin's agility and his use of his body, especially in the final sequence where he fights with the actor, is like no other comedian in films at that time. His split-second timing as he ducks punches, throws others, and skirts from one place to another have a style and rhythm that must have appeared especially impressive (and daunting) in 1915.

When Chaplin presents the harried director, he does so by having the actor (Charles Stine) exhibit gestures that would have the viewer assume this director was on the verge of apoplexy. Chaplin shows the leading man (Charles Hitchcock) as carrying himself in real life with the same haughtiness displayed by the actors in the film-within-a-film. As a director, Chaplin wanted the studio setting to be more than a backdrop for gags. He wanted to find areas in the moviemaking process that were ripe for satire. The securing of employment and carpentry scenes are filled with the expected slapstick, while the presentation of a movie being made relies almost completely on the overplayed gestures that separated artful movie acting from the broad theatrical style found all too often in early movies. In his second year behind the camera, Chaplin already noticed the difference.

Chaplin was pleased with his film, but not with his working conditions. Despite having initial misgivings about the Niles branch of the studio, the Chicago setup was little better and had the added element of harsh winter weather, disallowing any outdoor shooting. Chaplin was also dissatisfied with his cameraman, although Jackson Rose was said to be one of the best cinematographers on the lot. The decision was made to return to Niles. Chaplin took along Ben Turpin, with whom he especially enjoyed working, and Leo White, who would figure prominently in the Essanay story after Chaplin left the studio for the Mutual corporation.

Chaplin's use of Turpin in *His New Job* was the comedian's first big break. He would later become a leading star in his own right when he went to the Sennett studios a few years later, but up to this time Turpin had made little impact. Now he was being recognized as having appeared in a Chaplin film, with funny business of his own to perform. For the rest of his life, Turpin acknowledged Chaplin as giving him his first real opportunity in movies.

In the 1919 annual issue of *Motion Picture Classic*, Turpin recalled: "The very first time I met Charlie Chaplin, he laughed for two hours, couldn't act at all. They told him to straighten up and get to business, but he said, 'I can't — that chap's blank expression has me laughing so I can't stop. At that time I was getting twenty-five and Charlie was drawing twelve-fifty!"

Leo White had gotten only slightly more recognition than Turpin by the time he appeared as an appropriately hammy actor in *His New Job*. Chaplin saw potential; and, like Turpin, White was allowed opportunities in Chaplin's films that significantly boosted his status.

3. The Essanay Films

His New Job is unusual in being the only Essanay that is confined to indoor shooting. In Richard Schickel's documentary *Charlie: The Life and Art of Charles Chaplin,* one interviewee is quoted as saying that the Essanays are fascinating because they are very much "street comedies"—filmed on real locations, showing the areas as they were in 1915. This is true of all except *His New Job,* which is confined to indoor shooting due to the harsh Chicago winter weather.

His New Job was a sensation upon its initial release, as theater owners had been clamoring for the next Chaplin film, waiting rather impatiently during the time from the release of his last Keystone (*His Prehistoric Past*) to his first Essanay. It was also the first time Chaplin received onscreen billing, as the Keystones did not list the actors in their credits (although this writer's research has found several period movie ads from late 1914 Keystone films that very prominently display Chaplin's name with the title).

Chaplin was already established as a leading screen comic, and his Essanay tenure would only increase his popularity. Audiences and reviewers recognized that his work stood out among his peers, but could not always discern exactly why. The period film magazine *Bioscope* stated in its February 1915 issue:

> There is probably no film comedian in the world more popular with the average picture theater audience than that famous funmaker, Charles Chaplin, whose services have recently been secured by the Essanay company. The art of Charles Chaplin defies analysis, and disarms the critic. Just why he is so funny, it is almost impossible to say, and very probably he could not tell you himself. He possesses a naturally comic personality, and its humor is accentuated by the originality of the innumerable bits of "business" with which his work is so profoundly interspersed. And perhaps the funniest thing of all is his own complete imperturbability. While those around him are rolling in an agony of mirth at his extravagant blunders, he himself pursues his course unmoved, with an air of mild detachment and stolid indifference. Good humorists never laugh at their own jokes. They realize the value of apparent seriousness. And, in the same way, Charles Chaplin remains emotionless, and even absent-minded, in the very midst of his maddest escapades.

Chaplin was not the only movie comedian in 1915 that refrained from calling attention to his performance with over-the-top histrionics (the

Chaplin at Essanay

equally popular Roscoe "Fatty" Arbuckle comes to mind). But even as early as his second year in pictures, Chaplin had established himself through his Keystone productions as one whom moviegoers and critics would single out as having a special charisma that seem to transcend even the most popular comedians of the period.

Reviewing *His New Job*, the *Chicago Tribune*, in its February 2, 1915, issue, stated: "It is absolutely necessary to laugh at Chaplin in ten-ninths of his antics in his disaster-attended search for a new job — the small point in which is evidenced the only irony in the picture."

Film critic Margaret I. MacDonald stated in the February 20, 1915, issue of *Moving Picture World*:

> Judging from first impressions and the roars of laughter evoked by Chaplin's first Essanay comedy from a representative New York audience, *His New Job* is going to be popular. Strange to say, the production has no plot to speak of; but it would seem that Charles Chaplin has but to poke some other fellow in the stomach, pummel the seat of his trousers, or rattle his brains with anything that comes handy to call forth round after round of the heartiest laughter. And after all is said and done the whole production consists merely of slapstick comedy; nor does it seem to belong to any distinct school of comedy. The fact of the matter is that *His New Job* is rather a hard proposition to analyze, and the only thing that is certain, besides its assured popularity, is that it sets the fuse to the picture fan's bump in mirth. Ben Turpin proves a good foil for Chaplin. For him the comedy star has no respect whatsoever. He pushes his face and kicks him, slams the swinging doors in his face, and finally walks on the unfortunate's stomach. In fact, he abuses with sturdy vigor most people who happen to cross his orbit; and stepping on the leading lady's train, with the result that her shapely silk-stockinged calves, with the appendages of feet in French-heeled slippers continue on their upward way unconscious of the public gaze, is one of the least of the offensive committed by the clever comedian.
>
> What there is of the plot consists of his coming to a moving picture studio to look for work. From the position of carpenter's assistant he falls heir through stress of circumstances to the enviable role of the hero of a picture play which is in the course of production. The mistreated applicant whom he has pummeled to the queen's taste take his place as carpenter's assistant. Later, by a clever reversal of situations, the head carpenter, blamed for the

3. The Essanay Films

hero's misdeeds, is thrown bodily from the studio. It would be impossible in short space to recount the various atrocities committed by comedian Chaplin in these two vibrant reels; but, as indicated before, if the audience thinks it's funny, it must be so.

Critics did not suddenly notice additional subtlety in character and execution, but this is understandable. In assessing Chaplin's entire film career, we can now pinpoint subtle differences in his cinematic evolution, knowing the culmination at Mutual and subsequent feature work for First National and United Artists. While it was happening, the subtleties were too subtle to be discerned. The aforementioned assessment from *Bioscope* indicates the reviewer's inability to pinpoint exactly why Chaplin's work stands out. But stand out it did.

His New Job was Chaplin's biggest box-office hit to date, allowing Essanay to realize they made no mistake in offering so astronomical a sum to the comedian. Essanay was inundated with orders from theaters for prints of the film. According to the February 13, 1915, issue of *Motion Picture News*, orders were coming in for two and three times the usual number of distribution prints, while theaters that did not usually book through Essanay's distributor, General Film Company, were outbidding regular subscribers for the right to screen the Chaplin film.

Film preservationist David Shepard restored the Essanay Chaplins in the late 1990s. *His New Job* was transferred from a 35mm nitrate duplicate negative dating from about 1918. For years represented only by prints that were, at best, fair to good, *His New Job* is now available and accessible on VHS and DVD in as good a condition as can be had, as Shepard characteristically drew from the best existing materials for his restoration.

His New Job is certainly an interesting movie, and its place in cinema has obvious significance. Funny though it is, *His New Job* can perhaps be considered, in retrospect, one of the weaker Essanay pictures. Still, the small changes that were slowly being made to character and execution were already having an enormous impact on Chaplin's career, as well as on the development of humor in cinema.

According to Ted Okuda and Dave Maska in their book *Charlie Chaplin at Keystone and Essanay*: "*His New Job* is one of the lesser Chaplin Essanays, representing the comedian embarking on a journey rather than arriving at a destination. Fans will want to check it out for historical reasons."

With the massive success of this film, passionate requests were being made by theater owners to ship another Chaplin film, and Spoor wanted to capitalize on his investment as quickly as possible. Chaplin's second Essanay film, *A Night Out*, was shot at the company's Niles, California, studios. Once Chaplin was satisfied with the final product, the film was hastily printed up for release only two weeks after the release of *His New Job*, helping to meet the massive demand for more Chaplin product. Chaplin's stardom was suddenly about to reach an even higher level, and Essanay was more than happy to fulfill the demand that would net them top money.

Chaplin's contract with Essanay was no secret. While there was certainly jealousy in some quarters, Essanay had no problem advertising *His New Job* as starring "the world's greatest and highest paid comedian."

A Night Out

Cast

Charles Chaplin	Drinker
Ben Turpin	Fellow Drinker
Bud Jamison	Head Waiter
Edna Purviance	Head Waiter's Wife
Leo White	Frenchman and First Desk Clerk
Ernest Van Pelt	Second Desk Clerk
Charles Allan Dealey	Restaurant Manager
Eva Sawyer	Leo's Companion
Fritz Wintermeier	Cop
Frank Dolan	Waiter
Lee Willard	Customer Slurping Soup
Madronna Hicks	Woman with Veil
Danny Kelleher	Bellboy Carrying Suitcases
Earl Esola	Bellboy with Cigar Boxes
Eddie Fries	Bit
W. Coleman Elam	Bit

Credits

Charles Chaplin	Screenwriter, Director
Harry Ensign	Cinematographer
Ernest Van Pelt	Asst. Director

Shot at the Essanay Studios in Niles, California, and on location in Oakland, California. Released February 15, 1915. Two Reels

3. The Essanay Films

Chaplin's second Essanay short, *A Night Out*, is an especially interesting effort for many reasons. First, Chaplin works in a decidedly adversarial team situation with Ben Turpin. Second, it is a fleshed-out version of his Keystone one-reeler *The Rounders* (where Roscoe Arbuckle starred opposite Chaplin). Finally, it features drunk bits that have their genesis in his Karno days, had been done at Keystone (most notably in *Mabel's Strange Predicament*, and would be seen to even greater advantage in the later Essanay *A Night in the Show* and the Mutual production *One A.M.*

A Night Out is also fascinating as to the way Chaplin directs his characters, something that would stand out in each ensuing Essanay production. Chaplin had a very distinct vision as to how each character would be presented, and his exacting methods of direction would sometimes cause consternation among the actors whose improvisational ideas were thwarted by their director's puppet-like manipulation of their performances. But Chaplin the auteur knew precisely what he wanted, and our knowledge of these methods makes the performances, and how the actors play off of one another, of even greater interest.

Charlie and Ben Turpin team up here. While Chaplin would pair Charlie with other comedians in various sequences, this film is perhaps the most team-like of his career, even moreso than *The Rounders*. Charlie and Ben have a history, have issues between them, and feel the need to defend one another, but do not appear to trust each other. The complexity of their relationship is borne out in their reaction to each other, and to others they encounter.

A Night Out opens with a shot of Leo White and Ben Turpin standing on the street. White is a well-dressed, pompous sort, Ben just a sloppy street guy. Chaplin waddles up to the two men and is greeted by Ben. Charlie gestures with his cane and inadvertently knocks off Leo's hat. There is a bit of a tussle until a cop comes by and breaks it up. Charlie and Ben lock arms and enter a bar. Leo leaves in a huff and goes to a restaurant.

Chaplin immediately establishes his character-driven setups among the key individuals. We know that Charlie and Ben are friends, are drinkers, and are rebellious toward pretension. We see that Leo is pompous and condescending. This initial setup allows the characters to meet, to briefly interact, and to have the first rumblings of conflict.

Even the very first shot is just right. Chaplin frames Ben and Leo so that they appear to be somehow crowding one another, even though they are merely standing together on a sidewalk with ample room between them. They are disparate types, and ignore each other while still obviously being aware. When Charlie greets Ben and his gesture knocks off Leo's hat, these common folk have suddenly entered the uppity man's world, and he wants no part of this intrusion. They fittingly go their separate ways upon being separated by an officer.

Charlie and Ben leave the bar, clearly drunk and barely able to make it up the street to a nearby restaurant. Of course, it is the same spot at which Leo is having his dinner. So the conflict that started on the street earlier can now continue in this new establishment, but not before Chaplin the director allows the viewer to see just how drunk Charlie and Ben are. The movement of the actors, and the way Chaplin films them, serves to emphasize not only the drunkenness of the two characters, but the fact that they are as confrontational as they are happy, and not above battling even each other at the slightest provocation.

The two men enter the restaurant, staggering, still arm in arm, but more in an effort to maintain balance than any display of friendship. Charlie tries to lean against a water fountain, where there is nothing to lean against. They see Leo sitting alone and take the table next to him. It is not deliberate. It is their drunken shenanigans that are getting in his way. Leo puts his hat on the floor; Chaplin mistakes it for a spittoon. Chaplin, feeling playful, knocks Leo's hat off his head. When Leo reacts, Ben comes to Charlie's defense. A confused Charlie knocks Ben out of the way, which causes a drunken skirmish between the two friends. The two are warned by the waiter. Meanwhile, the other patrons look on with shocked expressions.

Ben and Charlie make a spectacle of themselves, acting drunk, boorish and disruptive. But somehow the viewer is on their side. Chaplin the director creates a set that needs little explanation as to its poshness, and the snobbery of its staff and patrons. This sort of cold, off-putting establishment appears to deserve having patrons like Ben and Charlie come crashing into their peaceful world. The duo's entry indeed causes immediate disruptions involving both inanimate objects (a fountain that appears to take on a life of its own) and people (Leo, with whom they'd argued on the street earlier).

3. The Essanay Films

It is not long before Ben and Charlie's behavior extends to other patrons. A big western-looking sort eating soup is hit by Leo, who had been pushed by Charlie. Ordering a cocktail, Charlie is slapped on the back by Ben and spits his drink on Leo, who finally has had enough and complains to the manager (Bud Jamison). Bud warns the boys, and Turpin stands up to him. Bud knocks Turpin around while Chaplin ignores them, casually sipping his drink. Ben is tossed out. Bud returns and gives Charlie a stern look of warning, while Charlie daintily tips his hat, indicating that he will be no trouble.

Here we establish another level of the Ben-Charlie partnership. They are buddies, they stick up for one another, but when Ben is tossed from the establishment, Charlie does not rush to his side. He wants to remain where he is, and even indicates compliance with the very person who threw Ben out.

Bud leaves the area, and Charlie promptly falls asleep at his table. He is awakened by a girl coming to join Leo. She casually twirls her handbag, hitting the nearby Charlie several times. She also, while gesturing, unwittingly rests her hand on his knee. Charlie takes this as flirting and returns in kind, insulting the woman, who stands away as Leo defends her. Chaplin knocks Leo down.

Here Charlie again overlooks all issue of territory. The woman is attractive, she appears to be giving him attention, and she is clearly there to see Leo. That does not stop Charlie from responding in a far more blatant way than her casual hand on his knee. That she was, in fact, doing so unwittingly and was not flirting at all makes Charlie's more boisterous reaction even funnier. Leo, of course, comes to her defense, but the brash, drunken Charlie finds the pretentious fop to be no match at all.

Charlie then staggers up to the fountain, removes his jacket, and starts washing up. He even takes the stalk of one of the water plants and uses it to brush his teeth. Splashing water under his armpits and wiping them with a handkerchief, Chaplin makes use of the fountain display as if it were a wash basin.

Many silent film comedians were adept at using objects. A fancy fountain in a classy restaurant is transformed into a lavatory wash basin simply by Chaplin's approach. Back in 1915 it was something of an innovation to place props in a different context by using them in a fashion other than

49

An inebriated Charlie brushes his teeth at the fountain.

that for which they were designed. With this move, Charlie is not only funny, he is clever. It is amusing to see his drunken body wavering about as he laboriously picks at his teeth with a plant stem and splashes water about his face and person. It is clever to see him transform this glitzy decoration that reeks of pretension into something that is utterly common and low.

Bud sees Charlie at the fountain and orders him out. He gives him his coat and knocks him down, expecting him to leave. Chaplin gets up and starts toward Bud, who begins to remove his coat, ready to fight; so Charlie leaves and joins Turpin, who is still sitting outside where he had been thrown out.

This quick bit is great for its rhythm. Bud accosting Charlie, Charlie reacting towards him, Bud's welcoming of any possible battle, and Charlie's backing down are all done with split-second timing that follows the same perfect beat that this two-reeler has maintained thus far. It is as impressive as it is amusing.

Charlie and Ben, reunited, return to the neighborhood bar where they had first become drunk. Soon afterward, they leave it in an even more inebriated state. Ben must drag Charlie down the sidewalk back to his place of residence. Charlie is unable to stand up. As Ben is trying to get in his room, Charlie waits, sitting on him.

Edna Purviance plays a pretty girl who rooms nearby. She comes up to her room and starts to casually flirt with Charlie. Charlie reacts to her flirting in kind, and suddenly kicks Ben into the room and out of the way. This is another example of perfect physical timing. The flirting is cute and coy, then suddenly Charlie turns and kicks Ben into the room (and out of the frame) to indicate that three is most certainly a crowd. To accent the light flirting with a bombastic kick is most effective.

Edna goes to her room. Charlie looks through the keyhole. A bellboy catches him, so he pretends to simply have the wrong room. Edna's husband leaves the room — it is Bud, the overgrown waiter with whom Charlie had issues at the restaurant. He threatens to hit Charlie, who goes to his room, packs a suitcase, and leaves the building as Bud watches.

For all of his drunken bravado, this is the second time Charlie shows he wants no part of Bud. He left the restaurant when a fight was likely to occur, and now is intent on leaving his place of residence.

Charlie travels to another rooming house and gets a room. Charlie falls down, gets his foot caught in a spittoon, and is ultimately thrown out by the proprietor. Meanwhile, Edna and Bud leave their place after Bud becomes angry with the establishment due to a laundry mishap. Charlie, with nowhere to go, tries to sleep off his drunk on a park bench. Bud and Edna go to the rival rooming house that Chaplin had just left.

While he would explore this sort of plotting to an even greater degree in his Mutual production *The Rink* (1916), Chaplin here wants more than merely a series of slapstick gags hung on a premise. He wants to do more with his characters and their conflicts, so he sets up areas of coincidence that would have them run into each other even as they are trying to avoid one another.

Ben finds Charlie on the park bench and demands half their room rent. He starts a fight with Charlie, who hits him with a brick and wanders back to the rooming house to get a room. While setting up a new room, Charlie flirts with a lady whose face is hidden by a veil. He approaches, removes the veil, sees that she is hideously ugly, and hurries away.

Here Charlie is extending his notions of character. His buddy, with whom he has clearly had an adversarial relationship, is now an enemy demanding money. The women with whom he has been flirting have been elusive, and the one who appears interested turns out to be less than adequate. Charlie, at the center of his world, is finding it difficult to get along with anyone.

Next we have another brilliant piece of comic business. Up in his room, the still drunk Charlie tries to get water from a phone. When no water comes, he decides it is a coat rack, and hangs his coat and hat on it.

Edna is seen playing with her dog. The dog wanders into Charlie's room. Edna, looking for it, ends up there too while Charlie is in the bathroom washing up for bed. Charlie staggers out and sits on the bed, just as Bud returns home. Charlie looks down and finds Edna peeking out from under his bed. Not realizing that Edna and Bud have already moved into this establishment, Charlie thinks at first that he is losing his mind. Meanwhile, Bud is wondering where Edna is. Charlie finally looks under the bed and finds Edna. She is clearly embarrassed, while he is clearly pleased. She punches him and proceeds to leave, but sees Bud in the hallway looking for her, so she hides. Charlie peeks out and recognizes Bud. While Bud inquires in the lobby, Charlie sneaks Edna back to her room. But then Charlie is locked out of his own room and must hide in Edna's as Bud returns. Bud finds Charlie and the two try to explain. Bud will have none of it. He pulls out a gun and shoots at Charlie, who jumps out of a second floor window and lands on the ground. Ben, meanwhile, comes along looking for Charlie and the rent money. Pajama-clad Charlie reenters the building and goes upstairs to find an irate Ben. The two fight. Bud comes out of his room and soon gets involved. Charlie is tossed into a full bathtub, and the film ends.

Despite a rather abrupt conclusion, *A Night Out* is a rather brilliant example of Chaplin's experimental phase at Essanay. He takes elements of various Keystone films, including *The Rounders* and *Caught in the Rain* (both 1914), and revamps them for Essanay, where he enjoyed the option of taking more time to explore ideas and possibilities. Slapstick gags and physical business maintain a beautiful rhythm, from the staggering drunkenness of Ben and Charlie, to their expertly timed fight of several missed punches. Chaplin's structure in directing the characters and causing a comedy of errors in which they run into each other by going to the same place in an effort to avoid one another is also very sound. It shows his interest in deriving humor from situations as well as from slapstick.

Rollie Totheroh, an Essanay cameraman who worked on the Broncho Billy films, and would later become Chaplin's chief cinematographer, told Timothy Lyons in a 1967 interview for *Film Culture*:

> After Chaplin finished [*A Night Out*] he wanted to rest and go to San Francisco for a couple of days over the weekend. Anderson decided he was going to cut the first reel of Charlie's picture. Charlie didn't go to San Francisco. He decided not to at the last minute and came walking in on us. We were cutting the first reel, and Charlie said, "Take your hands off that." At that time we never had a print made; we used to do the cutting on the negative. If we scratched it that was just too bad. So Charlie said, "And furthermore, I want a print." At that time we had our own little laboratory, but we never had a printing machine. So they had to send all the way back to Chicago to get one. By the time we sent out for it with express, it was two weeks before we got it. Then they went to make a print and they had forgotten to send the blower for the machine. The blower would contact each frame on the aperture when it went through the printing machine; it held the film firm. So this laboratory man made the print with everything going in and out of focus. So Charlie said, "How am I going to cut with that thing?"

Jess Robbins then had to make a quick trip to Chicago and get the necessary pieces so that a proper print could be made.

Chaplin apparently held no grudge against Totheroh for his part in trying to help Anderson edit *A Night Out*, as he hired Totheroh to be his own cameraman once Chaplin left Essanay for Mutual in 1916.

Edna Purviance here makes her first appearance in a Chaplin film. When casting *A Night Out*, Chaplin searched in vain for the right leading lady. Edna was brought in by an assistant director, and Charlie quickly approved. There are conflicting reports as to where she was found, some saying she was a secretary, others that she was a waitress in the Bay area. She is given little to do in *A Night Out*, but the spark is already evident. It would become even more evident with subsequent films, as Edna continued as Charlie's co-star over the next several years. And while

Chaplin at Essanay

Chaplin's subsequent leading ladies would include Virginia Cherrill, Paulette Goddard, and Claire Bloom, Edna remained his best. In a December, 1915 Photoplay interview, she stated:

> Perhaps I shall never be a great success, but whatever success that I may have I shall always attribute to Mr. Chaplin. It is Charlie who gave me my first chance. It was he who directed me over the rough spots, who always was patient and painstaking with me, who coached me, who encouraged me, and without whose help I never could have accomplished what I have.

Bud Jamison (nee: Jamieson) also made his first appearance with Chaplin in *A Night Out*, and would appear in most of the Chaplin Essanays thereafter. While today best known for his many films with the Three Stooges during the thirties and forties, Jamison was a 21-year-old man out of vaudeville when he was chosen by Chaplin to appear as the heavy in his Essanay comedies. Jamison was a large, imposing man, not unlike Mack Swain at Keystone, and even more similar in appearance to Eric Campbell, who would be Chaplin's heavy at Mutual.

This was Ben Turpin's chance to shine in a film that would be eagerly sought by moviegoers. Chaplin films were the top, and although Turpin had been in Essanay pictures since 1907, his success was only moderate at best. Along with being an actor, Turpin also worked as the studio janitor. *His New Job* brought Ben Turpin notice, and *A Night Out* gave him an even greater opportunity to shine. According to David Kiehn, in his book *Broncho Billy and the Essanay Company*:

> [Turpin] was someone who, if he didn't actually steal a scene from Chaplin, could collaborate with the Englishman in a way that no one else had done before, except perhaps Roscoe Arbuckle. It put Ben in a new comic class. Briefly.

With the exception of a very brief walk-on in *The Champion*, Turpin never worked with Chaplin again (his scenes in *Burlesque on Carmen* were added after Chaplin had left Essanay). But he never forgot. Turpin told Edwin Schallert for the *Los Angeles Times*, Oct. 19, 1919:

> As to my career in the pictures, I feel that I owe everything to Charlie Chaplin.... Charlie gave me a start when he was with

3. The Essanay Films

> Essanay. You remember *A Night Out*. I played the part of the brother-in-arms of Charlie, or rather it was more like a brother-at-the-bar. Charlie did everything but walk on my face in that film. However, I learned many things that I've never forgotten.

Five years later, Turpin was a star in his own right, working for Mack Sennett and appearing in such classics as *The Daredevil* (1923) and *Yukon Jake* (1924). By then his crossed eyes, never exploited properly during his early years at Essanay, had become such a trademark that he had them insured with Lloyds of London. Turpin told Neil M. Clarke, for the November 1924 issue of *American Magazine*:

> Charlie Chaplin brought me out here, and he gave me my start. I'll always feel grateful to him for it. Mack Sennett put me over big. He has never broken his word about one single thing.

Chaplin never forgot Turpin either. He told the magazine *Reel Life* in their May 6, 1916, issue: In my opinion, Ben Turpin is one of the few really good comedians in motion pictures. He earns every laugh he gets."

Turpin eventually made enough money in movies, and with shrewd real estate investments, to make him among the richest men in Hollywood. It got to the point where he only worked when he chose to. He took some time off to care for his ailing wife Carrie (who died in 1925), but remained at least sporadically active well into the talking picture era. Some of his two-reelers for the low-budget Weiss Brothers during the late 1920s, including *Idle Eyes*, *The Eyes Have It*, and *The Cockeyed Family*, are among his funniest. Chaplin had not seen Turpin in many years when he learned of Ben's death at age 70 on July 1, 1940, shortly after appearing with Laurel and Hardy in *Saps at Sea*. Chaplin did not attend the funeral, but sent a seven-foot spray of red roses.

A Night Out was very well received upon its initial release. *Bioscope* stated in a February 1915 issue:

> Chaplin goes out with Ben Turpin for an evening's entertainment, and the fun is certainly fast and furious. The sight of these two disreputable tramps mixing with the company in a gorgeous restaurant and behaving in a manner which would not be tolerated in an East-end bar house, is sufficiently amusing in itself, and by disregarding any pretense at realism adds to the absurdity

and enjoyment of a humor that is extravagant to the last degree. Chaplin appears in the old familiar costume, and does all the old familiar business, some of which might well be spared, but most of which is rendered even funnier by its constant repetition. The ease and apparent lack of effort with which Chaplin works his quaint tricks show him to be a very conscientious and hardworking actor in his own peculiar line.

The Cinema stated in a February 1915 issue:

> The hero [Chaplin] is magnificently and consistently drunk from first to last. Accompanied by his knockabout partner, Ben Turpin, he sets out to test the limits of a stupendous thirst.... This film gives Chaplin full elbow room for many extraordinary antics and touches of humorous detail, and the fun runs along at top speed. There is little or no actual plot, Charlie having very wisely been given his head, and we should imagine that, at the finish of the production, it was a very sore head. Turpin makes an excellent partner, and takes many a stunning knockout blow with paralytic indifference.

Spoor frantically wanted Chaplin to make more films, and was bothered by the time it took to complete *A Night Out*, especially including the time taken up by the editing fiasco. The release of *His New Job* not only garnered good reviews and requests for two and three times the number of prints usually made for distribution, theaters that didn't otherwise book with Essanay distributors General Film Company were trying to outbid the regular subscribers.

Chaplin, however, did not approach his work from a business perspective like Spoor did. He was purely creative, and wanted to make the best films he could. *A Night Out* may not, in retrospect, be among the best Essanays (it was, after all, only Chaplin's second film for the company), but it is perhaps the best paced film of his career up to this time. It features good, solid slapstick, as well as excellent characters in humorous situations that neatly dovetail from one sequence to the next. Within its two-reel running time it accomplishes far more than much longer efforts of the era.

3. *The Essanay Films*

The Champion

Cast

Charles Chaplin .... Challenger
Edna Purviance .... Trainer's Daughter
Ernest Van Pelt .... Spike Dugan
Bud Jamison .... Bob Uppercut
Leo White .... Dishonest Gambler
Lloyd Bacon .... Sparring Partner, Referee
Bill Cato .... Sparring Partner, Trapeze Man in Gym
Frank Dolan .... Man with Stretcher
Fritz Wintermeier .... Cop
Ben Turpin .... Vendor at Fight
G.M Anderson .... Fight Fan
Jess Robbins .... Fight Fan
Eddie Fries .... Fight Fan
Henry Youngman .... Fight Fan
Leo West .... Fight Fan
W. Coleman Elam .... Fight Fan
Spike the bulldog .... Himself

Credits

Charles Chaplin .... Screenwriter, Director
Harry Ensign .... Cinematographer
Ernest Van Pelt .... Asst. Director

Shot at the Niles Essanay studios. Released March 11, 1915. Two Reels.

The Champion is Chaplin's best film up to this time, and remains one of the most important of his early Essanay productions. With his third Essanay film, Chaplin offers noticeably more depth to his onscreen character, a practice that appears to have begun with his Keystone film *The New Janitor*. Chaplin the filmmaker's realization that Charlie the character is more than an active body for slapstick buffoonery had become evident some time before, but it is borne out in *The Champion* moreso than any of his previous films. This idea would manifest itself even stronger in his next two Essanay productions, but its emergence is quite clearly presented here.

The Champion opens with Charlie, broke and hungry, putting together a stale hot dog, but stopping to share it with his bulldog. The bulldog will not eat it until it is properly seasoned. After Charlie adds condiments, the dog responds favorably, and Charlie gives him half of the frankfurter.

This opening scene, with Charlie presented as more down and out than he'd ever been, sharing his miniscule meal of one frankfurter with an endearing little bulldog, immediately captures the audience's sympathy and displays a depth to his character. In an era when so many comedians were bombastic and outrageous, Chaplin's tramp always had a refinement in presentation, even in the most slapstick-oriented Keystones. A greater depth of character was coming along as a result of choices Chaplin was making regarding the execution of gags and a subtler approach to comic

A down and out Charlie and his faithful dog Spike.

sequences. The opening scene of *The Champion* is of a real heartwarming nature. The bulldog represents the only other being in Charlie's world. Amusingly, the dog's finicky reaction to the frankfurter shows that he, like Charlie, will not allow his poverty-stricken strata in life to affect his inherent dignity and self-esteem. Only seconds long, it says more than many comedians were able to offer in an entire reel.

Desperate for money, the hungry Charlie and his companion pass a sign which states: "Sparring partners wanted who can take a punch." Charlie starts to walk away, but finds a horseshoe, which he believes may bring him enough luck to handle being a sparring partner.

After the opening scene with the dog, the idea that Charlie would rely on an old superstition for good luck seems quaint. It forces the viewer to take his side, to hope that he will indeed find good luck as a sparring partner. This is not funny, wicked, slapstick Charlie from Keystone — this is sweet, downtrodden Charlie the tramp who loves his dog and wants to earn some money for food.

In the July 7, 1915, issue of *The New York Dramatic Mirror*, critic Arthur Swan tried to assess the opening scene of *The Champion*:

> It is in the little touches that this performer shows at his best. Take, for illustration, the opening of *The Champion* where Charlie sits eating his grub and confabulating with his faithful dog. There is no acceleration of action here; it is almost wholly a matter of physiognomy. This is Mr. Chaplin and movie farce at their best.

Chaplin was said to be a fan of prizefights, an affection he shared with Broncho Billy Anderson, who makes a cameo in this picture as a ringside fight fan. Chaplin likely came up with many ideas stemming from this interest, perhaps with Anderson's input (Anderson would claim, in later interviews, to have directed *The Champion*, with Chaplin directing a Broncho Billy film in return; but there is no evidence of this being true). Chaplin was also very obviously inspired by Roscoe Arbuckle's 1914 Keystone two-reeler *The Knockout*, in which he cameoed as a comic referee.

Not simply relying on milking humor simply from the climactic boxing match, Chaplin the director also explores that which leads up to the bout. Once in the training camp, Charlie sits on a bench with other potential sparrers, one of whom is a punch-drunk fighter continually fidgeting in his seat as he jabs at the air. The basic disheveled appearance that this has-been displays is accented by his wearing a larger-than-normal pair of boxing gloves. They are not huge and overbearing, but just large enough to offer another amusing detail to the scene without distracting from it. When the disruptive fighter continues to punch at the air, Charlie, in a neat bit of pantomime, counts out the man's imaginary opponent in an effort to curtail his outbursts.

The boxer training at this camp knocks off one sparring partner after another, including the punch-drunk fighter who, despite his bravado, lasts only one quick punch. Each sparring partner is carried out in a most gruesome state as Charlie looks on with trepidation, realizing that boxing is not just punching, but being punched as well.

Finally, it is his turn. Charlie takes the horseshoe out of his pocket and examines it, having second thoughts about its ability to offer good luck. He carefully places it in one of his boxing gloves, realizing that this is the one way the horseshoe can indeed help him in this situation. Charlie enters the training quarters to spar, smiling confidently. With his loaded glove, he effectively knocks the professional fighter out cold, and leaves the area triumphant. The fighter comes to and demands another shot at Charlie. Along with his bobbing and weaving, Charlie continues to knock the fighter around with the loaded glove, and even spin kicks him. It gets to the point where the fighter has had enough and hurriedly leaves. Not only does he leave the sparring area, he leaves the camp altogether, with Charlie chasing him down the street. After the fighter runs for his life, Charlie gets past a suspicious cop in the same violent manner and returns to the training camp. Meanwhile, the fighter hops a train and leaves town, while Charlie is triumphantly hoisted onto the shoulders of the other sparring partners.

During the 8mm and 16mm film collecting era, a distributor called Official Films released the aforementioned sequences as a one-reeler entitled *Sparring Partner*. This is significant in that the film up to this point does indeed set up the second reel with a unified story. It shows that Chaplin the filmmaker was structuring his two-reel comedies more carefully, not only adding greater depth to his character, but offering a solid narrative laced with slapstick sequences (rather than merely some thin idea that serves as a backdrop for twenty minutes of gags). Comic exaggeration is

3. The Essanay Films

quite effective in the sequence, with the fighter, after being pummeled by Charlie and the loaded glove, not only scurrying away, but actually leaving town on a train. To show the man merely fleeing is not enough for the cleverness and creativity of Chaplin. His idea to exaggerate the sequence makes it incredibly funny.

And there is a different take on Charlie as well. Keystone Charlie would certainly have loaded his glove and bopped away at an opponent. He would have done it with comic malice. But after the opening sequence establishing Charlie as sympathetic, the glove loading seems like a necessary method of survival to get needed funds rather than comical cheating.

The first reel of *The Champion* is so filled with interesting ideas and amusing moments that it would seem difficult for even a comedian so great as Chaplin to maintain such a pace for another reel. But despite *The Champion* offering two reels that could each stand on their own, it also works effectively as a unified whole. The second reel of *The Champion* not only maintains the artistic level of the first reel, it builds upon it, surpasses it, and offers a preview of material Chaplin would use much later in his career.

The second reel proceeds to the training quarters of champion Bob Uppercut, whom Charlie is now scheduled to face in a main bout. Uppercut is played by Bud Jamison, who, after *A Night Out*, had immediately settled into the role of heavy for Chaplin's Essanay period (as had Mack Swain in many Keystone films). Uppercut is a big, mean man who shows no mercy in the ring. It is unlikely Charlie will have a loaded glove in a championship fight, as the referee will check for such things. Chaplin wants his audience to wonder what Charlie will do to survive this situation. The viewer has become invested in the sympathetic nature of his character, and genuinely wants Charlie to win somehow. This, of course, underlines Chaplin's effectiveness at presenting a sympathetic character rather than merely one adept at clever gags.

After seeing the large Uppercut, who seems invulnerable next to the slightly-built Charlie, we are shown the tramp's training. Charlie trains for the fight by struggling with various weights, and attempting to find a rhythm with punching bags (but getting hit in the face by the bag more often than not). As nourishment to replenish his energy, Charlie drinks from a large jug that is clearly labeled as beer. His trainers offer little assistance, as Charlie wanders around the gym with a barbell, turning and hitting each of them in the head and stomach as he passes.

In a neat bit of filmmaking ingenuity, Chaplin chooses to cross-cut between the training methods of Charlie and those of Bob Uppercut rather than show each scene as a separate piece. Just as such cinematic pioneers like Edwin S. Porter and D.W. Griffith had discovered during cinema's infancy the beauty of cross-cutting to enhance audience suspense during action sequences, Chaplin uses it to show Uppercut as an intimidating force, and Charlie as the proverbial fish out of water. It is rather interesting to compare this to, say, Sylvester Stallone's choice to use cross-cutting when showing the differing training methods of Rocky Balboa and his Russian behemoth of an opponent (Dolph Lundgren) in *Rocky IV* (1985). Rocky is out in the snow, hauling giant logs on his back, while the Russian is in a warm gym working out with the latest equipment. It is unknown if Stallone was inspired by *The Champion* (or if he has ever seen it, despite the fact that the first *Rocky* [1976] is said to be the last film Chaplin saw in his lifetime), but the comparison is worth noting.

Charlie happens upon Edna, the trainer's daughter, and is immediately smitten. Charlie shows off his weight lifting prowess rather clumsily, lifting his leg as he lifts the weight. But Edna finds him charming, and his subsequent flirting makes her laugh. Edna Purviance, making her second appearance in a Chaplin film, maintains her pleasant, understated performance. She is again given little to do, but her presence is immediately striking, and the spark between her and Charlie is evident. With each subsequent film, Edna was used more extensively and became more and more comfortable and natural in front of the camera. As a performer, she was clearly nurtured by Chaplin the director, which is one of many reasons why she remains his greatest leading lady.

Edna watches as Charlie does his road work, which consists of him skipping about the yard, turning corners with a right-foot skid. It is all rather ridiculous, but Edna is clearly smitten and embraces him as he finishes.

Leo White hammily plays another bad guy role with melodramatic effectiveness as a gambler trying to talk Charlie into fixing the fight. Chaplin expresses no interest, but Leo is persistent and follows him into the exercise area of the gym. His persistence is not successful.

3. The Essanay Films

Leo White tries to get Charlie to throw the fight.

This exceptional sequence shows how Chaplin and Leo White have learned to effectively play off each other in an adversarial fashion. While Leo tries to persuade Charlie to throw the fight, Charlie keeps unwittingly hitting him. He turns and hits Leo in the stomach with a weight, drops another on Leo's toe, and bumps him with a punching bag. Fed up, Leo pulls out a gun as a persuader. Undaunted, Charlie douses him with water, then swings on a pair of exercise rings and kicks Leo out of the gym.

This delightful slapstick excursion is important for several reasons. First, Chaplin places Leo into the mix as another character and subplot, adding more to the situation and linear structure of the film. Second, the slapstick that occurs throughout this sequence maintains a steady rhythm, something Chaplin appears to have already perfected. Lastly, and perhaps most important, Charlie's refusal to relegate himself to fixing the bout for money shows him as more inherently honest than his character had been in most of his films. This adds another element of sympathy to his character, one that sets the Chaplin films apart from other comedies of the era.

Finally it is fight night. Charlie awaits his bout with his faithful dog as his only companion. He is worried, so he bids his dog farewell by shaking the canine's paw as if it will be the last he will see of him. Crooked Leo is prominent in the audience, his dapper figure standing out in the motley crowd, which includes vendor Ben Turpin and a cameo by Broncho Billy Anderson (playing an extra in the audience at ringside).

Chaplin's staging of the championship fight is delightfully funny, with big Bud Jamison doing a good job showing enough agility to keep up with Chaplin's ballet-like choreography. Chaplin swings and misses, spins, and hits the second time around. After each round he collapses in his corner. Their stances result in an abrupt embrace, and they end up dancing. Chaplin swings from the clench and knocks down the referee, who is taken to a corner and revived between rounds. Charlie foolishly takes a bow after inadvertently knocking down the champ, who gets up and pounds Charlie as he rises. The champ finally hits his stride and begins pummeling Charlie relentlessly. Charlie's dog at ringside acts upon instinct and charges the ring, literally putting the bite on the champion. Locking his strong bulldog jaws onto the seat of Uppercut's trunks, the champion is overwhelmed, and Charlie punches him relentlessly. This allows Charlie to emerge victorious. The reward is a kiss from Edna, which Charlie coyly hides from viewers with his large mug of beer.

In most studies of Chaplin films, when discussing his massive popularity, there is mention of theaters simply advertising "Charlie Chaplin today" in order to garner huge box-office returns. The first such evidence this writer's research could find was a March 1915 ad for the Virginia Theater in the *Washington Post*. The film showing was *The Champion*.

Thus, by this time Chaplin's popularity has reached legendary heights. His Keystone comedies had been so popular that they had generated a demand to know just who this unbilled funnyman was. Once his name was known, the Chaplin comedies became tremendously popular very quickly. First it was due to the brilliance of his comedy. Then, due to his progression as both comedian and filmmaker, his films drew even more notice. At this point, the mere mention of his name was all a theater needed to ensure strong box office. For 1915, it was quite amazing.

3. The Essanay Films

By his third Essanay film, Chaplin was billed as the world's greatest comedian.

In a spring 1915 issue of *Picture Play,* Chaplin explained how real-life situations and characters were the basis of his comedy:

> I study the screen closely now, and I am firmly convinced that everyone in the industry should do likewise. There are many things we can learn from it, even though we think we have perfected ourselves in our own line of the great industry. I endeavor to put nothing in my farces which is not a burlesque on something in real life. No matter how senseless a thing may seem on the screen, I think that if it is studied carefully it can be traced back to life,

and is probably an everyday occurrence, which the would be critic of the farce had never thought to be a bit funny.

Chaplin was making great strides in directing characters and situations, as well as adding greater substance to his own character and to his comedy. His first few Essanay efforts were spent exploring the possibilities greater creative freedom allowed him. Now, with this third film at the studio, the evidence of his ultimate goal became quite clear. Chaplin wanted his films to be more than merely funny. He wanted to have a point to each gag, create substance in the characters, and provide structure to the situations. Chaplin wanted to employ a steady rhythm and construct a proper pace to enhance the comedy as well as the plot. His cinematic work was evolving, his deeper talents emerging. It is a fascinating thing to observe. With only three Essanay productions, Chaplin was already able to explore enough to discover a method that resulted in a film like *The Champion*. It is no wonder that people flocked to theaters at the mere mention of his name.

During this rise in popularity, Chaplin considered some offers to return to the stage. An announcement in the March 21, 1915, issue of the *Washington Post* indicated that he was contemplating a vaudeville tour in the Fall. Only days later, that same newspaper indicated that Florenz Ziegfeld was trying to secure Chaplin for his *Follies of 1915*, but his offer of $1800 per week was not enough to secure his release from Essanay. Finally, Chaplin seriously considered an offer of $25,000 to appear live in Madison Square Garden. Spoor and Anderson were so concerned with this as a cinematic setback for their company that they offered to give Chaplin that amount simply not to go to New York, and to remain in California making pictures. This was detailed in the May 29, 1915, issue of *Moving Picture World*:

> Change will have to be made in the announcement that Charles Chaplin is to come to New York to appear at the new picture show at Madison Square Garden, New York, for two weeks for the sum of $25,000 for the engagement. Word comes from the coast that the deal is off, but that Chaplin will get the twenty five thou' just the same. The money was passed to him on May 14 in the form of a check drawn by Gilbert M. Anderson on the Fort Dearborn

3. The Essanay Films

National Bank of Chicago. George K. Spoor and Mr. Anderson were both in Los Angeles to put the deal through. Two weeks ago, Mr. Spoor in Chicago was called on the phone from New York by L. Presburg, Manager of the Arena Amusement Company. Mr. Presburg was very anxious to secure Mr. Chaplin's appearance at the opening of the Garden. Mr. Spoor said it was impossible, but that he was starting for New York and could be seen there. In New York, Mr. Spoor said the engagement was out of the question; that six figures would have no more influence than five. The releases had to be maintained and the head of the Essanay Company declined to listen to the suggestion that Chaplin could be working on pictures enroute and in New York City. Mr. Spoor returned to Chicago at the end of the week. Back in New 'York City on Monday, May 10, Mr. Spoor had a hunch the wires between New York and Los Angeles were too busy so he just boarded the midnight train and on May 13 met Mr. Anderson in Oakland. The report was then that Chaplin had decided his contract with Essanay would permit him to make the trip and return to the company. It was understood the comedian was to travel across country in a special train with observation platform appearances and a circus parade on arrival in New York. Mr. Spoor and Mr. Anderson were in Los Angeles on May 14, and on the same day there was deposited to Chaplin's account, the bouquet twenty five thousand dollars and there was executed a supplementary contract to the mutual satisfaction of the parties concerned. The transaction is probably without precedent in amusement history. On Sunday, Mr. Spoor returned to Chicago and Mr. Anderson to Niles.

The Champion was an artistic triumph for Chaplin. It explored the character with dramatic elements, and this led to further investigation of such possibilities with subsequent films like *The Tramp*, the Mutual production *The Vagabond* (1916) and the First National short *A Dog's Life* (1918). Charlie's bulldog in *The Champion* is a clear precursor to his similar canine friend in *A Dog's Life*, with this relationship later expanded upon in his feature *The Kid* (1921), wherein the dog was replaced by an abandoned child. It shows how Chaplin's cinematic exploration was such that an acknowledged classic like *The Kid* has its genesis in his short films, beginning with his third Essanay effort. Charlie and the dog are alone in the world in *The Champion*. He fights to raise money for each of them. The dog comes to his rescue in the end. It is the sort of relationship that elicits warmth and awe from the audience, something Chaplin had discovered and would use on several levels throughout his career. His creativity was exploding with ideas, but he needed enough time to present them most effectively.

The opportunity to take more time with his films was one of the perks allowed Chaplin upon joining Essanay. He no longer had his artistic freedom stifled by Sennett's limited schedule for films, being forced to grind them out as quickly as one per week. Chaplin took nearly all of February to complete *The Champion*, making sure the scenes were shot effectively and the pacing was edited properly. *The Champion* defies rhythmic structure. The opening scenes are relaxed and establish Charlie's relationship with the dog. The rest of the first reel explores the comedy that can be found within the sparring situations that lead Charlie to a championship bout after he KOs the fighter during practice. The second reel explores training methods for fighters, and leads directly to the fight. Chaplin's choreography of the fight reportedly took a great deal of time, and many takes, before achieving what he envisioned.

Time, however, was a factor that impeded progress on the business front. George Spoor was upset that it took Chaplin nearly all of February to complete *The Champion*, as the tremendous success of *A Night Out* even surpassed that of *His New Job*. Spoor realized Chaplin's popularity was not only going to pay back the company's huge investment in the comedian, but would become very profitable very quickly. But he also knew that the more Chaplin pictures available, the more his company stood to make. Therefore, he wanted the Chaplin movies to come out at a steady rate.

Realizing some level of the business perspective, despite his being almost completely focused on the creative, Chaplin agreed to dash off a quickie one-reeler to make up for the extra time he took completing *The Champion*. While studies of Chaplin's films dismiss his subsequent effort, *In the Park*, as a quick throwaway deserving little attention, this writer disagrees.

In the Park

Cast

Charles Chaplin . . . . Tramp
Edna Purviance . . . . Nursemaid
Bud Jamison . . . . Her Boyfriend
Leo White . . . . Nattily Dressed Man in the Park
Leona Anderson . . . . His Girlfriend

3. The Essanay Films

Ernest Van Pelt .... Hot Dog Vendor
Lloyd Bacon .... Pickpocket
Paddy McGuire .... Hot Dog Thief

Credits

Charles Chaplin .... Director, Screenwriter
Harry Ensign .... Cinematographer
Ernest Van Pelt.................... Assistant Director
Jess Robbins .... Producer

Filmed in San Francisco. Released March 18, 1915. One Reel (12 minutes).

There are some students and historians of comedy in cinema that carefully debate the merits of one-reel films versus those that run two or more reels (but not at the level of a feature, which would exceed four reels). Some will contend that a one-reeler is too brief—not enough time for solid comedy ideas. Others argue that a one-reeler is simply more compact and gets rid of any dross. They point out effective one-reelers that are now classics, such as Snub Pollard's *It's a Gift* or, for that matter, Chaplin's *The Rounders*. The debate has some sound reasoning on both sides, but this writer must argue in favor of one-reelers as effective entertainment. However, in most studies the consensus regarding Chaplin's Essanay two one-reel films is that they are dismissible aberrations in a more solid body of work. They are presumed to be less effective and far less significant because they have been made in haste to maintain contractual obligations. Not only is this inaccurate, *In the Park* is actually a rather formidable link in Chaplin's career progress.

Although *In the Park* is only one reel in length, uses the most basic of settings, and is filled with the sort of slapstick one finds more frequently at Keystone, it is Essanay Charlie in a Keystone setting, and it is Essanay Chaplin directing a Keystone-styled film. As far as its place in the development of Chaplin as a comedian and filmmaker, *In the Park* is certainly one of the most interesting efforts of this period in his career.

Breezing past this comedy as a brief one-reel stopping point during a great comedian's cinematic evolution is to overlook the details that are very evident beneath the surface. Chaplin the director's choices as to how to use the setting, present the gags, and structure the madness is precisely why *In the Park* is so much more significant than most other filmographic studies would have one believe.

The backstory has to do with Chaplin's massive popularity and the fact that exhibitors were not interested in waiting very long for new Chaplin product. After taking so long at perfecting *The Champion*, Chaplin found himself behind schedule and had to make a movie quickly. Retitled versions of the previous year's Keystone Chaplins were finding their way into theaters. Spoor, ever aware of his massive financial investment, and wanting to please the exhibitors, did not want his financial thunder stifled by old product from which he would not profit. At the same time, exhibitors with long memories resented being duped by year-old retitled Keystone Chaplins. Chaplin had to have his latest films ready for release at regular intervals, and if his creative vision took a bit longer on one project, as it did with *The Champion*, it was necessary for him to somehow compromise enough to produce another film in less time.

So Chaplin compromised as an artist by setting up a simple premise that he knew would be easily directed without stifling his creative spark. With little setup necessary, and needing material for only one reel, Chaplin could concentrate on the characters, situations, and gags within this smaller framework. *In the Park* does not maneuver the characters and situations with the same structure as *A Night Out*, nor does it have the depth of character found in *The Champion*. Instead, it takes a simple premise, a handful of characters, and the most basic of conflicts, and combines these to present a solid, enjoyable, and tightly structured comedy.

In the Park is very much like a Keystone film — or, more precisely, an Essanay version of a Keystone picture — even to the point of resembling the Sennett-produced *Twenty Minutes of Love*, which is said to be Chaplin's first solo directing job.

The first shot of *In the Park* features Leo White in his French Count costume on a park bench wooing an apparent girlfriend (played by Broncho Billy's sister, Leona Anderson, not Margie Rieger as indicated in some other sources). Edna is shown sitting on a nearby bench in a nursemaid's uniform, with a baby buggy at her side. She is holding a romance novel and watching the couple with an amused smile, rolling her eyes at their blatant romantic gestures.

Here Chaplin has his setup, which has clear Keystone similarities. But the actors here do not consume the camera with overplayed histrionics. Leo's florid mannerisms have a comedic point, while Edna appears relaxed

3. The Essanay Films

and exhibits subtle amusement at those very mannerisms. It is a pleasant, uneventful day in the park — until Charlie comes along.

Charlie is a pickpocket whose own pocket is picked by a clumsy crook who fumbles along the lining of Charlie's clothes while looking away, watching out for wandering cops. Charlie reciprocates by picking that man's pocket, coming up with a cigarette and a match, which he lights up by striking the match against the man's neck. Charlie then wanders up to the spooning couple, and although there is an empty park bench nearby, he chooses to sit next to them, alternately fascinated and amused by their romantic manner.

One can immediately react to the way Chaplin chooses to frame this shot. Having Charlie sit by the couple allows him to appear both interested and intrusive. But the scene is accented by the nearby appearance of an empty bench. Charlie could very well have sat nearby on his own bench, but he instead chooses to sit right with the spooning couple, mocking their manner and getting nudged off the bench onto the ground.

Here we see Chaplin's method of directing his actors. They do not appear to realize Charlie is there, nor does their nudging him away seem deliberate. They are consumed by their own relationship, while Charlie's amused mocking is on the periphery, despite the close proximity. It is only after he his nudged away that the couple appears to notice him. Charlie remains amused, nudging Leo and playfully knocking off his tall hat.

This could also be Chaplin the filmmaker's take on overplayed cinematic melodrama. Striving for a naturalness in his comedy, and gradually achieving it with each film, Chaplin could very well be making a subtle point by having two overplayed romantic characters in the center of the frame carrying on while others react with befuddled bemusement.

Leo and Leona are not the only romantic couple. Edna is soon joined by her boyfriend (Bud Jamison), who is a big, hulking brute. Chaplin chooses to direct Bud Jamison's performance towards the absurd. Bud, who was said to be over six feet tall and around 270 pounds, comes skipping and prancing up to Edna like a sissy, and soon leaves in the same manner to get them each a hot dog from a nearby vendor.

Chaplin always liked to use his body for comedy, and asked the same of other actors he directed. His direction of Jamison to contrast his large, imposing bulk with a light and dainty manner is inspired in its absurdity, and shows Jamison as a game actor who responded well to Chaplin's vision. His skipping and flitting about is completely at odds with his appearance. It wouldn't be the last time Bud would play the pansy. Even in his appearances some thirty years later with the Three Stooges, the imposing actor would play swishy butlers in such comedies as *Three Sappy People* (1939) and *Crash Goes the Hash* (1944). It is Chaplin who first thought of the comic possibilities of a big guy like Bud playing a pansy. Bud is clearly amused by the stereotype and gives it all he can.

Leaving the romantic couple, Charlie wanders over to Edna, who is again sitting alone, and flirts with her. She is amused by the attention, so he attempts to interest her further. She spurns him, of course, as her boyfriend will soon return.

Here, then, is the first in what would be several situations where Charlie is attracted to Edna, whom he cannot have. This would be revisited

Edna looks on, as a cop, played by an unknown actor, nabs Charlie (*In the Park*).

3. The Essanay Films

to a much greater degree in subsequent films like *The Tramp* and *The Bank*, but Chaplin is first trying it out in this quickly made one-reeler. Of course he had been thrown together inadvertently with her in *A Night Out* (where she was also paired with Jamison), and wooed her successfully in *The Champion*, but this is the first film in which he is interested and she is inaccessible. Little is made of it, but it sets a blueprint for later, more in-depth examinations of their relationship in subsequent Essanay films.

The pickpocket sneaks up to the spooning couple and steals Leona's pocketbook. The couple, still necking, do not notice. Meanwhile, Edna's boyfriend returns and chases Charlie away. Charlie notices a small man attacking the hot dog vendor, trying to steal his wares. Charlie comes to the rescue and chases the crook away. The vendor thanks Charlie, who then steals the hot dogs for himself.

Here is Chaplin condensing his vision to the one-reel limitation by having several things happen at once. The stealing of the pocketbook propels the narrative. Edna's boyfriend chasing Charlie away continues the conflict. Charlie's saving of the hot dog vendor is merely a ploy for him to steal the same goods. It comes off as sly and clever trickery rather than an off-putting criminal act. Chaplin somehow keeps the viewer firmly in Charlie's corner. To cap this bit of amusing trickery, Charlie hangs the string of hot dog links from his breast pocket and moves his body to swing the wieners up to his mouth as he bites at them.

The pickpocket steals the hot dogs from Charlie, while at the same time Charlie steals Leona's pocketbook. Charlie sees Edna's boyfriend daintily picking flowers for his girl, so he sells the purse to him for $2. The nearby pickpocket angrily hurls bricks and hits Edna's beau, but not Charlie. Charlie then gives the purse to Edna as a gift and receives a hug from her. Bud awakens and returns to claim the purse and Edna, while Leona finally discovers that her purse is missing. Leo tries to play the hero and confronts Edna's much larger boyfriend, and is soon pushed back and intimidated. Leona is ashamed of him, and walks away. Leo is so distraught he decides to commit suicide. He first pulls a gun, then has second thoughts and wanders over to the lake to jump in and drown himself.

Charlie comes by and helps him out by booting him in the backside. Once Leo is in the water, Bud and a policeman get the purse back from

Charlie. Soon, however, it is they who fall into the lake, while Charlie freely walks away and leaves all this behind.

The conclusion offers many interesting elements. First, Charlie has some fun with romantic melodrama by having Leo overplay his decision to end it all by dramatically jumping into the lake. Charlie boots him in, but not impulsively. As Leo crouches over to jump, working up the nerve to do so, Charlie goes through a series of stances and setups to get himself, and Leo's derriere, in just the right position before booting him in.

Second, Chaplin has Charlie cleverly achieve the upper hand over everyone. When he rescues the vendor from the hot dog thief, he steals the franks for himself. When the pickpocket steals the franks, Charlie steals the pocketbook. When Bud is knocked out after purchasing the purse, Charlie not only has Bud's money, but receives a hug from his girl for presenting her with the very purse that Bud purchased. And when confronted by Bud and the cop, Charlie maneuvers in such a way that they are both in the lake, while he is free to go. Charlie leaves this situation without a care for the pocketbook, or for Edna. It was just another misadventure on the road of life, and Charlie fittingly leaves it all behind after disrupting each situation and, ultimately, emerging victorious.

Chaplin has more fun with the incongruity of a physical image versus its action. Bud Jamison's large frame skipping along and daintily picking flowers is at odds with the stereotype of a big man or "heavy." He also presents the attractive Edna as a nursemaid who gives no attention to the baby buggy for which she is responsible (when Charlie backs into it and knocks it to the ground, Edna is more interested in the stolen purse). She also offers a fickle reaction to both Bud and Charlie, appreciating whatever attention she can get from either.

On the surface, *In the Park* appears to be just a quickie knockabout one-reeler dashed off as a mere stepping stone from one important film (*The Champion*) to another (*A Jitney Elopement*). But the ideas that Chaplin presents within the simple context of a one-reel park comedy clearly displays his evolution thus far. *In the Park* can be so closely compared to Chaplin's Keystone roots, given that it has the general setting and structure of a Keystone one-reeler, it allows us to see the areas of refinement that Charlie already displayed as a comedian and filmmaker. While plenty of knockabout slapstick is presented, Chaplin also does more with visu-

3. The Essanay Films

als, with his characters, and with interrelating situations than what one would find in a typical Keystone short. Edna's more nuanced performance as the one sane factor among Bud's sissified prancing, and Leo's over-the-top melodramatics nicely offsets the characters and their relationship to her and each other. Charlie is able to infiltrate each of these separate factions by merely passing by (and continuing to pass by once his disruptions are complete). Chaplin the director was continuing to make real strides in cinematic structure.

There are elements of Keystone Charlie still in existence within his present character at Essanay. He does flick ashes into an unconscious Bud's open mouth, and steals sausages from a vendor after chasing away another thief. But even in a scene where he knocks off Leo's top hat, he does so more playfully than maliciously, and Leo is presented as the sort of pretentious fop who deserves such a comeuppance.

At the time *In the Park* was filmed, Chaplin was still shooting in Niles, a suburb of San Francisco, but for this film he traveled to a San Francisco park area to use its setting.

In the Park is fast-paced and filled with comic incidents, yet somehow all of this material crammed into one reel does not seem cluttered. It is a tribute to Chaplin the director that he was able to structure this film so that it emerges as another step in his evolution at Essanay, and not, as frequently reported, merely a Keystone revisitation that can be dismissed in our journey through this portion of his filmography. The cleverness of *In the Park* puts it at the top of Chaplin one-reelers, and its effectiveness clearly indicates a continued progression in his Essanay films, showing outstanding development even when revisiting older structures and ideas.

There is one rather confusing thing regarding this film's title. A 1914 Keystone one-reeler, *Caught in the Rain,* was retitled *In the Park* when released to the home movie market by Official Films in the 1950s. Available for years under that title in 8mm, Super 8mm, and 16mm versions (the latter with a specially made soundtrack), *Caught in the Rain,* while a funny Keystone one-reeler, is not at the level of the Essanay picture. However, despite the fact that home movie collecting has been completely eclipsed by home video, the confusion with *Caught in the Rain* continues. The Keystone film can be found on budget VHS and DVD collections under the title *In the Park*, as these distributors of public domain material simply released the old Official Films print (albeit with a different soundtrack than the 16mm version). So, on any number of cheaply made VHS or DVD Chaplin collections, a film called *In the Park* may very well be *Caught in the Rain*.

A Jitney Elopement

Cast

Charles Chaplin .... Charlie
Edna Purviance .... Edna
Ernest Van Pelt .... Edna's father
Leo White .... Count
Lloyd Bacon .... Butler, Cop
Paddy McGuire .... Butler, Cop
Bud Jamison .... Cop

Credits

Charles Chaplin .... Screenwriter, Director
Jess Robbins .... Producer
Harry Ensign .... Cinematographer
Ernest Van Pel .... Assistant Director

Shot in Niles and San Francisco, California. Released April 1, 1915. Two Reels (26 minutes).

Film historians nearly always cite Chaplin's sixth Essanay, *The Tramp*, as the most important of the Essanays in terms of adding depth to his characterization and embarking on a distinctly unique style. However, it was with his fifth Essanay, *A Jitney Elopement*, that Chaplin goes beyond mere nuances or refinement of Keystone situations to present an original idea that is far more subtle and substantial than his earlier work.

A Jitney Elopement is one of the most interesting films of Chaplin's career, especially within the context of his Essanay productions. Chaplin had been striving for some time to find a greater richness in his films, and now that he had more freedom for creative expression, he revisited some old Keystone ideas and improved upon them for his first few Essanay comedies.

Chaplin had already established the idea that a comic character could have more depth than that provided by merely making faces and taking

3. The Essanay Films

pratfalls. Now that the Little Tramp was an established figure in cinema, Chaplin wanted to venture into storytelling with the same creative fervor. He wanted to take a more dramatic approach to his stories, with the characteristic gags accenting a straight story rather than being the focal point. This was becoming somewhat evident as early as *The Champion* when Chaplin used the poignant setup of Charlie and his dog as outcast companions. With *A Jitney Elopement*, Chaplin attempted to rely on the suspense of the situation and the depth of the characters as much as on physical gags.

Perhaps one of the reasons *In the Park* is considered merely a one-reel aberration, despite its having so many interesting elements, is that it stands directly between two rather extraordinary Essanay productions. It comes after *The Champion*, which shows great promise in the direction Chaplin seems to be going with his work. And it precedes this film, which looks further into refining Chaplin's presentation as both an actor and a director.

A Jitney is the era's slang for a Model T Ford, and this car was quite popular among the masses in 1916 when *A Jitney Elopement* was made. So Chaplin's naming the car in his title was a definite nod to this pop culture icon.

The plot for *A Jitney Elopement* has Edna's father arranging for her to marry a count (Leo White), even though she loves a commoner (Chaplin). Charlie poses as the Count, whom the father has not met, in order to win Edna's hand. Of course, the real Count shows up, and Charlie must find another way to keep his romance alive.

Chaplin again establishes his characters during in the opening scene. Edna's father delightedly and greedily arranges the union between daughter Edna and the Count, then demands, with flailing arms, that Edna cooperate.

Edna informs her beau, Charlie, in a delightful Romeo and Juliet bit where she is standing on the second floor balcony of her home while Charlie stands below. She tosses down a note:

> "My Hero
> Father wants me to marry Count Florid de Lime. Won't you save me?"

It is worth pointing out Charlie's very first appearance in *A Jitney Elopement*. The film irises in on his standing on the street in front of the

Charlie against the wall plotting to rescue Edna in *A Jitney Elopement*.

brick building. As the dark picture expands to show Charlie, he is facing the camera, with only a brick background behind him. This is a good indication of Chaplin's popularity at this point. While the Keystones were heartily enjoyed, the Essanays raised Chaplin's popularity with critics and moviegoers to extraordinary levels. Thus, a showy entrance such as this was warranted, and likely generated applause in theaters throughout the world.

Charlie has now been designated as a hero by Edna, so he plans her rescue. But there is no indication of Keystone Charlie here, as was evident in some of the other Essanays. He does not run in and kick the others, with Edna carried out on his back. Instead, this Charlie is more pragmatic, and he creates a scheme to impersonate the Count and win her father's good graces.

Charlie's relaxed, shabby appearance belies who he is, but he stiffens up and changes his demeanor and mannerisms once he is with the father. Chaplin's pantomime is exceptional here. Without the benefit of dialog, Chaplin communicates through Charlie with body language to convey his ruse. He stands straighter, his mannerisms are more fluid, and his facial expression haughty. It is convincing enough that the father does not question his shabby manner of dress.

Charlie is placed in the living room and surrounded by two servants.

3. *The Essanay Films*

He asks one to pour him a drink, pushing up on the servant's elbow to make sure his glass is filled. He offers some to the servants, being blissfully unaware of the class system that forbids such a thing. He is offered a cigar, and happily takes a handful. He gargles his drink and belches. But because he is perceived as titled and monied, his boorish behavior is considered merely eccentric.

A luncheon is served. Charlie cuts the bread in a circular motion, ending up with a spiral — a gag that dates back to his music hall roots and that found its way into other comedies. He tears the loaf of bread apart and passes unwieldily hunks to the others. The diners eat their soup in close quarters, engaging in all manner of small talk.

At this point it is clear that *A Jitney Elopement* is much more refined in its approach than any other Chaplin film to this point. Slapstick is at a minimum, with the humor being driven by characters and situations. The anticipation builds as the audience awaits the inevitable exposure of Charlie's ruse. Little appears to happen during the luncheon sequence, other than some delicate gags with the cutting of the bread. But Chaplin the director is keeping things quiet in order to build up the suspense of the situation. When will Charlie unwittingly reveal himself as a commoner? Will the real Count show up and spoil everything? Will the father accept Charlie despite his common status?

Beans are served, and Charlie does not know the proper way to eat them. He casually covers his mouth as he chews. The meat is tough. He tries hard to cut it by rapidly running a knife over it, but gets absolutely nowhere. Through it all, Charlie continues smiling and bantering as he runs the knife rapidly over the uncuttable steak. Finally, he chances gnawing on his food whenever the others look away. Then a sip of hot coffee results in smoke spewing from his nostrils.

Charlie tries to remain subtly refined throughout this rather tumultuous luncheon. And, in effect, the humor is much more subtle and refined as well. Chaplin continues with this approach so that wild slapstick does not detract from the comic situation at the forefront. This is perhaps the first instance in which Charlie tries hard to be like everyone else, rather than lashing out against them; and the fact that he is failing while gamely trying puts the audience on his side. He is a misfit, but one with a background. At the very outset of the film he and Edna know each other, and are romantically involved. There is a backstory to their relationship.

The Count's inevitable arrival is amusing in that he differs little from Charlie in his manner, simply being more pretentious. Once the father realizes Chaplin is an impostor, he removes him from the dining area by the ear. Charlie tries to maintain the ruse, but he quickly realizes it is of no use. He bends over and allows Edna's father to literally kick him out.

Edna remains devoted to Charlie, and her reaction to the actual Count is very cold. A drive to the park is suggested, and heartily endorsed by Edna's father, who joins them. Once at the park, there is an amusing bit where the father stands between the Count and Edna, his expression fluctuating back and forth from smiling at the Count to angrily ordering Edna to respond favorably. The couple goes to a nearby park bench, while Edna's father remains within earshot, greedily rubbing his hands together. As Leo gallantly wipes off the bench, he bends over to reveal that the seat of his pants are patched. Realizing his aristocracy makes him no better than her common boyfriend, Edna laughs derisively.

Charlie happens by. Perhaps Keystone Charlie would have scurried up to the couple and kicked the Count in the stomach, causing the park bench to fly backwards. But this is Essanay Charlie, whose method and character are being carefully refined. Charlie pauses and rolls a cigarette. He does so carefully, but not effectively. His mind is elsewhere, and he dazedly allows the tobacco to fall out of the loosely rolled cigarette. He lights the paper, which quickly burns up to his mouth. While this scene does not blend with the film's plot, it is an effective aside. It adds suspense, while further indicating that Charlie is stunned and preoccupied over his situation with Edna.

Finally Charlie confronts the Count, who is willing to fight. The relaxed pace of the two-reeler speeds up as Charlie pulls the hat over the Count's eyes and shoves him into Edna's father, who is sitting nearby. Two policemen come along and begin following Charlie closely. They keep walking as Charlie takes a step backward and sneaks between them, effectively evading their watch. The two cops spend several seconds wondering where Charlie has gone.

In considering Sennett's boisterously hilarious attack on law enforcement with his delightful Keystone Cop escapades, it is impressive to see how Charlie makes the same statement with a shorter scene and in a far subtler fashion.

Charlie then gets into a comic fight with Edna's father and hurls two bricks to hit the two cops. Another cop comes along and Charlie retreats. This is followed by a car chase that is very uncharacteristic of Chaplin. However, despite it being the sort of sequence he usually didn't employ, Chaplin does a magnificent job setting up and filming the chase. There is none of the crude back projection often found in such scenes. Chaplin has the camera follow the cars, and cross-cuts from clasps to medium to long shots, allowing the suspense to build, just as it had risen throughout the narrative portion of the two-reeler.

When the film concludes, Chaplin borrows from his own *The Champion* and acts coy about the kiss he is about to give Edna. Noticing the camera (or, in effect, the prying eyes of the viewing audience), Charlie takes the car out of gear and leans over to kiss Edna. The "end" title pops up just before their lips meet. Chaplin rarely used film's technology for a gag, especially a closing one, so his decision to have some fun with the editing process makes this a most interesting final shot.

A Jitney Elopement is a true milestone in Chaplin's career. While his first four Essanay productions were essentially refining Keystone ideas and allowing for his character and filmmaking technique to develop, this fifth effort is a culmination of sorts. Chaplin appears to have decided on a particular approach to his comedy, one that did not completely eschew slapstick, but which gave greater concentration to character and situations while refining the physical comedy.

A Jitney Elopement also has a greater narrative structure than Chaplin's previous films, one that moves slowly and builds suspense for the viewer. The plot is standard and simple, but Chaplin's presentation and the elements he chooses to use are what enhances it beyond that which can be considered ordinary. Chaplin was learning that drama and comedy could coexist in a short subject, and that films could offer more than simply a succession of gags. The gags are there, the film is still a comedy, but the structure allows for what is essentially a serious story as backdrop.

A Jitney Elopement follows the same pattern set by the previous Essanay productions, where Chaplin's art as a filmmaker discernibly evolved. By this film, it appeared Chaplin was ready to create a situation from which he could derive comic possibilities through the characters.

Edna is at her winsome best as the object of Charlie's affections. She is warm, attractive, and given the opportunity to display her natural charm. Since she had no real acting experience, Chaplin directs her so that her natural qualities emerge. It's often noted how comparatively little she has to do in her first few Essanays. With *In the Park*, Chaplin allowed her a bit more; and with *A Jitney Elopement*, her natural ability really shines forth. Perhaps it can be concluded that Chaplin did not feel, instinctively, that Edna was quite ready in *A Night Out* or *The Champion*, and needed this experience before breaking out in *A Jitney Elopement*. While Edna was certainly noticeable in the first two films, and is gradually given a bit more screen time in each successive appearance, *A Jitney Elopement* features her strongest performance to date. Some believe the romantic element found in *A Jitney Elopement*, and most of Chaplin's subsequent films, is due to Chaplin's offscreen relationship with Edna Purviance, which was in full swing while filming these comedies.

Leo White is once again the personification of classic bombast in his role as the Count. What is interesting is that Charlie's impersonation of the Count is more refined and disciplined than the actual Count himself. Leo White made a career out of playing pretentious fops, and Chaplin used White's skills effectively in many of his Essanay productions. *A Night Out* is especially notable in that Leo is pitted against both Charlie and Ben Turpin. In *A Jitney Elopement*, White once again employs the florid gestures and snobbish bent, exhibiting a perfectly ridiculous character that Edna finds laughable. She has no interest in him at all, preferring the down-to-earth Charlie.

Chaplin used conflict differently here than he had in his previous Essanays. Here the situations put Charlie on the defensive. He is dismissed as a lesser prospect for Edna by Edna's father, who prefers she marry wealth and power, despite her own personal interests. Charlie must somehow prove himself, and does so by employing the ruse of pretending to be the Count. The father goes out of his way to make this supposedly important person feel at home, and Charlie relishes the preferential treatment. While his tramp instincts are evident at a marginal level, he plays the Count as a generally likable individual. Charlie does not change while pretending to be the Count — he is still himself, but merely saying he is someone else. He responds to the special treatment in kind, but he does not take on gestures or manners that would stereotypically befit royalty. Leo White, however, plays it up big, and the revealing shot of his patched-up trousers indicate his ruse is just as empty. It is Charlie who is the better man at every level.

Chaplin's decision to conclude the film with a Keystonesque chase sequence shows how much he learned at his former stomping ground. The sequence is choreographed beautifully, as artfully as a ballet, with cars weaving about, near misses, and the necessary cross-cutting to enhance the rhythm of the action. It is the sort of territory Chaplin did not frequent, *A Jitney Elopement* being one of the very few times he chose to direct a car chase climax. Interestingly, several cutaways are medium shots, allowing not only the movement necessary to the scene, but the viewer a better look at the characters' expressions. Acting was still going on; these are not merely stunt people in long shots.

A Jitney Elopement is a very strong film, and a decided milestone in Chaplin's career. That it leads neatly into something as important as *The Tramp*, which came next, has caused other filmographers to overlook its significance. But there is a great deal about *A Jitney Elopement* that causes it to rise to the level of the truly important. It is subtle, its humor is gentle and delicate, it delves more deeply into its characters, and it allows for other levels of Chaplin the actor (and Edna the actress) to propel the narrative.

At this point, only five films into his Essanay tenure, we can clearly see how Chaplin was evolving from brilliant comedian to an equally brilliant filmmaker. With each new production, a bit more of his innate sense of comedy and filmmaking was revealed. This is especially true of his very next film. While *A Jitney Elopement* is important in many ways, Chaplin's next picture made even greater strides towards a serious story in the context of a comedy short.

Note: Another Essanay production was copyrighted March 31, 1915, the day before *A Jitney Elopement* was released. The film is now lost, so we have no idea as to the contents of *Introducing Charlie Chaplin*. It is a bit curious that Essanay would want to introduce an actor who was about to release his fifth movie for the company, but perhaps we can make an assumption. It may be that Essanay needed to have a few Chaplin films produced before they could get a director (in this case Wallace Carlson) to put together some highlights to help promote the films. While Chaplin was already quite a major attraction, it may be that the money-conscious Spoor wanted to use every promotable opportunity to recoup his massive investment. Although there is a director credited, it seems very unlikely that any new footage of Chaplin was shot. Whether or not such a film ever existed (and one would think it must have since a copyright exists), it deserves at least a footnote in a study of Chaplin's Essanay period.

The Tramp

Cast

Charles Chaplin	A Tramp
Edna Purviance	Farmer's Daughter
Ernest Van Pelt	Farmer
Lloyd Bacon	Edna's Boyfriend & Thief
Paddy McQuire	Farmhand
Leo White	Tramp/Thief
Bud Jamison	Thief
Billy Armstrong	Poet

Credits

Charles Chaplin	Director, Screenwriter
Harry Ensign	Cinematographer
Ernest Van Pelt	Assistant Director
Jess Robbins	Producer

Filmed in Niles and Sunol, California. Released April 11, 1915. Two Reels.

In every performer's filmography there are certain efforts that stand out as especially significant, even moreso when we concentrate on a specific period in an actor or filmmaker's career. Among the Chaplin Essanay productions, it is *The Tramp* that stands out as the checkpoint at which we can assess the development of Chaplin as a comedian and filmmaker. It is this two-reeler that effectively coalesces all that had gone before; and it embarks on a journey toward subsequent films with ideas that stem from those presented here.

The Tramp is one of the finest films of Chaplin's career. Much has

3. The Essanay Films

been said about its importance to Chaplin's development as an actor and filmmaker, with studies often citing it as the first film in which Chaplin significantly uses pathos to add greater depth to his character.

We have seen in the previous Essanays that a real progression was being made towards *The Tramp*. Chaplin spent his first two Essanay films, *His New Job* and *A Night Out*, defining his style and refining its structure. While both of his first two pictures were essentially reworked versions of Keystone ideas, they each displayed a discernible evolution in Chaplin's cinematic vision through pacing and presentation. His third Essanay, *The Champion*, revealed, via its opening scene with Charlie and his dog, that a deeper level of character definition was being explored. *In the Park* made further strides by showing how a typical Keystonesque idea could be structured to a level of slapstick perfection that used all of the standard elements — setting, characters, and gags — resulting in a more inventive one-reel comedy. And, finally, *A Jitney Elopement*, the film just previous to *The Tramp*, offered subtlety and situational humor at a more refined level than any Chaplin film to date.

Therefore, *The Tramp* is indeed a milestone, but one reached only through the progression offered by Chaplin's Essanay tenure up to this point. It is not an amazing work that suddenly appears out of nowhere like an oasis in the desert. It is not even really a culmination, since further strides were made in ensuing Essanay productions. *The Tramp* may very well be Chaplin's finest film to this point in his career, but its conception is evident through all of the films which came before. Furthermore, the subsequent Essanay films would maintain a consistent high quality, and many of them, including *Work*, *The Bank*, and *Police*, would be among his finest.

The very first scene in *The Tramp*, which is only seconds long, shows a farm girl (Edna) being given a few dollars by her father for an errand. The scene quickly cuts to Charlie, from a distance, walking up a dirt road through a woodsy area. Charlie is, of course, the title character. He is tired, and as he checks his shoes for wear, cars come by one after the other, from either direction, knocking him down both times. His Tramp is a downtrodden victim of the elements, but retains an inherent dignity. As he rises from being knocked down, he pulls out a whisk broom to carefully dust himself off. Chaplin makes it funny by pulling out his baggy trousers to whisk them off, and bending over to put the broom through his legs and dust off his backside.

He finds comfortable shade tree, sits beneath it, and prepares to eat his meager lunch of bread and water, likely gotten from a handout. Another tramp, lurking behind a tree, steals his food. He must then try to gain nourishment by eating grass. It is outrageously funny and oddly poignant at the same time.

A farm girl, walking home through the woods with a few dollars in her hand, is robbed by the same tramp who took Charlie's food. She is chased to the area where Charlie is sitting, and he defends her by hitting the thief over the head with his hobo sack (tied to a stick for effect), which has been fortified by a brick. Charlie recovers the money and gives it back to Edna. He considers keeping a bill, but changes his mind and gives it all up. Meanwhile, the other tramp goes to another area of the woods where two of his friends are waiting. It appears he is part of a trio, and they decided to seek revenge on Charlie.

Immediately Chaplin establishes the fact that while Charlie the tramp is good and noble, despite his strata in life, the other tramps are more victimizer than victim. Chaplin does not point out that the other tramps are also victims of societal circumstances that force them into a life of petty thievery. These are bad people. Charlie is a good person. All are tramps.

Edna is approached by another, taller member of the bad tramps, and he is conked on the head, in like fashion, by Charlie. Finally, the biggest of the group (Bud Jamison) decides to exact revenge, while Charlie walks off happily with Edna. Bud is no match for the now-confident fighter Charlie has become, however. Without the use of his brick-filled sack, Charlie jumps up and drop-kicks Bud, who makes a hasty retreat. In his hurry he bangs into his comrades and all go falling into a nearby river. Charlie, the noble tramp, the honest one, remains triumphant over the unsavory examples.

A grateful Edna brings him home, where he is given food and put to work by her equally grateful father. Here is where Chaplin the comedian's comic ingenuity gets a real workout. The farm setting is good for slapstick comedy. It begins with Charlie continually poking the other farm hand with a pitchfork. The farm hand turns the pitchfork around in Charlie's hands, but soon Charlie bumps him in the eye, knocking off his hat.

3. The Essanay Films

The farm hand again turns the fork around in Charlie's hands, bends over to pick up his hat, and is once again poked in the backside.

While this is the sort of uproarious slapstick that resulted in gales of laughter coming from every neighborhood theater, we can now, through more careful scrutiny, see a real method to the madness. Knockabout slapstick in the Keystone tradition is as much about the rhythm and execution as it is about the superficial amusement of the proceedings. But at Essanay, there is also the element of character. Charlie is not so much

Charlie and Paddy McGuire as farm hands in *The Tramp*.

deliberately poking the farm hand out of malice — it is mostly accidental. He is, at first, doing what he believes is the equivalent of tapping his shoulder to get his attention. He is completely clueless as to farm work and what to do with its tools. When the pitchfork is turned around, he hurriedly follows the farm hand, who abruptly stops and turns, therefore causing Charlie to bump him in the eye with the blunt end of the implement. It is turned around again, and as the farm hand picks up his hat, one final jab results from Charlie simply not paying enough attention to what he is holding onto. The timing of this scene is brilliant.

In his biography *Charlie Chaplin*, John McCabe stated:

> Charlie's infinite ease in doing everything, simply everything, is literally marvelous. When Charlie does these things they are not done as a stunt. Charlie does not "pull" the gag or "do" the gag; he *is* the gag.

Charlie goes into the hen house and emerges with two eggs. Both he and the farm hand react to the stench of rotten eggs, and blame it on the chickens. They want to get rid of them, and decide that the best place is in the booklet of a nearby pastoral poet, who stands reciting about the beauty of his surroundings.

The film maintains its rhythm, and the slapstick inspiration continues. Large, heavy sacks are carried down a ladder and dropped on the farmer standing below. Charlie waters rows of fruit trees with a paltry hand sprinkler, gently and ineffectively wetting the trunk of each. He then tries to milk a stubborn cow (after first approaching a bull and quickly realizing his error). With no idea as to the process of obtaining milk from a cow, he puts the bucket under the udders and cranks the animal's tail like a pump. These sequences are funny, beautifully performed and feature Chaplin the comedian at his most inventive. But through the humorous sequences there are brief stops to show a blossoming friendship with Edna. While Edna is graciously friendly, Charlie is quite obviously smitten with her natural beauty and charm. Without allowing the disparate elements of drama and comedy to clash, Chaplin the filmmaker neatly blends the inspired slapstick with gentle touches of romance. These sequences season the film perfectly and never appear obtrusive.

The trio of crooks from the woods have followed Edna and Charlie.

3. The Essanay Films

Sneaking into the house, they see her father in his kitchen counting a substantial amount of money. They run into Charlie and approach him as a downtrodden comrade. They want his help in stealing the money from Edna's father, and offer to split the cash with him. Charlie agrees to help them, while obviously thinking of a way to thwart their intentions.

Inside the house Charlie lights a candle while standing too close to Edna's father, who is reading a newspaper. The newspaper goes up in flames. When he and the farm hand retire to their room, he helps the farm hand remove his stubborn shoes by placing his own foot on the farm hand's face and pulling. As the farm hand removes his sock, Charlie quickly opens a window.

It is nightfall, and the farm hand goes to sleep. Charlie finds a mallet and waits by the window for the crooks, whom he plans to attack as they enter the house. He first bops the sleeping farm hand, just to make sure he stays asleep.

Edna's father wanders outside quite casually and notices the ladder going up to Charlie's room. Curious, he climbs up the ladder and, of course, is bopped by Charlie's mallet. The father dazedly goes down the ladder, and Charlie decides to wake the farm hand to help with the incoming crooks. The father comes upstairs, sees the farm hand with the mallet, and blames him.

Finally the crooks arrive. Charlie takes off after them. During the fracas, which includes gunfire, Charlie is shot and injured. He is nursed back to health by Edna, who pampers him until his complete recovery, and his affection for her increases. Finally, as Charlie is almost fully recovered, Edna's boyfriend comes calling. Realizing he has no opportunity with Edna, he decides to move on. Charlie writes a farewell note and is on his way.

The final shot is the now iconic image of Charlie walking down the dirt road on which he had arrived. Only this time he is sadly going in the other direction. After a few steps, he suddenly shakes himself off and changes his stride to a more jaunty gait, confidently prepared for whatever misadventure comes his way.

Enhancing this final sequence is the impressive way Chaplin handled the scene in which Edna picks up and reads Charlie's farewell note. She has no real time to respond. Chaplin the filmmaker does not choose for her to segue into melodramatics. She looks at the note, looks up from it, and then Chaplin the director immediately cuts to the Tramp walking away down the familiar path upon which he arrived. The sequence is edited perfectly. Any other way, even a hold on Edna's face that was only seconds longer, would have been less effective.

As indicated, *The Tramp* has always been lauded as a true milestone in Chaplin's career, other studies commenting on this film as if it was a sudden change from Keystone slapstick to a dramatic structure with pathos and a moving finale. Chaplin does employ pathos here, which is significant, but much of *The Tramp* offers more boisterous slapstick than *A Jitney Elopement*.

Curiously, a review in the April 28, 1915, issue of *The New York Dramatic Mirror* was fine with the rough-edged comedy, but less impressed with the pathos:

> You would really be surprised to see how much fun Charles Chaplin gets out of a brick, or a pitchfork, or whatever he takes up. And later, when he is sent out to milk the cow and, by mistake, meets the bull, as in the old yarn, the house rocks with laughter. Certainly the work of Charles Chaplin has never been any funnier than here, and that is saying as much as is, within the circumstances, possible. One laughs at the other characters, but only when they are being knocked down, or when he plays some trick on them. He is represented as a tramp, and in helping save the farmer's daughter, earns the gratitude of the farmer who puts him to work. This allows the whole range of fun he may create in trying to reconcile himself to his new and distasteful environment. The very end is rather dramatic, in comparison, and falls flat by reason of its contrast with the tempo of what had preceded. Also, the photography at times might have been clearer, and there were instances where working closer to the camera would have brought the comedy of his expressions out better.

Most reviewers, however, were impressed with Chaplin's dramatic seasoning. In the July 7, 1915, issue of the same periodical, another writer states:

> It is the little touches that [Chaplin] shows at his best. Take, for illustration, the opening of *The Champion* where Charlie sits eating his grub and confabulating with his faithful dog. There is

3. The Essanay Films

no acceleration of action here; it is almost wholly a matter of physiognomy. This is Mr. Chaplin and the movie farce at their best. So, also, is the finale of *The Tramp*, than which, as a whole, a more fatuously sentimental farce-melodrama can hardly be imagined: here, Charlie is shown wearily trudging away from us up a long hilly dusty road; he has been disappointed in love, poor chap, and his every step speaks of the bitterness of his sorrow. Then, suddenly, there is a carefree shrug of the shoulders, and the old familiar gait is once again his own. But a "moving" episode like this must be seen to be appreciated.

Another of the many innovations seen in *The Tramp* is the way Chaplin incorporates the pathos. It is merely the framework to bracket the comedy. He introduces Charlie as the ultimate victim, not only of poverty and the elements, but of his fellow tramps as well. He is almost immediately shown as honest and noble in his rescuing of Edna. He is then presented as willing to work rather than steal.

The subsequent body of the film is slapstick, and rather rough slapstick at that. But it is some of the most inventive slapstick that cinematic comedy could boast by 1915. And its pacing, its rhythm, and Chaplin's performance all enhance its inventiveness. Slapstick can be, and often was, elevated to an art form. Chaplin perfected its presentation, so that in *The Tramp* it is not only riotously funny, but impressively executed. When approaching the Chaplin cinematic canon in retrospect, the brilliance of his inspired comedy's execution should be of little surprise to anyone who has even marginal knowledge of his working methods.

Stan Laurel told John McCabe for his book *Charlie Chaplin*:

> Leo White, a friend of mine, worked on *The Tramp*. He said they repeated some gags until the actors felt that if they did it one more time they'd blow their corks. He said the business of the crooks going up the ladder was done so many times and in so many variations that they just couldn't tell what the hell the fuss was about. But they were wrong. That's just what made Charlie a great creator of comedy. He knew that sometimes you *have* to do a thing fifty times in slightly different ways until you get the very best. The difference between Charlie and all the rest of us who made comedy — with one exception, Buster Keaton — was that he absolutely refused to do anything but the best. To get the best he worked harder than anyone I know.

The Tramp has great definition in its character. David Robinson, in his book *Charlie Chaplin: His Life and Art*, stated: "Made in only ten days, this remarkable film shows a staggering leap forward in its sense of structure, narrative skill, use of location, and emotional range. Charlie is now clearly defined as the tramp."

The Tramp is not the cinematic equivalent of an oasis in the desert. It stands out for several reasons, but not because it is far and away the greatest film of Chaplin's career, or even of Chaplin's Essanay tenure. What the film indeed is, and what it remains, is a perfect career checkpoint in the Chaplin filmography. The flashes of brilliance in his often exceptional Keystone productions, his gradual refinement within the evolution of his Essanay comedies, and the experimentation that became especially evident in the films immediately leading up to it, make *The Tramp* a good stopping point for career assessment.

Chaplin was learning that the cinematic process benefited from his taking a great deal of time, shooting a tremendous amount of takes, and pragmatically approaching his work. The actors would balk at the numerous takes (as per the earlier Stan Laurel quote), but Chaplin's vision was clear, and he examined every nuance of every sequence to bring it in line with that vision.

The Tramp benefits from this especially, and it appears to have been a creatively, physically, and emotionally draining experience for its creator and star. Chaplin not only performed in the title role, he supervised the performance of each character with even more precision than in his previous films. There was more to *The Tramp* than there had been with *A Jitney Elopement*. For *The Tramp* also had long, inventive slapstick sequences that took advantage of setting, props, and characters equally. They had to play just right to fit comfortably within the brackets of a more serious story, especially since Charlie was at the forefront of each.

It is the ending of *The Tramp* that has enjoyed the most discussion. According to Ted Okuda and David Maska, in their book *Charlie Chaplin at Keystone and Essanay*: "The entire sequence is positively heart wrenching, and Chaplin performs it with stunning sincerity." The authors also note that Edna's presence serves to enhance the pathos of the final scene, and conclude by stating: "At any rate, *The Tramp* establishes the motif of Charlie wandering into the lives of certain people, then, at the end, wandering off alone, a theme that recurs in *Police*..."

3. The Essanay Films

Gerald D. McDonald, Michael Conway, and Mark Ricci stated in their book *The Films of Charlie Chaplin*:

> We most often think of Charlie was the one who loses, as the one whose hopes must go down in defeat. Charlie first showed us this side of his nature, and his destiny, in *The Tramp*.... This was the best picture he had made since entering the movies.

With all he had put into *The Tramp*, it appears Chaplin felt himself in need of a break. Just as the time and effort he put into *The Champion* led to a backup in the production schedule and resulted in his hastily making a one-reeler, this same situation presented itself after *The Tramp*. However, the one-reel film that followed *The Champion* (*In the Park*) was filled with ideas that were interesting and enlightening in our study of Chaplin's Essanay period. The one-reeler made after *The Tramp* (*By the Sea*) was interesting in another way. Unlike *In the Park*, which showed Chaplin perfecting and refining established ideas and setting the bar a bit higher for future efforts, *By the Sea* tried a few new things within its one-reel running time. It was something of a stepping stone for the remainder of Chaplin's Essanay tenure, and the final one-reel film he would make.

The Tramp is also the last film Chaplin shot at Niles, a suburb of San Francisco. He discovered that he needed new studio space for his work, and a search for new quarters was on. He made his next film on location at Crystal Pier, and another at the Bradbury Mansion in San Francisco (a location used often for Essanay productions), but would then move his production company into a new studio setting in Los Angeles. He would finish out his Essanay contract at the Los Angeles studios, creating his films without interference and continuing to build on the ideas and innovations found in *The Tramp*.

This is really another turning point in Chaplin's career, especially at this transitional stage. Chaplin's filmography has its share of checkpoints, where one must stop and examine the film and those that have gone before. With *The Tramp* we reach a checkpoint for assessment that allows one a proper appreciation for Chaplin and his work. We have already discussed those films that lead up to *The Tramp*, and will now see that all his subsequent films were based on the format Chaplin had now established as most effective. *The Tramp* is not only one of Chaplin's best films, it is one of the most important, pivotal movies in motion picture history.

By the Sea
Cast

Charles Chaplin	Tramp
Billy Armstrong	Husband
Margie Reiger	Wife
Edna Purviance	Girl
Bud Jamison	Jealous Boyfriend
Harry "Snub" Pollard	Ice Cream Vendor
Ed Armstrong	Tobacconist
Ernest Van Pelt	Policeman
Paddy McQuire	Policeman

Credits

Charles Chaplin	Director, Screenwriter
Harry Ensign	Cinematographer
Ernest Van Pelt	Assistant Director
Jess Robbins	Producer

Shot at Crystal Pier in Santa Monica, California. Released April 29, 1915. One Reel.

Charlie Chaplin's final one-reeler (except for *The Bond,* a World War I fundraiser he would appear in later on) is a largely improvisational, gag-filled slapstick comedy shot on location at Crystal Pier in Los Angeles. Once again we come to the argument that a one-reel subject is somewhat less effective than a longer film, that its brevity precludes any ability to offer a proper amount of creativity. And, as with the previously discussed *In the Park*, such an assessment of the one-reeler is wrong. Chaplin uses the beach and the boardwalk as his setting for character conflict and slapstick gags, and it is one of the most inspired comedies of his career.

It is easy to dismiss a film like *By the Sea* as merely a gag-filled one-reel aberration, just as one could approach *In the Park* with the same expectation. An assessment of *In the Park* has already determined that there is far more to its conception and presentation than a one-reel excursion hastily assembled to make up for lost time spent on *The Champion*. And the same

3. The Essanay Films

can be said for *By the Sea*, which was reduced to one reel due to the time and effort spent on producing *The Tramp*.

Chaplin did not hastily throw films together. Decreased production time may have simply resulted in a shorter movie, half the length of the previous one, but this does not mean the film was a rush job that proceeded with lessened creative thought. Chaplin limiting himself to a one-reel running time did not allow much in the way of dramatic plotting, but the depth and substance that emerged naturally from his character was always evident in the gag sequences. And Chaplin continues to do a great deal with character, especially his choices for burly Bud Jamison, whose placement in the frame and facial expressions perfectly enhance the situations in which he is directly involved.

By the Sea was shot on location on a windy day at the Crystal Pier beach, and Chaplin makes the most of this setting and the elements. The beach, the boardwalk, and the strong winds are all incorporated effectively. There is no real plot, just a series of characters who find themselves in each other's company, engage in conflict, and move on. Within the course of this setup, Chaplin gives us some of his funniest and most creative comedy, further presenting his development as a comedian and filmmaker during this quintessential period in his cinematic career.

The film opens with a couple (Billy Armstrong and Margie Reiger) at the beach on a windy day. Margie leaves the area, and Billy waits for her. The location filming is immediately noticeable, and a nice pale backdrop to the opening of the man and woman bickering.

We cut to Charlie's entrance. He is walking up the street in the beach area and eating a banana. At this point in Chaplin's career the anticipation of Charlie happening upon any situation is one for celebration. We know he is going to create a disruption. We know it is going to be funny. For some time, his very entrance would net applause in the theaters where his films were shown. Chaplin realized this, and had been staging Charlie's entrances accordingly. For his entrance in *By the Sea*, Chaplin shows Charlie waddling up the seaside street, with the banana as an amusing prop. It works, as eating a banana is somehow more amusing than an apple or pear. Chaplin emphasizes this choice by having Charlie casually toss the banana peel away and then immediately slip on it himself.

Charlie soon walks up to where Billy is standing. The blowing wind causes their hats to blow off. The elastic strings attached to their hats are very noticeable, and Chaplin makes them a part of the gag, allowing them to become entangled. The hat battle soon escalates into a fight between Charlie and Billy that is both frantic and hilarious. Fighting on the sand allows for some delightfully spectacular pratfalls, including tumbles over park benches. At one point there is a close-up of Charlie looking at Billy and indicating he's crazy by circling his finger around his temple. Billy wants to continue the battle. Charlie tricks him into looking down, then puts him in a headlock and starts pummeling him with all the gusto of a modern day pro wrestler. He then picks at the dazed Billy's hair, and several fleas jump onto Charlie's arms. Chaplin then performs a precursor to the flea circus routine seen in his much later talking feature *Limelight* (1952).

At this point in *By the Sea* Chaplin has worked out a discernible rhythm for the slapstick brawl between Charlie and Billy. This battle is abruptly interrupted by a cutaway to big Bud Jamison waiting impatiently on a nearby park bench. Chaplin enjoyed using the heavies in his pictures for comic effect. A guy like Bud Jamison (or Mack Swain, or Eric Campbell) was an imposing presence, especially when surrounded by comparatively diminutive characters like Chaplin, et. al. Bud could be, and had been, effectively used as the big, overbearing threat, or the incongruous pansy. Here he is merely the snarling, impatient boyfriend of sweet Edna, who is keeping him waiting because she has just noticed Charlie.

As Chaplin cuts back to the beach, Edna comes by and reacts to his crude antics, but somehow finds him endearing in spite of them. Charlie flirts vigorously and humorously, with Edna becoming more and more attracted to Charlie as he continues his silly flirting. Billy staggers up, still ready to fight. Charlie tells Edna to look away, and he shoves Billy out of the frame.

Throughout this scene Chaplin periodically cuts away to a still-waiting, still-fuming Bud Jamison. Bud is big and pretentious in his top hat and ill-fitting suit. He also has romantic intentions towards Edna, but appears more ridiculous and less endearing than Charlie. Meanwhile, Billy and Charlie are still battling when a third party comes along. They team up and accost him, and then decide to be pals. Thereafter, every time Charlie and Billy accidentally bump or poke one another they immediately and vigorously shake hands. It is all so simple, so charming, and yet so brilliantly done and so wildly hilarious.

3. The Essanay Films

Billy and Charlie get ice cream cones, but neither has money. While they argue over who is going to pay, each keeps eating his ice cream cone. This evolves into an argument. It builds slowly and gradually until the point where they start splattering ice cream in each other's faces. Soon they're back to where they had previously burns.

A thrown cone hits Bud, and he joins the fracas. He steps up just as Charlie holds Billy in a backwards headlock, kicking him in the face. When the intimidating Bud enters the fray, Charlie escapes to leave Billy and Bud to fight. The timing of this entire sequence is quick and beautiful, with each missed shot, each pivot, and every twist and twirl choreographed with incredible precision. The laughs are there, but often one's reaction to viewing this sequence is slack-jawed astonishment. One cannot help being awestruck by the marvelous technique.

A cop breaks up the fracas and takes Billy away. Bud discovers Charlie flirting with Edna and chases him away. Charlie then approaches Margie, who is searching for the missing Billy. When all of the characters meet up, Charlie tips over a park bench and makes his getaway, once again leaving the tumult he has caused by casually infiltrating the lives of others.

It can be argued that the ending to *By the Sea* is rather abrupt. But this abruptness is, in fact, effective. Charlie is a wanderer, one who makes trouble even if it is not purposeful, and we enjoy his audacity, his ability to get himself in and out of situations. He is a more attractive mate for Edna than the burly Bud Jamison, and also a better choice for Margie than the repugnant Billy. Charlie handily dances his way through the humdrum lives of these people, adds a bit of subversive excitement to their day at the beach, and then disappears.

Chaplin does a brilliant job with the characters in *By the Sea*, highlighting what was to become a hallmark of his evolution as a filmmaker. Billy Armstrong is the bothersome scamp that Chester Conklin or Paddy McGuire had been in other films. Edna is again the sweet object of his desire. Bud Jamison is a wonderfully effective heavy, used perfectly as part of the ensemble. Bud's performance is outstanding, as he conveys just the attitude that works within the grouping of characters. Jamison would only work with Chaplin at Essanay, but he would continue to impress for the remainder of his career, especially as the frequent nemesis for the Three

Stooges in many of their Columbia Pictures comedies. Chaplin uses him most effectively, and it is likely that Bud learned an immeasurable amount from this experience, developing insights that would serve him well as his career continued well into the talking picture era.

As has been indicated, films like *By the Sea* are often assessed unfairly. Those engaged in film analysis frequently dismiss a gag-oriented comedy as having less depth than something like *The Champion* or *The Tramp*, both of which use dramatic elements as well as comedy. Chaplin's ability to create a one-reel comedy like *By the Sea* with such brilliance is what makes this overlooked film appear so formidable in context. Like its fellow Essanay one-reeler *In the Park*, *By the Sea* is a very funny and very effective comedy that continues to establish Chaplin's evolution as a comedian and filmmaker.

At this point in Chaplin's career his Essanay development was easily discerned. The experiments of his first two films, the strides made in *The Champion* and the milestone that is *The Tramp* were further augmented by both *In the Park* and *By the Sea*. It is not so much that these are one-reelers made necessarily shorter due to scheduling needs; it is what Chaplin was able to do within the one-reel context that is significant.

By the Sea is a one-reel gag-filled comedy. The gags are creative and inspired. The performances are uninhibited and committed. The pacing is fast and maintains a solid rhythm. That its running time does not permit the dramatic element Chaplin was blending with his comedy does not make *By the Sea* automatically a lesser film. Chaplin was first and foremost a master comedian, and how he took his stage-trained comedy to the screen is one of the keys to his genius. He honed his comedy with each ensuing film, especially at a studio that allowed more time to experiment.

Along with character, another of the interesting aspects of *By the Sea* is how Chaplin uses the beach setting — the way his characters respond to a location different from the norm. Chaplin did not close down the beach while filming, as we see other people, even dogs, in the background. They are minding their business, seemingly unaware that a film company is shooting a slapstick comedy several yards away. As a backdrop to the slapstick gags, the casual beachgoers serve as an enhancement for the wild rhythm of the action. Since they take place on soft sand, pratfalls can be even more daring.

3. The Essanay Films

As with *In the Park*, everything occurs within several yards, either on the beach or the boardwalk. Chaplin happens along, disrupts two couples on their day at the beach, extends this to vendors, and leaves when the disruption peaks.

The frequent critical dismissal of Chaplin's Essanay one-reelers overlooks the fact that comedy, which is compact, which relies on gag situations, and which uses various characters effectively, is, in fact, an art unto itself. Chaplin elevated knockabout slapstick to the level of art as early as his Keystone tenure. Lavishing greater care on his Essanay productions, Chaplin was able to maintain what made him great at Keystone and present it in an even better one-reel comedy, as evidenced by both his Essanay single-reel films. Without exploring characters in great detail, Chaplin assembled various types and allows for their interaction, with humorous results. And throughout the situations the gags are creative, carefully placed, and beautifully performed. The supporting cast, all seasoned veterans, responded to Chaplin's exacting method of direction, resulting in a wonderfully funny comedy. When Chaplin made films that had no pretensions beyond generating laughter, the results were every bit as rewarding as those films where dramatic elements were explored. One can only assume that those who approach Chaplin films without enthusiasm for his essential Essanay comedies, including those of one-reel length, are perhaps limited to enjoying to his later feature-length productions. Certainly one cannot get as much into a one-reeler (or two-reeler, or three-reeler) as in a feature picture. But Chaplin's features are only as good as his best short films. He was a comedian first, and his comedy could be brilliant at any length, even as short as one reel (or, if we harken back to his second Keystone, even a split reel!). Chaplin would extend the gag-oriented comedy to a full two reels with his next film, and it would result in yet another of the finest films of his career.

Work

Cast

Charles Chaplin . . . . Charlie, the Paperhanger's Assistant
Edna Purviance . . . . Maid
Charles Inslee . . . . Boss Paperhanger

Chaplin at Essanay

Marta Golden .... Wife
Billy Armstrong .... Husband
Leo White .... Lover

Credits

Charles Chaplin .... Director, Screenwriter
Harry Ensign .... Cinematographer
Ernest Van Pelt .... Assistant Director
Jess Robbins .... Producer

Filmed at the Bradbury Mansion in San Francisco, California. Released June 21, 1915. Two Reels.

While Chaplin's brilliance extends beyond merely performing gags, he was primarily a comedian — perhaps the greatest one in motion picture history. Thus, when a film is brilliant because of its humor, when it is perhaps the Chaplin short with the greatest laugh content up to this time, it stands out as a classic in the same sense as the more subtle *A Jitney Elopement* or the more dramatic *The Tramp*. It is perhaps not quite the milestone that is *The Tramp*, and not the same sort of checkpoint for career assessment, but *Work* is still a magnificent Chaplin film filled with comic invention and ideas, further demonstrating the significance of his Essanay output.

Chaplin's level of performance sophistication and his ability to place his actors in the frame was already evident by the time he filmed *Work*. Chaplin again concentrates on how parallel situations among groups of actors can combine to create a discernible energy, punctuated by slapstick gags. He also shows a flair for interesting visuals, especially in the oft-discussed opening shot.

Biographer David Robinson has singled out this opening sequence as rivaling the filmmaking level of D.W. Griffith's *Birth of a Nation*, released that same year:

> It is the introduction to this delirium of destruction that makes the film most memorable. Our first sight of Charlie is as he advances towards the camera down a busy city street, harnessed to a cart piled high with ladders, boards, and buckets. The boss sits on the driver's seat, flicking at him with a whip. The cart gets stuck on the tram lines: Charlie drags it clear in the nick of time. He attempts a hill, but the cart again slides back into the path of an oncoming tram. In silhouette, we see Charlie hauling the cart

3. The Essanay Films

up the side of a 45 degree incline. The weight of the cart raises the shaft in front, with poor Charlie dangling helplessly in the air. The boss thoughtfully offers a heavyweight friend a lift, and Charlie must now drag the two of them. He disappears down an open manhole, but is hauled back, hanging onto the shafts and counterweighted by the cart. It is a series of haunting, grotesque, horror-comedy images of slavery, with a degree of audacity and invention in the visualization that was hardly to be challenged until the Soviet avant-garde a decade later.

To show diminutive Charlie pulling a large wagon filled with debris and his overfed boss, Chaplin chooses a long shot, careful to get all of the imagery in the frame. It may seem commonplace in these more enlightened times, but during cinema's infancy such an idea was impressive. The backdrop of the other traffic, moving swiftly behind this large, lumbering wagon, adds greater depth to the shot. Charlie is the ultimate proletariat worker, made to represent mule-like service in a blue collar job. His employer is completely without sympathy, even to the point of picking up a passenger on the way to their destination.

Charlie and his boss are set to redecorate the house of an upper-class couple. The home is occupied by an impatient man (Billy Armstrong), his haughty wife (Marta Golden), and an attractive and well-meaning servant girl (Edna Purviance). The man of the house is harried about every marginal inconvenience, while the neglected wife is having an affair with another man (once again played by the delightfully hammy Leo White), who shows up unexpectedly and must hastily pose as one of the paperhangers. Meanwhile, the servant tries to avoid the tumult and go about her business, despite the advances of well-meaning Charlie.

Class systems are evident in the sequence where the woman, suspiciously eyeing the paperhangers, carefully locks her valuables. Charlie and his boss, no less suspicious of the haughty woman, put their own watches and meager coins together and carefully safety-pin their pooled belongings into Charlie's front right pants pocket. It is a wonderfully clever dig at class distinctions. Chaplin would later make veiled political statements more regularly, but in *Work* he is merely creating a clever gag out of the pretensions of rich homeowners.

The act of paperhanging is a very easy setup for slapstick gags. It is immediately messy and requires both balance and proper placement. Chap-

Charlie gets in the way of his employer (Charles Inslee) in *Work*.

lin, who had performed similar paperhanging sketches on stage in the Karno Music Hall troupe, reached back into his past for some of the gags, but also felt inspired by his cinematic surroundings. Essanay prop men were, in fact, instructed by Chaplin to round up as many different tools as possible. Chaplin did not know what he would do with them, nor whether he would use all of the materials he was presented, but he wanted

3. The Essanay Films

the props as creative inspiration. Some of them indeed inspired new ideas, while others reminded him of gags he had done in Karno sketches. Chaplin actually had little mapped out ahead of time, and filmed *Work* with only the sketchiest of ideas as to what he wanted on film. Hence, the project evolved constantly during shooting.

According to John McCabe, in his biography *Charlie Chaplin*:

> The film, like its Karno source, has for its best moments Charlie and his boss trying to paper the house and each other with thick white paste. This is all highly predictable and immensely funny in spite of it. The things making the predictable funny are two — Charlie's attitude and his overwhelming mimetic virtuosity. These two elements were cardinal to his work. This double compound, as exemplified in *Work*, creates outside laughter of a kind not heard in film theaters before or since.
>
> In addition to attitude, Charlie's infinite ease in doing everything, simply everything, is literally marvelous. When Charlie does these things they are not done as a stunt. Charlie does not "pull" the gag or "do" the gag; he *is* the gag. And the gags are mostly very old stuff.

In his book *The Comic Mind*, Gerald Mast describes one particularly inspired sequence:

> In the rich lady's house, Charlie notices a plaster statuette of a woman. He tips his hat to her. What else do you do to a lady? He eyes her. She is "artistically" bare. So he takes a lampshade and delicately hangs it over her bottom half. Charlie stares at this now proper plaster lady, then he pushes the lampshade and we suddenly see it turn into a hula skirt; the plaster figurine, as if by magic, dances the hula (better yet, the "hootchy kootchy"). Then Charlie's curiosity gets the best of him; he lifts the lampshade-skirt, which he himself added, to peek at the lady-figurine's forbidden parts. In this action, Chaplin endows an inanimate object with life; he miraculously raises the dead and converts the corpse into the most wayward of women; and he confers sex appeal on the sexless. There is magic in this metamorphosis, indeed.

Charlie's response to Edna plays off of their already established cinematic chemistry, which had been clearly evident, especially after *A Jitney Elopement*. Subtleties, such as the way the two look at each other, convey

Chaplin at Essanay

Edna and Charlie only have eyes for each other in *Work*.

a real romantic spark that comes through even ninety-some years after production. The real-life affection between Chaplin and Purviance likely played some role in the effect, but within its context the relationship is very successfully presented here.

The wife's dalliance with another, and his inopportune appearance, allows Chaplin to direct conflicting situations among his characters, something he was doing in the past few Essanay productions with steadily increasingly results. Chaplin liked to pace his actors so that a discernible rhythm was evident in the near-misses and awkward situations, which he did to great effect in *Work* when the homeowner chases his wife's lover throughout the house. Not being the catalyst for the situation, Charlie is this time one of the innocent people caught up within it. It is an interesting attempt to place Charlie somewhere other than the center of the trouble, and is no less effective.

3. The Essanay Films

Work runs two reels, but has the same sort of energy as *By the Sea*, the compact one-reeler immediately preceding this effort. With the extra reel, *Work* has more time to establish characters and maintain its comic rhythm. And while *By the Sea* is a marvel for successfully presenting a myriad of situations and characters within the limitations of a one-reel format, *Work* makes full use of its longer running time to add layers to the gag situations, even if the characters remain caricatures.

Chaplin observes the class system as basically corrupt and full of mistrust. But he does not exhibit any real malice in his presentation. His caricatures are enhanced for our amusement, and the stereotypes are recognizable and accepted.

The pace of *Work* is very brisk, but still offers a sense of artistic control that would separate it from the more free-form Keystone productions. Chaplin was learning the rudiments of filmmaking as he made movies, exploring as he accomplished. With a film like *Work* his presentation and his performance are matched only by his keen direction of the supporting players. With confused identities, attempts to mislead, and clandestine meetings going on throughout the massive house, Charlie's worker infiltrates this collection of confusion in the same way he intruded onto the situations taking place in parks or on beachfronts in previous films. The ending, an explosion that results in Charlie emerging from a destroyed oven and smiling, has been called "awfully contrived" by Ted Okuda and Dave Maska in their book *Charlie Chaplin at Keystone and Essanay*, but this writer finds it a rather fitting culmination. Each element in *Work* is a special ingredient, the combination of which results in one of the most remarkable films in Chaplin's career.

Work was shot at the Bradbury Mansion in San Francisco, which Essanay frequently used. The house faced 147 North Hill Street, with a side entrance at 406 Court Street that led to offices. An open air stage occupied the back yard. This area was concurrently being used by a young producer named Hal Roach, who, in the 1920s, would become one of the most important comedy film producers, with productions featuring Harold Lloyd, Charley Chase, Laurel and Hardy, and Our Gang. Roach had been hired by Jess Robbins to direct one-reel comedies with actors in Chaplin's stock company who were currently not working. Filming such players as Margie Rieger, Bud Jamison, and James T. Kelly, all of whom figured prominently in most of Chaplin's Essanay films, Roach produced a one-reel comedy for Essanay each week.

During the production of *Work*, Chaplin sent Spoor and Anderson a telegram requesting a two-week vacation. The demand for Chaplin films was at its absolute peak, so neither Spoor nor Anderson were interested in their biggest star being away from production for what at that time seemed quite a long period. They discovered that Chaplin wanted to travel to New York and appear live at Madison Square Garden. Chaplin had been contacted by I. Presburg, manager of the Arena Amusement Company, who asked that the comedian appear fifteen minutes in the afternoon and fifteen minutes at night over a two-week period, for a fee of $1,250 per week. Madison Square Garden had apparently put in a massive projection system and wanted Chaplin to help fill its 13,000 seats with a personal appearance. Chaplin was interested, and his Essanay contract allowed it.

In order to keep their star at home and working, Spoor and Anderson not only gave Chaplin the $25,000 he would have received for the engagement, but also a new contract calling for him to receive a $10,000 bonus (on top of his $1,250-per-week salary) for each film he completed. The films would be produced between June 1, 1915, and January 1, 1916. The new deal included *Work*, which was the film he was working on at the time.

There is an interesting side note regarding *Work*. According to the Internet Movie Database, in September of 2001 a Chaplin program was scheduled at the New York Historical Society. In the wake of the terrorist attacks at the World Trade Center, however, this film, and one other, the Keystone production *Dough and Dynamite* (1914), were pulled from the program because each one ends with Charlie emerging from the rubble of a destroyed building.

Work is another solid example of how straight comedy with no pathos or attempts to explore dramatic elements of a character can be every bit as artistic and rewarding as those films with headier elements. The film's sense of timing, location of characters and objects within the frame, and precision of movement all serve to elevate *Work* to a most lofty status among Chaplin films. Other factors, including how the comedy sequence settles into the backdrop provided by the film's setting, how reaction shots are handled, and the level at which editing plays a part in the success of the gag,

3. The Essanay Films

also to the picture's overall effectiveness. Chaplin's filmmaking expertise was in how to present broad comedy for the intimate movie camera, and too often a film like *Work* is summarily dismissed (as are the aforementioned one-reel subjects) because the viewer believes the dramatic elements found in *The Tramp* and later films (like Mutual's *The Vagabond*, First National's *A Dog's Life*, or the features *The Kid* and *City Lights*) offer a more fulfilling experience. *Work* is certainly every bit as magnificent a subject as any Chaplin classic because of its complete concentration on comedy, and not in spite of it. Chaplin continued to experiment, to challenge comedy, and to offer wonderful examples of his comic creativity with his next film.

A Woman

Cast

Charles Chaplin	Charlie
Edna Purviance	Daughter
Charles Inslee	Father
Marta Golden	Mother
Margie Reiger	Girl in Park
Billy Armstrong	Father's Friend
Leo White	Dandy in Park
Jess Robbins	Soft Drink Salesman

Credits

Charles Chaplin	Director, Screenwriter
Harry Ensign	Cinematographer
Ernest Van Pelt	Assistant Director
Jess Robbins	Producer

Filmed in Los Angeles, California. Released July 12, 1915. Two Reels.

Men masquerading as women for comic effect is as old as the legitimate theater, originating with the ancient Greeks and Romans. Of course, in the days of Shakespeare, when women were not even allowed to attend a play, males played female roles (causing no small measure of confusion with a production such as *As You Like It*, which would feature a man playing a woman masquerading as a man).

Chaplin himself had done such a burlesque on two occasions at Keystone in 1914, including his split-reel comedy *A Busy Day* and the later one-reeler *The Masquerader*. *A Woman* would be Chaplin's final venture into dame masquerade, and is another Essanay two-reeler attempting to improve upon older ideas that Chaplin felt needed repeating and refining.

It could perhaps be argued that *A Woman* more closely follows a Keystone pattern than any of Chaplin's other Essanay productions that attempted to hone what he'd learn with Sennett. In fact, Ted Okuda and Dave Maska, in their book *Chaplin at Keystone and Essanay*, make just such a claim.

Chaplin continued his concentration on comedy stemming directly from characters and situations, as he'd been doing in his most recent Essanay productions. With each new film, one can clearly see how Chaplin was evolving this style by trying new ideas and situations in which the various characters play off one another. He approaches *A Woman* in the same fashion, choreographing characters and situations; but this time he concentrates more on character than situations. He allows established Keystonesque caricatures to propel the situations more specifically.

A Woman opens with a camera pan showing a family sitting on a park bench. In close-up, Chaplin reveals a grumpy, scowling father; his passive wife, who is sound asleep; and his long-suffering daughter. This quick pan establishes the characters immediately, and Chaplin waits only a couple of beats before having an attractive woman pass, immediately attracting the father's attention. Now all smiles, the man joins the woman on another park bench and offers to go get her a drink. Just then Charlie wanders by, sees the woman sitting alone, and does a bit of flirting himself. The fickle woman enjoys the attention and responds with smiles, but when Charlie gets up to leave, he accidentally hooks her ankle with his cane and pulls her off the bench. Sitting her back down, he is confronted by the returning father, who breaks a pop bottle over Charlie's head. The father and the woman wander off, the man insisting the woman feel his flexed bicep, while Charlie lies dazed at the bench.

Two foppish, top-hatted sorts come to sit on the bench with Charlie, who diverts their attention, drinks out of a soda bottle one is holding, and ends up in a melee. Charlie walks away and confronts the father once again, who is now blindfolded and in the midst of a hide-and-seek activity. Charlie drags him by the neck with his cane, bringing him to the lake. Testing the water to make sure it is deep enough — and chilly

3. The Essanay Films

enough — Charlie finds just the right spot to shove the man into the drink. A police officer comes by and Charlie flips him into the water, tipping his hat as he wanders away.

These opening moments do a superb job of establishing the rhythm that Chaplin had been using since arriving at Essanay. And while the Keystone setting is quite evident, Chaplin's presentation here is even more refined than in his most recent ventures. The conflicts build gradually to a finish, they do not immediately erupt into wild punches and kicks. The situations play into each other very naturally, they do not clash in a furious Keystone manner.

The scene where Charlie prepares to push the father into the lake is a perfect example of his elaborating on Keystone gag ideas. Falls into the lake were rather common in slapstick comedies, and Keystone is responsible for many a splash. But Charlie is methodical. The blindfolded father does not realize it is Charlie guiding him about, he thinks it is his playful conquest. Charlie brings the father to the lake and carefully measures the water's depth with his cane. Dissatisfied, he brings his victim to another area and does the same. It takes a few tries before Charlie is satisfied that the water is deep enough, and chilly enough, for the father to make a splash. Just as he has found the right spot, the father touches Charlie's face and feels his mustache. Reacting, he pulls off the blindfold just in time to have Charlie break a pop bottle over his head, the perfect retaliation, and kick him into the water. This elaborate scene is staged perfectly, Chaplin wringing several laughs out of a longer sequence rather than merely getting one laugh out of a quick, obvious gag.

Wandering through the park again, Charlie discovers the sleeping mother and daughter, and sits by them. Meanwhile, the father, more irate than ever, rises, soaking wet, out of the lake without realizing his nemesis is effectively charming his wife and daughter, so much so that they invite him back home with them.

Enjoying the hospitality, as well as the wealth of material goods which surround him, Charlie makes himself at home. He settles quite comfortably into a lifestyle to which he would not likely be invited, and is especially delighted with the pretty daughter.

Chaplin does a neat job of cross-cutting between the father and his friend back at the park, and Charlie enjoying the hospitality of the mother and daughter. The father attempts to buy a lemonade, but realizes his wallet has gone missing during the sopping melee. Charlie, on the other hand, is enjoying the father's household immensely. He is scooping up donuts with a knife and sloppily gargling his tea, eliciting bemused laughter from his two enamored hosts.

Of course, the father returns, and Edna wants to introduce him to her new friend. Once they see each other, a slapstick brawl is inevitable. Chaplin uses all of the classic comic knockabout methods, but artfully choreographs the sequence with that delightful rhythm. The free-form method of Keystone slapstick battles is adapted to a slower beat and more effective pace, but the violence remains at full force. The father grabs Charlie by the face and throws him out of the room. The father then runs into that room, again grabs Charlie by his face, and throws him back into the original room. Charlie fights back with kicks and slaps, ducking those attempts by the father. He finally is able to battle out of harms way and runs upstairs.

Charlie must somehow continue his dalliance with the daughter and still hide from the father. The only way he can imagine doing so is by disguising himself. He is caught in an upstairs dressing room, so he removes women's clothing off a dummy, carefully doing so as if the dummy were an actual person. He puts on the clothes, applies a hat, picks up a fur, and camps it up as a woman.

Again Chaplin cross-cuts his action. A frantic argument, which erupts into physical actions, is going on between the father and mother. Meanwhile, Charlie carefully and delicately dons women's garb upstairs. Chaplin cuts between the two sequences beautifully, the differences in pacing somehow blending within his inimitable comic rhythm.

Edna goes upstairs to find him, and laughs uproariously, her hysterics causing her to collapse to the ground. She decides to help Charlie with his charade, shaving his mustache, applying makeup, and giving him a pair of women's shoes. (*A Woman* shows Chaplin performing on film without a mustache for the final time until *Limelight* [1952], not including cameos like *Show People* [1928], or newsreel footage.)

Once the metamorphosis is complete, Charlie is recognizable as a woman. The father is attracted to "her" and immediately begins flirting. A friend of father's is similarly smitten, and Charlie finds himself as the

3. The Essanay Films

woman in the middle of a love triangle. The mother and daughter, watching on the sidelines, find the whole thing terribly amusing. Of course, the father eventually discovers the ruse and another melee ensues, but now the mother and daughter intervene, and Charlie proclaims his love for Edna. The father remains stubborn, but the finally is forced to come around when Charlie threatens to divulge information about father's flirting ways. He and Charlie shake hands, but father is not at all sincere. Charlie is immediately tossed out of the house.

A review in *The New York Dramatic Mirror* from the summer of 1915 stated:

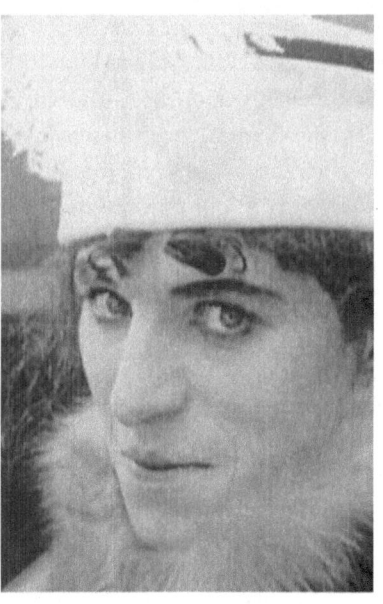

Charlie appeared in drag in *A Woman.*

> This picture is a refutation of the belief held by many that Charles Chaplin can only do the kind of comedy that he has more or less created, for he opens up a new field of humor for him, and one that should be as successful as the peculiar style that has gained him his immense popularity.

A Woman is another remarkable film, continuing his evolution at Essanay. Chaplin carefully constructs his comedy so that each character has a point in the conflict, and each sequence neatly leads into the next. Most effectively, he cross-cuts between two sequences with vastly different rhythms and successfully plays them against each other. It all works perfectly.

The Keystone influence exists only in the most basic structure of the story. This two-reeler is most assuredly an Essanay film, with Chaplin's modified, refined style and the comic rhythm he had developed being only some of the major reasons why *A Woman* is one of the best two-reelers of his career.

While this is the last time Chaplin did dame masquerade, it was hardly the last time cinema visited it. Scores of dismissible efforts involving this idea are overshadowed by more significant examples, such as Laurel and Hardy's *Twice Two* (1933) or Billy Wilder's *Some Like It Hot* (1959). Even the Don McGuire-Larry Gelbart script for *Tootsie* (1982) features a similar sequence whereby a man masquerading as a woman falls for a girl while the girl's father is smitten with him. In the later film, however, the girl is not in on the ruse.

A Woman is Chaplin's first film at the former Majestic Studios at 651 Fairview Avenue in Boyle Heights, Los Angeles. The company had moved there during the first week in June. Of course, Echo Park was used for location filming during the first sequences of *A Woman*, but interiors were at the new studio. All subsequent Essanay films would be shot there as well.

According to *My Autobiography*, Chaplin was done filming at Niles:

> I made four comedies at Niles, but as the studio facilities were not satisfactory, I did not feel settled or contented there, so I suggested to Anderson my going to Los Angeles, where they had better facilities for making comedies. He agreed, but also for another reason: because I was monopolizing the studio, which was not big enough or adequately staffed for three companies. So he negotiated the renting of a small studio at Boyle Heights, which was in the heart of Los Angeles.

Chaplin's popularity was at its height. By March of 1915, theaters were simply advertising a photo of Chaplin with the indication "He's Here Today," and they could count on packed houses, even to the point of factories being shut down and schools being closed. Theaters had Chaplin imitators frolic outside their establishments to entice potential customers. Soon other businesses followed suit.

According to David Kiehn, in his book *Broncho Billy and the Essanay Company*:

> Essanay, overwhelmed by their self-distribution of the Chaplin films, turned over the task to the General Film Company, which promptly boosted the price to nearly double its rate for first-run films, and tied their release to the less desirable General Film product line. There was an immediate outcry from exhibitors, but no one dared to start a boycott and risk being left behind. Even if they put the other General Film releases aside, and refused to show them, they could still profit from the Chaplin films.

3. The Essanay Films

An article in the June 26, 1915, issue of *Moving Picture World* stated:

> Mr. Chaplin has made a thorough, painstaking study of comedy in pantomime and this was a sort of preparatory course for his moving picture work. He is the exponent of realism and spontaneity in moving pictures, and his work has made him the best known actor on the screen today. This does not bar the serious stars of the silent drama. Wherever there is a Chaplin booking, the public flocks.

In concluding our discussion of *A Woman* it is necessary to point out how Chaplin was able to not only effectively draw from his own experiences with Karno or Sennett, but also from longtime traditions in comedy performance. In an act that can be traced back to ancient Greek and Roman theater, Chaplin dons a female masquerade. It reminds us that most of his comedy is steeped in tradition, including pantomime and slapstick, two valid forms of comedy performance that are a significant part of theater history. Chaplin's ability to elevate movie slapstick to fine art had a lot to do with traditional theatrical elements, all of which are clearly presented in *A Woman*. This further justifies the importance of Chaplin's transitional Essanay films during the course of his motion picture career.

The Bank

Cast

Charles Chaplin	The Janitor
Edna Purviance	The Stenographer
Charles Inslee	The Bank President
Carl Stockdale	Charles the Cashier
Billy Armstrong	Another Janitor
Lawrence A. Bowes	Bond Salesman
Leo White	Bank Officer
Paddy McQuire	Clerk & Robber
Fred Goodwins	Clerk & Robber
Lee Hill	Robber

Credits

Charles Chaplin	Director, Screenwriter
Harry Ensign	Cinematographer

Chaplin at Essanay

Ernest Van Pelt . . . . Assistant Director
Jess Robbins . . . . Producer

Released August 9, 1915. Two Reels.

While yet another reworking of a 1914 Keystone idea (*The New Janitor*), *The Bank* is another of Chaplin's finest two-reelers, maintaining the successful streak of consistently brilliant efforts he had been producing for Essanay since *A Jitney Elopement*. Of course, this is not to negate the significance of those Essanay films made previous to *A Jitney Elopement*, nor are the favorable comparisons to Keystone productions an attempt to put down the work Chaplin had done with Sennett. But while *The New Janitor* is certainly one of the finest Keystone films, *The Bank* is one of the very best of Chaplin's entire career, and, as is the case with all of his better films from this time, further indication of the strength of his Essanay output.

Just as with the previous Essanays, Chaplin appears to be keenly aware of Charlie's initial entrance in *The Bank*. The first shot is from behind, with Charlie walking away from the camera into his place of employment, tripping on unseen debris as he approaches the building. Chaplin then has Charlie entering the bank from the background through a revolving door. He spins around a few times before finally making it inside.

Chaplin is subtle. He does not have Charlie make a point about the door. It is not used as a central gag. He simply enters in a comical manner. Reportedly, Charlie's initial entrance had always been met by laughter, even if he was simply walking up the street. In *The Bank*, Chaplin has Charlie earn the laugh with a revolving door gag. It is quick, unassuming, and delightful.

What follows is a great bit that sets the pace for this particularly remarkable film. Charlie walks into the bank with an air of importance, enters the main vault as if he were in a managerial position, and comes out with a mop and bucket. He is the bank janitor, but respects his position as if it were among the most well-paid and important at the bank.

The difference between Chaplin and other comedians is his attention to even the tiniest of character details. When Charlie enters the vault, he does not simply turn the lock to the correct combination and walk in. Charlie stops and thinks, placing the numbers and their order in his head

3. The Essanay Films

Charlie is the proud janitor on duty in *The Bank*.

before venturing on. It is a very human trait, very natural, and something that would easily be overlooked by virtually any other actor. Chaplin's attention to details such as these adds substance to every scene.

Charlie's pride in his status is offset by fellow custodian Billy Armstrong, a sloppy, disheveled sort who carries himself about in a very lumbering manner that stands in sharp contrast to Charlie's sprightly steps.

Charlie the commoner loves the more refined office girl Edna from afar. He gives her a flower and note, but her dismissal of him is so complete that she simply discards it in the trash the minute she believes he is out of sight (he is not; he sees her do this). She loves one of the higher level bank officers, and Charlie is barely within her peripheral vision.

Charlie's interest in Edna, his boldness in expressing that interest, and her cavalier dismissal of him are all key here. Just as the establishing few moments of his character in *The Bank* show him exhibiting an air of importance over his custodial position, he continues the same attitude in his approach to Edna. She immediately reveals her belief that she is clearly above his blue-collar working-class status, while his initial approach continues his own lofty perspective of his position. It is one of many examinations of the class system that Chaplin would subtlety make with his comedy, as well as one of the strongest.

The depth of character that Chaplin had been attempting with his Essanay films, especially since *A Jitney Elopement*, is taken to a greater level in *The Bank* than in any of his other efforts from this period, even *The Tramp*. Charlie is a proud and honest member of society's lower working class, endearingly amusing, and sadly found to be unworthy by the woman he loves. The audience is immediately drawn to the pathos of his character.

Chaplin explores Charlie's relationship with Edna in deeper terms here. Charlie is very seriously smitten, not playfully attracted. It is not comedy that stems from this situation, but the sort of heavy drama that concludes *The Tramp*. And while *The Tramp* maintains slapstick comedy throughout nearly all of its two reels, *The Bank* uses comedy to introduce, and to accent, what is essentially a serious story.

Chaplin does not avoid gags or comedy situations, and there many very funny moments in *The Bank*. When Charlie mops up near a desk clerk and a waiting customer, his wet mop drips into the customer's upright top hat. As he turns to apologize, the wet mop flings over his shoulder into the faces of each man. Walking back near seated coworker Billy, Charlie turns again, and the wet mop skirts across the top of Billy's head, effectively parting his messy hair. The mop over his shoulder is a veritable weapon for Charlie, and with each turn and thrust he unwittingly pummels all who are nearby.

The Bank features several bits of inspired comic business within the context of janitorial cleanup. Charlie lifts a filled wastebasket and carries it upside down, spilling its contents across the floor. Charlie and Billy, in separate rooms, continue to sweep the floor's messy contents into each other's area. Armstrong, himself, like Chaplin, a former Karno trooper, is most effective playing off of Chaplin at this level.

One very funny idea has Chaplin continually picking discarded papers off the floor and putting them onto a desk where a small fan blows them back. It is a very quick throwaway gag, but the sort of inspired comic business that makes *The Bank* such an exceptional two-reeler. In an even more outrageous sequence, Charlie uses a customer's tongue to moisten a stamp, and when he finds that his envelope is too large for the mail slot, he rips it into pieces and sends it through a little at a time.

While it contains many very funny scenes, Chaplin's presentation of Charlie's feelings towards Edna is truly the focal point of *The Bank*. Much of this idea's success has to do with Edna's performance and how Chaplin presents her. She is not an ingenue, a victim, or flashy in any way. She is a very ordinary, attractive office girl with a comfortable relationship, a good job, and a very relaxed, satisfied manner. Edna does not overplay her role, and Chaplin does not make her character more than it needs to be. Therefore, Charlie's attraction also appears very natural, and is more effective within the context of the film. This helps capture the audience's sympathy, especially during a bit in which the disappointed Charlie stands outside of Edna's office; just as she walks by, Edna looks at him with disdain and chuckles. He truly means nothing at all to her.

His infatuation with Edna, his deeply disappointment by her dismissal, and his longing for a way to impress her results in a dream sequence wherein he imagines himself a hero. Criminals enter the bank, plotting a robbery. The group of crooks take control, but Charlie thwarts their attempt with a series of slapstick heroics. He punches, kicks, slips and slides out of the way, and ultimately locks the crooks in the vault. Edna, overcome, faints in his arms. He flings her across his shoulder and picks up a dropped pistol, effectively subduing the remaining criminals. Charlie gently sets Edna on a chair so he can battle a particularly tough crook, and when he starts to lose this fight, Edna awakens and rescues him by attacking the criminal from behind. Charlie soon has all under control, phones the police, and is congratulated by the bank manager as his foppish romantic rival comes crawling out from under a desk. Charlie's fantasy not only bolsters his own assessment of himself, it also imagines his rival as a sniveling coward whose manner is revealed as terribly unattractive. He even throws Edna to the ground in order to save himself from the pursuing criminals.

In the dream, Charlie's slapstick heroics are delivered with a certain seriousness that makes them as poignant as they are funny. Charlie's dream

Charlie dreams of being Edna's hero in this shot from *The Bank*.

features him prominently as Edna's hero, the bank's hero, and one who not only overshadows Edna's beau, but creates a context where the rival's true cowardice is on display. It is the perfect fantasy of the peripheral person, the outcast, one whose well meaning ways are overlooked by a segment of society that feels itself above his station in life. He is not only their equal, he is their savior.

Alas, it is all a mere fantasy. Charlie awakens and is once again alone in his very real world. Edna and her foppish beau are together, look upon Charlie with typical disdain, and wander off together Charlie sniffs his flower, tosses it behind his back, and wanders off by himself.

The comedy in *The Bank* is so delightful, and its drama has such depth, it is especially impressive that Chaplin was able to combine the two elements so effectively. He would continue to do so with subsequent films, especially his best feature-length silents, but it is at Essanay where this quality was honed. Chaplin uses a few parallels here, something he would do

3. The Essanay Films

with greater frequency in later films. One in particular begins with the sequence in which Charlie sees the bank clerk putting on a tie that Edna has purchased for him as a gift. Later he sees Billy putting on a tie himself, preening in a similar fashion. Charlie gives him a swift kick that sends him across the room, and Billy is more confused than injured by the sudden violence. It is a wonderful parallel, and an equally wonderful example of how humor and pathos can blend so effectively in Chaplin's cinematic world.

The Bank is truly one of the finest short comedies of Chaplin's career. Of course, the best Essanay films all exhibit the strength of this pivotal period and the great work found therein. But *The Bank* is especially significant in that it contains elements of all of the experiments Chaplin had been conducting in films, and even surpasses the milestone *The Tramp* by being a better structured film. When one takes into consideration the evolution that had taken place in Chaplin's Essanay films up to this point, *The Bank* can be considered a culmination of those ideas, and another career checkpoint. With *the Bank*, Chaplin's cinematic basis was firmly established. Any further experimentation he would make would be to explore different levels of comedy and filmmaking. The most obvious would be his burlesque via two different versions of *Carmen*, a comic idea that was unlike anything Chaplin had attempted up to this point, and a truly inspired and courageous undertaking. This would happen a few films later, but unfortunately, the making of the film, its re-edit by Essanay once Chaplin left the company, and the subsequent legal ramifications would overshadow its artistic success.

However, with his next Essanay production, *Shanghaied*, Chaplin decided to make yet another competent two-reel comedy before exploring even more challenging ideas.

It is hard to pinpoint just how completely Chaplin responded to the way he was assessed in periodicals. While his work was embraced as brilliant in most circles, there were some who continued to look disdainfully at slapstick comedy, even when performed expertly. Period drama critic Heywood Brown tried to sort it out in a Fall 1915 article printed in *The Moving Picture World*:

> The vulgarity of the Chaplin pictures cannot be denied. They are altogether lacking in subtlety and their appeal must be directed

toward a low order of intelligence. They are a scathing indictment of public taste, these Chaplin pictures, and that is why we blush for shame in confessing that we laugh our head off when we see one.

Brown later indicated his choices for good film players:

> The best comedy work we have ever seen in moving pictures was done by Sidney Drew in *Playing Dead* ... and, in our opinion, no comedienne untrained in picture work could hope to realize anything like the possibilities which Mary Pickford makes actualities in *A Girl of Yesterday*.

One of Chaplin's supporting players, Fred Goodwins, stated in *Pearson's Weekly* at the time:

> His fame was at its zenith here in America when suddenly the critics made a dead set at him. They roasted his work wholesale; called it crude, ungentlemanly and risqué, even indecent. The poor little fellow was knocked flat. But he rose from his gloomy depths one day, and came out of his dressing room rubbing his hands. "Well boys," he said with his funny little twinkly smile, "Let's give them something to talk about, shall we? Something that has no loopholes in it!" Thus began the new era in Chaplin comedies — clean, clever, dramatic stories with a big laugh at the finish.

But there were many who balked at the vulgarity tag placed upon Chaplin by more pretentious reviewers. Chaplin had elevated the comedy film to incredible levels in only a year, something that is commonly understood now, in retrospect, and from a historical and cultural perspective. Brown's comments are included here only to indicate that, despite Chaplin's extraordinary work at this time, a handful of critics still didn't get it.

Meanwhile, newspapers and film journals continued to comment on how Chaplin's massive popularity kept soaring to new levels. Onscreen for just over a year, he had become the biggest star that the infant motion picture industry had ever known, and was the first to be heavily imitated and talked about at every age and class level.

In the August 7, 1915, issue of *Motography*, Journalist Captain Jack Poland indicated:

3. The Essanay Films

> Charlie Chaplin, the half-a-million-a-year comedian of Essanay fame, is the star of Broadway in this city. All the kids are aping him by becoming miniature Charlie boys, and every time his name appears over a picture house it means full crowds.

The public's affection for Chaplin became a different sort of cause for concern, as per this article from the same time in *The Washington Post*:

> Beckie Hoffman told Judge Graham today she wanted a divorce from Sam Hoffman, a furniture dealer, because he is insanely jealous of Charlie Chaplin. "I like to go to the movies," Mrs. Hoffman declared, "but when my husband hears me laugh at Chaplin he becomes insanely jealous."

Judge Graham took the case under advisement.

And in another *Washington Post* article, a London priest expressed these concerns:

> "Charlie Chaplin is more to some people than Almighty God," said Father Watt, a priest, who is recovering from wounds after a year spent on the battlefield.
>
> "Although the best blood in the world is being spilled at the front, a nation here has gotten itself into the clutching hand of the cinematograph shows," he added. "Many people seem to know more about Charlie Chaplin than God. Chaplin is silly, but the people who want to see him are sillier."

It is interesting to compare this reaction to the one John Lennon would receive some 50 years later upon announcing his belief that the Beatles were more popular than Jesus Christ. Of course, Chaplin did not make such a claim, but as late as the rock and roll era we have had clergy insisting that youngsters who championed the likes of Elvis Presley or the Beatles were elevating them to the level of God.

It appears Chaplin's massive stardom was a harbinger of things to come.

Shanghaied

Cast

Charles Chaplin . . . . Tramp
Edna Purviance . . . . Daughter of the Shipowner

Billy Armstrong	Shanghaied Seaman
Fred Goodwins	Shanghaied Seaman
Lawrence A. Bowes	Mate
Paddy McQuire	Shanghaied Seaman
John Rand	Ship's Cook
Wesley Ruggles	Shipowner
Leo White	Shanghaied Seaman

Credits

Charles Chaplin	Director, Screenwriter
Harry Ensign	Cinematographer
Ernest Van Pelt	Assistant Director
Jess Robbins	Producer

Released October 4, 1915. Two Reels.

Chaplin's choice to make another straight comedy without a dramatic element or pathos would initially seem curious following the artistic triumph of *The Bank*. One would think Chaplin would want to maintain this style and investigate other ways it could be used effectively.

Chaplin would later do just that, but with *Shanghaied* he instead explores how the cinematic process can enhance physical comedy, making *Shanghaied* one of his funniest pictures from this period, as well as one of his most intriguing. The very first appearance of Charlie is one of the best shots in this film. Charlie is seen facing a very nice piece of scenery, apparently marveling at nature's beauty. Suddenly Edna walks into the frame, and we see that he was actually watching *her*. It is a perfectly framed shot and opens the film with a solid laugh.

Charlie is soon recruited by a ship captain to help shanghai a crew by hitting them on the head while they are distracted. This same gag was reworked (arguably more effectively) by Laurel and Hardy in their 1934 talkie two-reeler *The Live Ghost*. Chaplin does use variations on the gag, however. At one point, for instance, he carefully removes a distracted potential crewmember's hat before conking him.

Once enough men are assembled for a crew, Charlie is paid off in bills (which he bites to test their authenticity), and, of course, he is distracted and conked himself. He is a most unpopular crewmember because of his role in shanghaiing the others. This was the setup in the later Laurel and Hardy film as well, but in the duo's two-reeler they are protected

3. The Essanay Films

Charlie returned to slapstick in *Shanghaied* (seen here with Charles Inslee).

by the captain, while Charlie must fend for himself. Thus, whenever Charlie sees the captain, he grabs a mop and starts frantically swabbing the deck. If there is no mop handy, he simulates with his cane, his overzealous productivity borne out of fear.

Most of the first half of *Shanghaied* features gag situations on deck, while the second half shows Charlie helping the cook. One of the best gags in the first half of the film features Charlie attempting to rescue a man from the ocean by pulling him up with a rope. He gets the man almost to the boat, then stops to spit on his hands for a tighter grip, letting go of the rope as the man plummets back into the water. When another crewmember comes to help, Charlie rests his foot on the man's backside for leverage, and ends up kicking this man into the ocean.

To simulate the rocking of the boat, Chaplin employed a set that could be gently rocked. When the rocking becomes more violent, however, he is merely tipping the camera and directing the actors to play accordingly. Decades before playing to a green screen (with special effects added later) became commonplace, Chaplin has his actors respond on a still set as if it were a rocking boat. Chaplin's own expertise at body movement allowed him to demonstrate how he wanted the other actors to respond, and their background in slapstick pratfalls and knockabout served them well. As a filmmaker, Chaplin appears to realize that the rocking of the ship would be good for gag situations, and that such an effect is possible with little effort. But the ship's rocking isn't so much a gag unto itself as it is an effect that allows for gag opportunities. The stumbling and the falling down is amusing, and despite being slapstick silliness, is carefully choreographed and has its own discernible rhythm as per Chaplin's usual structure by this time. But the real cleverness comes from the dining difficulties (a routine revisited to similar effect in the later Mutual short *The Immigrant.*). Chaplin's acrobatics are on display when he does a complete somersault while carrying a full tray — without dropping or spilling anything (he does this not once, but twice).

Edna is a stowaway, and it would not be the last time she would appear undercover, known only to Charlie. In the Mutual production *Behind the Screen*, Chaplin would revisit the situation, having Edna disguise herself as a boy, with only Charlie aware of her ruse.

There is a plot to blow up the ship for the insurance. Charlie discovers the bomb and throws it overboard. It lands on the lifeboat of the men who planted the bomb and explodes. Charlie is a hero. Edna's father shows up with a rescue ship, and Charlie and Edna board it. Charlie is ordered off, despite frantic explanations that he saved daughter Edna's life and saved the ship. The pleas fall on deaf ears, so Charlie kicks the father off the ship and embraces Edna for the fadeout.

Shanghaied is certainly one of the funniest Essanays, with some of the cleverest gags and most interesting cinematic comedy enhancements. That it does not use pathos or a dramatic base isn't indicative of its being a stopping point in Chaplin's evolution as a filmmaker. *Shanghaied* is another step in Chaplin's progress, allowing him to explore different ways to use cinema for comedy, and cinematic effects to enhance the slapstick ideas.

Shanghaied is also an interesting prelude to Chaplin's Mutual comedy *The Immigrant*. The later film features a seasickness bit, a rocking ship, and Edna as the ingenue. *The Immigrant* is generally considered one of the finest films of Chaplin's entire career (going beyond gags to make statements about immigration in early twentieth century America); but with *Shanghaied* we see the genesis of many comedy ideas used in the later film.

Shanghaied was well received by audiences at the time of its initial release, and helped maintain Chaplin's enormous popularity.

Despite this consistent success, word was that Chaplin was getting a bit restless. His contract with Essanay was inching toward its end, and a renewal was set. But Chaplin was aware of his tremendous popularity and realized he may be worth even more than the massive salary he was already enjoying. Other studios were beckoning him, and he was certainly weighing other offers.

Chaplin's exploration into various realms of cinematic comedy and narrative required that he take even more time on his films. The budget-minded Spoor wanted to please his exhibitors, who clamored for the popular Chaplin product. Spoor was also concerned about losing potential revenue to reissues of old Keystones with new titles (to fool moviegoers). There was some indication that Chaplin was searching for a better deal, not only for more money (despite his current pay being astronomical by 1915 standards), but for even greater creative control and the time to do as many takes as he felt necessary until a sequence was exactly as he wanted it to be. Essanay allowed that in theory, but Chaplin still needed to adhere to some semblance of a schedule that would satisfy both exhibitors and Spoor.

Spoor and Anderson were not at all interested in losing their prize acquisition. Chaplin, wanting any business negotiations to be private, issued a statement to the press that all was well. In the October 9, 1915, issue of *Moving Picture World*, an article, headlined "Chaplin Will Stick," claimed:

> Charlie Chaplin, Essanay comedian, whose latest comedy, *Shanghaied*, has just been completed, denounces the reports that he is planning to leave Essanay as "vain imaginings." It is stated both on the authority of George K. Spoor, president of Essanay, and Mr. Chaplin himself, that he will continue with Essanay indefinitely.
>
> "There have been many ridiculous rumors circulated about my leaving Essanay, which was news to me," said Mr. Chaplin. "One story I read said I was going into vaudeville on Broadway; another that I was going with other film companies. There is no truth to any of them. I am engaged under a long-term contract with the Essanay company and, as far as I am concerned, I intend to remain with it, and to produce no pictures for any other concern, nor go on the stage. Not only am I under contract, but my associations with the Essanay company have been most cordial and pleasant. Mr. Spoor and myself are in perfect harmony in regard to the work so why should I leave even if I had no contract?"

Of course, like today, the public (even those in the industry who read the trades) were being told one thing while something else entirely was going on. By this time Chaplin was well aware of his massive stardom and had set his brother and manager, Sydney, shopping around for other studio offers. Although he was still the highest paid comedian in films, Chaplin always sought greater creative freedom, and would stipulate on any subsequent contracts that he be given enough time, within reason, to complete a two-reel subject at the level of perfection he had already established for himself. Watching Chaplin's best films is a marvelous experience, but seeing his work evolve from slapstick fun to great art within the course of a year is an especially fulfilling experience. Audiences were enjoying the films at a greater level than any other comedian was able to generate at that time (except, perhaps, Roscoe Arbuckle). Producers were taking notice. It was time for Chaplin to investigate his possibilities outside of the studio.

A Night in the Show

Cast

Charles Chaplin .... Mr. Pest/Mr. Rowdy
Fred Goodwins .... Audience Member

3. The Essanay Films

Paddy McQuire	Musician
James T. Kelley	Musician
Edna Purviance	Woman in Audience
Charles Inslee	Audience Member
Bud Jamison	Dash (Singer)
Loyal Underwood	Dot (Singer)
John Rand	Orchestra Leader
Wesley Ruggles	Audience Member
Leo White	Man in Stalls and Black Man in Balcony
Dee Lampton	Fat Boy
Charlotte Mineau	Audience Member
May White	Fat Lady in Stalls, Exotic Dancer

Credits

Charles Chaplin	Director, Screenwriter
Harry Ensign	Cinematographer
Ernest Van Pelt	Assistant Director
Jess Robbins	Producer

Released November 20, 1915. Two Reels.

Another of the very best Essanay productions, *A Night in the Show* allows Chaplin to visit his music hall roots, to embellish an established sketch from his past, and to attempt playing the sort of character that would otherwise be his adversary.

While touring with Fred Karno's troop early in his career, Chaplin appeared in a popular sketch called "Mumming Birds" in which he portrayed Mr. Pest, a drunken wealthy socialite who attends a music hall show and effectively disrupts each performance. Committing this idea to film, Chaplin embellished it first by playing two roles. The second role is Mr. Rowdy, a sloppily attired lout who hoots and howls among the lower classes up in the balcony. Chaplin the director edits between the two characters, their world, and their disruptive behavior, indicating that while each is from a very different strata in life, both are the same sort of inebriated troublemaker.

Mr. Pest is the first Chaplin character to which we are introduced. He is clearly inebriated. He does not smile. His expression is one of effete snobbery. Mr. Pest is similar to the Leo White–type characters with whom Chaplin's Little Tramp was at odds in most of his films. But this time it is Charlie as the pest. Well dressed, with his hair slicked back, and sporting a permanent scowl, the tipsy Mr. Pest is demanding, meddlesome, and

Charlie, as the stuffy patron amidst society snobs, revisits his music hall beginnings in *A Night in the Show.*

a real threat to the safety of the show people and their audience. But because he is a man of wealth, he is allowed the privilege of eccentricity. If his rowdy counterpart in the balcony dared cause a disruption from somewhere other than his segregated area, he would likely be ejected from the theater. Not so Mr. Pest.

Mr. Pest first tries to cut in line because he dislikes having to wait. Once he enters the theater area, his expression shows that he does not expect to even enjoy the show. He casually strikes a match against a bald man's head, reacts negatively to an unattractive woman, and changes his seat frequently without regard to the other audience members. He gets in a shoving match with a woman in the adjacent seat over the joint arm of a chair.

Mr. Rowdy is also clearly inebriated, but he is at one with the others in the balcony seating. They are all rather rowdy, and appear to be excited to see a show. They react forcefully and boorishly to the entertainment, from applauding and hollering for those acts they enjoy, to pelting a less interesting performance with a barrage of vegetables, including some very ripe tomatoes.

Chaplin the director makes good choices that allow the viewer to take in all of the action. He cuts from what is happening onstage to the balcony, and then to the action in the floor seats. Closeups are used for the more intimate comedy on the floor, and closer shots of the acts are occasionally presented. The balcony remains in medium shot, Chaplin framing it so the action of the entire balcony can be seen, with Mr. Rowdy front and center. Chaplin's directorial rhythm helps a great deal with the pacing of the short. Even though he is cutting from a sequence featuring rapid movement to one that features slower action, the rhythm of the film remains consistent.

Chaplin also does an interesting job framing the action. He wants to show the acts performing while keeping Mr. Pest in the frame, thus capturing both the performance and Mr. Pest's reactions.

During a snake charming act, a barefoot woman straddles the stage with her feet near Mr. Pest, who reacts with disgust, attempting to fan the scent away. He then strikes a match on the sole of the snake charmer's foot, causing her to jump and angrily scold him for intruding on her performance. The patrons are not impressed, including the tumultuous spectators in the balcony, led by Mr. Rowdy.

One of the acts is a fire eater, whose handling of fire, as well as his general satanic appearance, intimidates Mr. Pest, who trades seats with an obese boy (Dee Lampton, who was actually a man in his twenties playing a much younger character). Meanwhile, the balcony rowdy turns a hose on the stage to put out the fires that are part of the act, and the entire house gets drenched (a throwback to a similar gag Chaplin had used in the Keystone one-reeler *The Property Man*), thus effectively ending the show.

A Night in the Show is an extraordinary comedy, one of the finest of Chaplin's career. It offers us a clear look at his music hall roots, allows him to act against type, and features some of his funniest moments. The structure of the film is also different than other Chaplin comedies up to this time. It presents stage acts, balcony rowdies, and higher class audience members on the lower level all performing within their own niche, but having a linear connection as well. As Chaplin films can be measured, it is clearly one of his most impressive.

It is interesting to take into account the approach of Chaplin the director, reminding ourselves that he is not merely in charge of choreographing himself in two different, unrelated roles, but also for directing each separate stage act within the film. The acts must all look authentic, yet also appear offbeat enough to fit within Chaplin's vision. He wants to present this show as a form of satire, and the acts are slightly more outrageous versions of what one would find in an actual music hall. Chaplin's own history gave him the ideas, of course, but with the cinematic process he is able to call attention to more intimate details. The close-up of hapless Bud Jamison and his diminutive partner venturing on with their unpopular singing duet while getting pummeled by the audience is just such an example.

Chaplin has found a way to merge his music hall roots with his work in cinema. He presents a show, a variety of different types of acts, and uses it as a backdrop, despite each act having its own level of movement and performance. In the forefront is the stuffy patron who has some elements of Keystone Charlie in his personality, but who is an upper level snob rather than a rebellious tramp. The similarities exist in the character's reactions to his surroundings, despite it being from another perspective. And, on the periphery, Chaplin's balcony character rowdily causes commotion in the audience by generating more noise than that emanating from the stage. Chaplin may be pointing out that the tumult caused by the lower classes in the cheap seats, led by Mr. Rowdy, is every bit as amusing as the succession of amateur talent parading onstage. Chaplin's tipsy snob character, Mr. Pest, is as bewildered as he is pretentious. Ted Okuda and Dave Maska, in their book *Chaplin at Keystone and Essanay*, point out:

> If the Tramp had created this much commotion, he would have been promptly ejected from the theater—that is, if he even made it past the foyer. But because of Mr. Pest's refined appearance, most audience members are willing to tolerate his annoying antics. Here, Chaplin touches upon the hypocrisy of perceived social status.

And the stuck-up central character of the piece acts just as uppity towards other rich patrons as he does towards those "beneath" his social status, condescending with everyone in his audience section—with the exception of the attractive Edna. Mr. Pest's amusing flirtation, which abruptly ends as Edna's husband enters, makes it unfortunate that Ms. Purviance appears so little in *A Night in the Show*.

Chaplin's exploration of characters is one of the many impressive elements of his transitional Essanay evolution. With *A Night in the Show*, Chaplin unifies many disparate elements — the show, two separate audience areas, and two separate characters — into a single theme. It is a daunting exercise, and Chaplin pulls it off remarkably.

A Night in the Show is one of Chaplin's finest films, certainly among the very best from his Essanay tenure. By this time, all that he had gained from his experimenting with his transitional Essanay output had settled into a method that would capably produce brilliant films. Along with being funny and timeless, they allow us to see Chaplin stretching his creative prowess into areas that extend beyond mere knockabout two-reel comedies with occasional pathos.

A Night in the Show is also an impressive tour de force for Chaplin, not only allowing him to play two different characters, but also to cut between the situations in the audience and those occurring onstage, offering the right amount of time for each cutaway to register effectively and play off of the next. This shows Chaplin's understanding of cinematic language from a comedian's perspective. It is all about framing the gag properly, timing the sequences effectively, and allowing the overall presentation to make its comic points without being abrupt or protracted. *A Night in the Show* has a great deal of historical significance in its cinematic presentation of Chaplin's previous stage career; but it is also a consistently brilliant film that uses elements of cinema effectively to present its comedy. Chaplin's work, in the course of only a year, had evolved so quickly and to such a level that it remains quite remarkable, even in the wake of what would be accomplished in the future.

There is much more going on in a complex Chaplin film like *A Night in the Show* than in other comedy shorts of the period. But, unfortunately for Essanay, now that he had refined his approach and was at the height of his creative powers, Chaplin was moving on. Brother Sydney had shopped around carefully, weighing several offers from many interested parties. Of course, negotiations with Essanay continued, but Chaplin's chief interest was creative control and the ability to explore cinematic possibilities without limitation or studio tampering.

Chaplin had only been in films for two years, and in that very brief time he had helped to make movie comedy into an art form that crossed age and demographic boundaries Sydney, a talented comedian in his own right, who scored in such films as *A Submarine Pirate* and *The Better Ole*, had a keen business sense and realized that even greater financial recompense and creative freedom was possible. So, along with being one of the most innovative and artistic comedians in films, Charles Chaplin also set a new standard for movie star salaries.

But unlike those celebrities whose work does not merit the large sums they are paid, Chaplin was indeed worth the money. The public clamored for his films to such a point an extent that even his old Keystones, released with new titles, were booked into first-run theaters and embraced by moviegoers.

Chaplin would, of course, fulfill his immediate obligation at Essanay, but it was soon announced that he was to become an employee of the Mutual Films Corporation.

4

Chaplin Signs with Mutual

Chaplin's Essanay films had evolved into bonafide classics by the time he began studying offers from other studios. His contract was about to end, and despite telling the press he was quite comfortable with his current surroundings and creative freedom, the monetary offers outside of the studio were at least worth considering. So Chaplin's brother Sidney, now acting as his business manager, sought another, more lucrative deal.

Upon the completion of two more films—*Burlesque on Carmen* and *Police*—Chaplin left Essanay to make films for Mutual studios. *Burlesque on Carmen* was to be released simply as *Carmen* on December 18, 1915, following the November release of *A Night in the Show*. It was a finished film, and Chaplin intended it to be released as a two-reeler. However, Essanay became aware that Chaplin was likely leaving the studio when his contact expired in January. Essanay was cagey with the press, indicating to Kitty Kelly of the *Chicago Tribune* that they were still waiting for the negative on *Carmen* to be processed for release (when Chaplin had, in fact, readied it and another film by this point). Then the January 21, 1916, issue of *Variety* claimed that Chaplin had been receiving $125,000 yearly from Essanay, with a $10,000 bonus for each release, but that Essanay had netted $1,380,000 from his films. Therefore, Chaplin was getting offers from other studios. Chaplin was revealing little at this time, telling reporter Mabel Condon of the *Dramatic Mirror*, "As far as I know I'm still with the Essanay company and my understanding at present is that I will be for the next year." He also indicated an interest in shooting some films overseas.

Chaplin wanted $10,000 per week. Anderson was inclined to accept, but Spoor refused, despite the amount that could be made from the Chaplin films. Spoor told Kitty Kelly for the February 18, 1916, issue of the *Chicago Tribune*:

Chaplin at Essanay

> Unless Chaplin comes down on his demands he is out of the running for Essanay. He is asking altogether too much for the company. He now wants $626,000 per year, which is $12,050 per week. If I could get the $12,000 for him I couldn't raise the $50!

On February 26, 1916, Chaplin signed with Mutual. He would receive $10,000 per week and a $150,000 signing bonus. Chaplin told *Reel Life* in their March 1916 issue:

> Money and business are very serious matters and I have to keep my mind off them. In fact, I do not worry about money at all. What this contract means is simply that I am in business with all the worry left out and with the dividends guaranteed. It means that I am left free to be just as funny as I dare, to do the best work that is in me, and to spend my energies on the thing that people want. I have felt for a long time that this would be my big year and this contract gives me my opportunity. There is inspiration in it. I am like an author with a big publisher to give him circulation.

Reel Life reported that the organizing of the Mutual Chaplin Company would involve the sum of $1,530,000, which was a staggering budget in 1916, and that Chaplin would begin shooting his first film for Mutual, which was to be released on March 20.

Anderson, livid with Spoor over his handling of the Chaplin matter, sold his interest in the studio to Spoor and offered to make films with Chaplin on his own. Chaplin liked Anderson, and reportedly considered it, but in the end took the offer generated by his brother Sidney, who had found him a home at Mutual studios.

Essanay withheld the release of their last two Chaplin films, and also hoarded Chaplin's various outtakes and the scrapped footage he had shot for a proposed feature-length picture entitled *Life* (referred to in some press accounts as *Nine Lives*). They extended *Burlesque on Carmen* from a two-reeler to a four-reeler by adding new footage with Ben Turpin (which some sources indicate had been directed by Leo White), releasing it as a longer Chaplin film in April of 1916 after Chaplin's Mutual films had already started coming out. *Police* had been released a month earlier, in March of 1916. In September of that year, Essanay strung together three

Chaplin films in an attempt to form a cohesive feature-length story, releasing it as *The Essanay-Chaplin Review of 1916*. In 1917 they took isolated scenes from Chaplin Essanays and attempted to edit them into a feature length story, this one being released first in London, and then in the United States, as *Chase Me Charlie*. Finally, Essanay took the discarded footage from the abandoned *Life* project, some outtakes and clips from other Essanay pictures, and had Leo White shoot some new footage. This conglomeration was edited into a two-reeler entitled *Triple Trouble*, which was released as a new Chaplin film in August of 1918, despite his not having been with the company for two years.

This practice embittered Chaplin towards his important Essanay films, and he spoke little about them for the remainder of his life. The films themselves fared poorly as well. Essanay encountered financial troubles after Chaplin left the studio, so his movies were endlessly re-released, duped, and re-edited over the years. Eventually they fell out of copyright and into the public domain, causing further copying and editing for the 8mm home movie and toy projector market, as well as 16mm films with soundtracks consisting of obtrusive music and sound effects for television broadcast. Despite distributors such as Blackhawk Films attempting to release the best quality and most complete prints of the Essanay films to the 8mm and 16mm collectors market, the films were not in good enough shape to appreciate at the level they deserved until the David Shepard restoration in 1999.

The following films, released by Essanay after Chaplin had left the studio, are approached with the understanding that they were tampered with, reconstructed, and even reinvented by the studio without Chaplin's consent. And each analysis will comment on the subsequent lawsuits involving their release.

Police

Cast

Charles Chaplin . . . . Tramp
Edna Purviance . . . . Girl
Wesley Ruggles . . . . Thief
Billy Armstrong . . . . Fake Preacher and Policeman
Fred Goodwins . . . . Real Preacher and Policeman

Bud Jamison . . . . Flophouse Patron
Paddy McGuire . . . . Flophouse Patron
Harry "Snub" Pollard . . . . Flophouse Patron
James T. Kelly . . . . Drunk with Pockets Picked
John Rand . . . . Policeman
Leo White . . . . Fruitseller and Doss House
                                              Owner and Policeman
George Cleethorpe . . . . Policeman

Credits

Charles Chaplin . . . . Screenwriter, Director
Harry Ensign . . . . Cinematographer
Ernest Van Pelt . . . . Assistant Director

Released March 27, 1916. Two Reels.

Police is the Essanay film that the majority of critics and historians point to as being most like Chaplin's Mutual output, indicating that the transition from Keystone is complete and that he is now at the very height of his creative powers. *Police* indeed draws upon all of the subtle nuance that Chaplin had perfected during his transitional Essanay period. And it successfully culminates this period in his film career by being one of his strongest two-reel comedies.

Police opens with Charlie being released from prison. Leaving through the prison gate, Charlie looks around at the open air and stretches, pondering the endless possibilities of his freedom, despite having only a dollar to his name.

As previously stated, Chaplin understood the importance of the entrance. Sometimes it involves quietly arriving among surrounding turmoil. At other times, Charlie is at the center of the frame immediately. In every case, his entrance befits that particular film's story, and makes a discernible impact. In *Police*, Charlie's entrance is especially significant. Showing the prison in the background, the shot focusing on the gate in the foreground, we see the unmistakable figure of Charlie walking towards this gate and his subsequent freedom. He is accompanied by an armed guard. We realize he has been in prison, that he is leaving it, and that he must abide by societal rules in order to avoid returning. Charlie's stretching upon entering succinctly shows a relaxed and positive attitude towards his first steps into a future that allows the freedom and possibilities lost in

4. Chaplin Signs with Mutual

the prison situation. We do not know specifics, but we do know enough of Charlie's backstory to understand his character and situation immediately upon his entrance. From this starting point, Chaplin can take Charlie in whatever direction necessary within the context of the introduction. So with *Police*, we will expect Charlie to respond to freedom and avoid trouble. It is a promising premise and immediately draws the viewer in.

A man in a clergy outfit emerges from behind a building and approaches Charlie. As the minister reads from his bible, Charlie is visibly moved. The minister indicates that he would like to see Charlie go straight. After a warm handshake, Charlie is on his way. He notices a drunken man with an expensive watch hanging from a chain. This clearly visible trinket is very attractive. Charlie considers stealing the watch from the intoxicated patsy, but decides against it. He is happy with his freedom. He has embraced the clergyman's message. The words from scripture have inspired Charlie, have led him from temptation. All seems right with his world when the movie cuts to the clergyman, showing this proponent of the Good Book in possession of Charlie's sole dollar, having picked his pocket during the faux sermon.

The beauty of this sequence is how it is played. The most noticeable area of comic subtlety occurs when Charlie approaches the drunken man with the visible watch chain. The man sways, staring straight ahead, seemingly oblivious to Charlie's presence. Charlie carefully lifts the watch and examines it. He casually looks around. He holds the watch, thinks briefly, then releases it and walks away. When he walks away, it is noticeably brisk, as he tries to get away from temptation as quickly as he can without arousing suspicion. It is performed beautifully and elegantly, displaying the subtlety that was now an inherent part of his work. The more blatant Keystone nuances are effectively overshadowed by this more graceful approach.

Even this early in his career Chaplin was noted for doing many, many takes of any given scene. This held up production, but Chaplin insisted on this as a most basic level of creative freedom. He would perform the scene several different ways, finally arriving upon the one that had the greatest comic effect. He would also carefully direct the others in minute detail. The drunk is obviously coached to perfection by Chaplin, while Charlie's long series of fidgety ponderings while deciding whether or not to steal the watch are the result of many different ideas. Interestingly enough, it is the action itself that Chaplin concentrated on via numerous variations and takes. He never changed the camera location or the lighting of the scene. Unlike with the later approach of Buster Keaton, whose use of the camera redefined the approach to comedy in cinema, to Chaplin the technology was secondary. His creativity was all about the performance.

The scene immediately following this one is another brilliant display of subtle pantomime. Charlie, realizing he has a dollar to spend, approaches an outdoor fruit and vegetable display and begins sampling the wares by biting into each one. It should be noted that produce such as this was only a few cents per item in 1915, so a dollar would buy several pieces. Charlie is particular about his choices, but the store owner fumes, reminding him that each piece is adding up. Chaplin is marvelous here. He is haughty as he tries each piece of fruit, emulating the style of a big-money consumer. His snobbery is borne from the power he feels as a recently freed man. He has money. He has a right to make a purchase. And, as a consumer, he may have anything he wants in whichever way he pleases, as long as he is able to pay. Charlie's reaction is superb when he eventually searches his pockets for the dollar. The initial concern turns to panic as the money fails to turn up in any portion of his jacket, vest, or pants. He searches through them slowly, then more rapidly, finally trembling with the realization that his meager savings has vanished. The store owner, meanwhile, gets madder and madder.

Charlie retraces his steps to see where he may have lost the money. While doing so, he runs into the faux clergyman, who is now sermonizing the drunken man with the watch. Charlie notices that when the minister leaves, the drunk's watch is gone. Irate, he searches in vain for the clergyman, then is approached by another, actual, reverend. Charlie reacts in anger and takes his frustrations out on the man.

Charlie's reaction to this actual minister is wonderful. He fumes during the sermonizing, slowly clenching his fist and carefully pushing up his sleeve. His expression builds, exhibiting greater and greater levels of anger. He then bursts into violence and chases the clergyman down the street.

In less than six minutes of running time, *Police* already has enough highlights to rank it among Chaplin's finest work. His subtle nuance has been perfected to a level that surpassed all other noted comedy from this

4. Chaplin Signs with Mutual

period. Even the better comedians active in 1915, such as Roscoe Arbuckle, who was enjoying success near Chaplin's level, were more bombastic (and would remain so, even while making some of the greatest comedies of all time). But this first six minutes of *Police* is only an introduction, an extension of the aforementioned entrance.

Still attempting to adapt to free society, Charlie wanders to a flophouse advertising clean beds for ten cents per night. There is only one man waiting, but Charlie still tries to cut in front. The man balks, and an argument starts. Meanwhile, several tramps wander into the flophouse ahead of both of them. Chaplin presents this scene with his usual timing and rhythm. He plays it out so that the man with whom Charlie is fighting is among those who get into the flophouse before Charlie does. The attempt to cut in line netted him the position of dead last.

Even more nicely presented is the very next scene, where the various tramps walk past the flophouse proprietor and hand in their dime admission. Chaplin gives us all manner of the downtrodden here, but none of them seem at all tragic or pathetic. All seem amusingly scruffy, and each possesses a discernible character. There are some attempts at irony (burly Bud Jamison plays a pansy, while another actor stuffily comes in with a battered top hat and a snobbish demeanor as if he represented some form of upper class society within this context).

An obviously ill man with no money is permitted a bed, so penniless Charlie pretends to cough, but is refused. For good measure, Charlie yanks the proprietor's hanging beard as he hurries away, then runs into the suspicious policeman who'd been chasing him before. Charlie trips the copper his cane as he continues to run.

Charlie is accosted by a burglar who intends to rob him, but the two recognize each other as former cell mates. The man asks Charlie if he'd like to help him rob a house. Charlie, desperate, tentatively agrees to be an accomplice. A house is chosen, and Chaplin uses a nice silhouette image to show Charlie and the criminal approaching the home, their shadows cast by the street light. This is followed by another neat bit where, after a long, fruitless struggle trying to pry open a window, Charlie discovers the front door is unlocked.

The next footage of Charlie concentrates on his futile attempts to keep from making noise and alerting the homeowner (Edna Purviance). Edna does hear him, and sneaks to a phone to call the police. Chaplin shows a concerned Edna in close-up, quietly but forcefully talking into the phone. He then cuts to the police station, where three cops are lazily drinking coffee. Unlike the immediate and frantic behavior of the Keystone Cops, Charlie presents these officers as relaxed, uninvolved, disinterested. The cop who answers the phone leans as he talks and patiently listens, while the cutaway to Edna shows the frightened, desperate victim of a crime. The cops then leave without hurrying, showing no concern. This portrayal of the police as anything but heroic becomes even more interesting when, as events unfold, the hero turns out to be Charlie himself. While Sennett poked fun at authority by showing them as clumsy and bombastic, Chaplin goes in another direction entirely. It is most interesting and highly effective.

Charlie sees Edna and realizes that the homeowner has been alerted. He is quietly removing a basket of various stolen items when he spots her; he slips and falls, sending the loot flying into the air. Charlie then hurries out of the room, knocking down his accomplice.

Charlie accosts a cop in *Police*.

4. Chaplin Signs with Mutual

Edna attempts to use psychology on the two criminals by offering them something to eat, while another cutaway to the cops shows them yawning sleepily as they take a leisurely ride to the crime scene. Charlie becomes smitten with Edna, while the criminal continues on his quest to rob the house. Charlie, still desperate and with no other immediate means for money, does not have a problem robbing the comparatively wealthy woman to whom he is attracted. But when his accomplice starts to rough up Edna, Charlie suddenly finds himself on the side of the law. He defends her physically, and a slapstick brawl ensues. This is where Chaplin the director is at his best, choreographing fights featuring wild swings, ducking from punches, attempts to flee, and other quick physical bits of business. One bit, where Charlie runs to the side of the steep stair railing and climbs over it so he is on the steps above his opponent, able to kick him down the stairs, is particularly creative.

The cops nab Charlie, but Edna lies and states that he is not one of the criminals, he is her husband. Charlie pops a cigar into his mouth and stands loftily, immediately playing up the ruse. The cops leave, Edna gives Charlie some money, and his faith in humanity is restored. He realizes there is good in the world, and that freedom is good. He wanders off. The last shot shows Charlie walking down the street, triumphantly stretching his arms and headed for a new tomorrow.

But while this is a classic Chaplinesque ending, Chaplin throws the audience a curve this time. As the film appears to reach fade-out, the cop who had been pursuing Charlie for most of the movie shows up. Charlie scurries away, and the scene fades out on the grimacing cop shaking his fist. Freedom comes with some limitations.

Walter Kerr, in his book *The Silent Clowns*, called *Police* Chaplin's best Essanay effort, stating:

> I cannot pretend to know when Chaplin discovered for himself what his true, all-embracing, ultimate, and indivisible comic character was. I only know when I [saw] it for the first time — fleetingly, but with the force of a thunderbolt.... With no transition at all, Charlie *becomes* Edna's husband. Affable, outgoing, utterly at home, digging his hands into his pockets and flexing his knees as though he were bonhomie, the host par excellence, eager to show his guests about.... The impression lasts for only a moment

or two, but, for me, its implications are immense. It is entirely clear that Charlie could have been this man at any time he chose to adopt the role.... No barrier stands between his talents and the assumption of a role in which they might be exercised. He is no natural tramp.

Police is believed by some historians to have been tampered with by Essanay, but this does not appear to be the case. There is no evidence that anyone other than Charles Chaplin supervised the production. Perhaps the fact that *Police* was released after Chaplin had left Essanay, and the fact that the studio did indeed tamper with *Carmen* and later used Chaplin footage in an exploitative manner (especially with the release of *Triple Trouble*), would cause some to conclude that this film also underwent some tampering.

Ted Okuda and Dave Maska, in their book *Charlie Chaplin at Keystone and Essanay*, call *Police* "Chaplin's last official Essanay film (i.e. the last one he personally supervised)," adding that it "represents a quantum leap from earlier Essanays like *His New Job* and *A Night Out*." However, as has been documented in this text, there is a very discernible artistic progression from those earlier Essanays to *Police*, with Chaplin not only learning more about comedy and filmmaking, but able to experiment with offbeat ideas.

One of the most impressive things about *Police* is Chaplin's use of the camera. Chaplin was not a technical craftsman like Buster Keaton. He is not noted for interesting camerawork. But, along with the aforementioned shot of the shadows, Chaplin allows the camera to enhance certain scenes. As Okuda and Maska point out, "Chaplin reveals a firm grasp of the cinematic language. The photography is impressive and Chaplin uses irises, close-ups, and panning shots to heighten the impact of a scene, both comically and dramatically." Perhaps this is more experimenting on Chaplin's part, his attempts to use cinema's technology in ways that he would later ignore (during the period when making his talkies, his cinematic technique was constantly dismissed as old-fashioned). Chaplin has been quoted as saying that he doesn't need interesting camera angles, that he himself was interesting. It stands to reason that if Chaplin did indeed say this, he was referring to the importance of the character and the narrative over any technological enhancement.

4. Chaplin Signs with Mutual

The present study of Chaplin's Essanay films has indicated that *The Tramp* was a good checkpoint at which one could assess his career. *The Bank* is another good checkpoint, allowing us to see further growth and refinement. Finally, *Police* is an appropriate checkpoint to show just how far Chaplin had progressed in only a year. His development happened very quickly, contained many experimental ideas, and faced an abundance of creative challenges. Charlie was now firmly established as a celebrated Everyman. The world with which Chaplin surrounds this subtle character includes corruption, mistrust, and disillusionment. While such an outlook may appear cynical in discussion, it was Chaplin's intent to show Charlie the downtrodden persevere in the direst of circumstances. With *Police* there appears to be no hope. Charlie is released from prison, wanting to go straight, but finds that freedom is futile without funds, and is

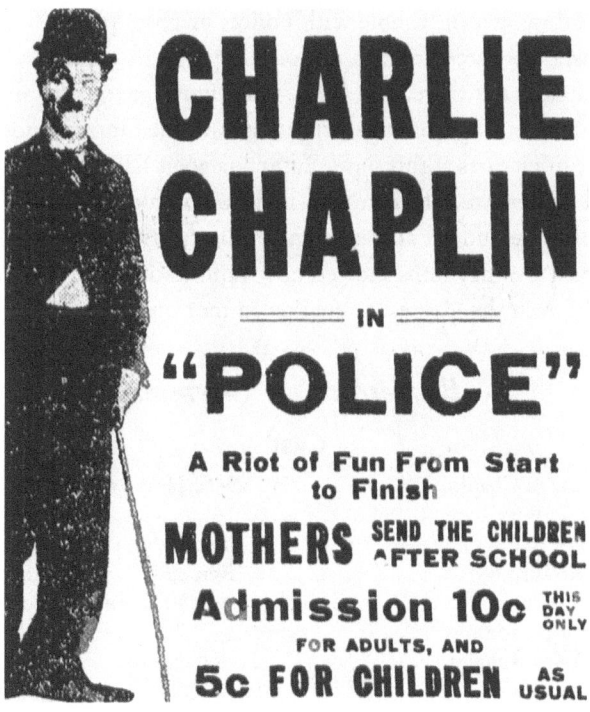

Mothers are urged to send the children to the latest Chaplin film in this newspaper ad for *Police*.

ultimately talked into reverting back to his criminal ways. But in Charlie's halfhearted execution of the robbery, and thanks to the cooperative and understanding Edna's charm, Chaplin presents an effective moral. Charlie does not want to be a criminal — he is a victim of a cold, cruel society that forces him to rob in order to survive. Charlie is won over by Edna's charm — she is the first truly honest and altruistic person he has met since being released from prison. His crooked accomplice, a career criminal is not smitten; he is there for a job. All of these elements are important to Chaplin's cinematic evolution. While he transitioned away from the pure slapstick raucousness of Keystone Charlie, we see a discernible metamorphosis that concludes with *Police*. Charlie is now a character with a soul. He is society's victim. And while he has the ability to fight back when the battle reaches down to his level, he is powerless against the all-encompassing futility of a tramp in an industrial world. If he is to commit a crime, get in trouble with police, or go to prison, it is because his circumstances forced him to do so. It is played for comedy, of course, but the statement is there, and it attracted moviegoers. Chaplin's popularity stemmed chiefly from the fact that he was the funniest and most creative comic in pictures at this time. But moviegoers fell in love with Charlie because he represented the common man so completely.

Chaplin was indeed at the height of his creative powers here. However, the next Essanay films showed how exploitation practices could mar the work of even the greatest comedian in motion pictures.

Burlesque on Carmen

Cast

Charles Chaplin	Darn Hosiery (Don Jose)
Edna Purviance	Carmen
John Rand	Escamillo, the Toreador
Ben Turpin	Remendado, a Smuggler
Leo White	Officer of the Guard
Jack Henderson	Lilas Pastia
Wesley Ruggles	Vagabond
May White	Frasquita
Bud Jamison	Soldier
Lawrence A. Bowes	Gypsy
Frank J. Coleman	Guard

4. Chaplin Signs with Mutual

Credits

Charles Chaplin . . . . .Director, Screenwriter
Leo White .Director (added material)
Harry Ensign . . . . .Cinematographer
Ernest Van Pelt . . . . .Assistant Director
Jess Robbins . . . . .Producer

From the novel *Carmen* by Prosper Mèrimèe, and the opera by Georges Bizet. Released April 16, 1916.

Another one of the truly interesting developments during Chaplin's Essanay tenure came in the form of his *Burlesque on Carmen*. Deciding to eschew the Little Tramp and engage in deeper satire for a headier production, Chaplin's burlesque promised to be his most impressive film to date. Along with tapping into areas he had not yet exhibited in his previous films, Chaplin would also use most of his familiar supporting players, allowing them to stretch as actors in roles not usually found in knockabout Essanay comedies.

The December 11, 1915, issue of *Motography* offered a tantalizing pre-release article:

> Charles Chaplin has nearly completed another Essanay-Chaplin comedy and it will be released shortly. The title is *Charlie Chaplin's Burlesque on Carmen* in two acts. Again, Chaplin is found in an entirely new role. There is less of the slapstick variety of fun and more of the subtle points of genuine humor. Mr. Chaplin apparently is able to put over something new in almost every production. You look for him as he appeared last and you find that his makeup has disappeared and a new one donned. But it is the same Chaplin underneath; you find the same personality that has made him beloved all over the world. It is largely this element of surprise that makes this fun of the top notch variety. You expect to see one thing and you are confronted with an entirely new phase of the mysterious Chaplin. But the surprise is always pleasing as the fun is always there.

In the December 25, 1915, issue of *Motography*, Chaplin's film was already being hailed as a potential masterpiece:

> *Carmen*, the classic tale of love and passion, written by a Spaniard and so appealing that it has been translated into every

language in the world and made into a play and into an opera and finally into a photoplay by two different companies, is the vehicle that Charlie Chaplin has chose for his next offering to the world of mirth

All the world knows the story. A young lieutenant goes into a province of Spain to stop the smuggling that yearly costs the government thousands of dollars. He proves adamant to bribes and is the despair of the smugglers. But Carmen, a gypsy girl, beautiful, alluring, and unscrupulous, guarantees that she will make the lieutenant Jose see reason. So the young soldier falls to her arts, kills a brother officer because of her, and joins a gypsy band.

But he finds that Carmen is an individualist. She doesn't love him. She goes to Madrid with the popular toreador and accepts the plaudits of the multitude as her just due. Jose follows and kills her as she scorns him. Then he stabs himself. The thing is so big that it lends itself to burlesque. And Chaplin, as the smitten soldier, uses Edna Purviance and the situations made by the story to such effect, that the play is a continuous laugh. The situations aren't changed. But it is Chaplin, as the lowbrow in the part, that makes it ridiculous. Edna Purviance is a beautiful, passionate Carmen, and Chaplin is a well-meaning, and therefore extremely funny lover.

Chaplin's film actually was a parody of two different 1915 releases of the story—one directed by Cecil B. DeMille, the other directed by Raoul Walsh.

It has been stated that in order to fully appreciate Chaplin's burlesque, one should screen the DeMille or Walsh originals. Then the specifics of Chaplin's parody can be appreciated. However, if the DeMille or Walsh pictures are not available, the Chaplin film can stand alone as the most ambitious project of the comedian's career up to this point. Once again Chaplin explores the characters for comic possibilities. But this time it is not characters of his creation, but those of Mérimée and Bizet. He realized that the pretensions of the actual story were perfect for parody and uses his seasoned supporting cast to burlesque the roles.

Carmen was completed by Chaplin and carefully prepared as a two-reeler at around the time when he decided to leave Essanay for Mutual studios. Upon his completion of *Carmen*, Chaplin shot the comedy *Police* and then left for Mutual. It was up to Essanay to release the subsequent Chaplin comedies after his departure.

4. Chaplin Signs with Mutual

Essanay released only *Police*, and then waited. They wanted to get the most possible benefit from their remaining Chaplin film now that he would no longer be making new products for the company. He was at the absolute height of his career, so Essanay stood to lose a great deal by losing Chaplin's services. It was several months after the aforementioned December publicity in *Motography* when Chaplin's *Burlesque on Carmen* finally hit theaters. But it was not the way Chaplin had prepared it. It had been decided by the studio to revamp Chaplin's completed *Burlesque on Carmen* by expanding it from a tightly structured two-reeler into a bloated, confusing four-reeler.

For years only the longer version of this Chaplin film was available. It was not until the end of the 20th century when film preservationist and archivist David Shepard created, from Chaplin's own notes and film materials, a reconstruction of the original two-reel version as Chaplin had intended. Quite frankly, the two-reel version is one of the finest films of Chaplin's career, while the four-reel incarnation is an incomprehensible mess. And since the four-reel travesty is in the public domain, it has been duped and re-released by dozens of small-time video distributors on various Chaplin collections, making it quite accessible. The two-reel original edit, carefully assembled by David Shepard, shows Chaplin tapping into areas of his ability that had not been evident up to this point, not even in his best work. The film is handsomely mounted on lavish sets with appropri-

Edna as Carmen, and Charlie as Darn Hosiery in *Burlesque on Carmen*.

ate costumes. Despite being in costume, Charlie is still Charlie within the framework of a classic story. Edna Purviance impresses greatly, playing the title role with relish. It is a far different portrayal than the supporting characters she had played (and would continue to play) since *A Night Out*. Chaplin's creativity is at a real high. His previous dabbling with dramatic elements are extended to the serious scenes here, while his comedic creativity insures it also remains a very funny film. This blending of comedy and tragedy in an Essanay two-reeler was a solid harbinger of what Chaplin would do in the 1920s with films like *The Gold Rush* and *The Circus*. The story structure is more polished, and the comedy set-pieces are among Chaplin's best. Among the film's comedy highlights is the choreographed battle between Darn Hosiery (Charlie) and Captain Morales (Leo White), which takes on a variety of different challenges. Another impressive bit is the scene where Hosiery must stab Carmen. Chaplin and Edna Purviance play it effectively, only to suddenly reveal that the knife is rubber and nobody has been hurt. Chaplin would continue to use tragic scenes and then suddenly hit his audience with a laugh. Jerry Lewis, clearly inspired by Chaplin, is one comedian who would also have fun with the staging of a movie and its props.

Essanay's padding of *Carmen* from two reels to four allowed it to be booked in theaters as a feature picture, generating higher rental fees for the company. In so doing, however, the film is saddled with an intrusive subplot featuring Ben Turpin, who shares no scenes with Chaplin. Some performers, such as May Reeves, appear in the Chaplin original *and* in the later footage, which is rather interesting. What is also interesting is that when we compare the four-reel version and the two-reel Chaplin cut, there is Chaplin-directed footage in the longer version that does not appear in his own edit.

While it is important to note that the December 11 *Motography* issue indicated that the Chaplin film was "a comedy in two acts," the April 15, 1916, issue stated otherwise:

> The mystery in regard to the Essanay-Chaplin photocomedy *Charlie Chaplin's Burlesque on Carmen* has been solved and exhibitors who have been wondering what had become of this film, announced several weeks ago, have had their inquiries answered. For the film is now being released as a four part fea-

ture. The care with which this picture was taken is shown by the footage of film, there being 16,000 feet in all. The picture was trimmed to 4,000 feet in the finished picture.

Chaplin is seen in an entirely new makeup in this comedy. Gone are his old tramp clothes, his dress suit, and his overalls. He appears in the uniform of a soldier, but of such a disreputable type that a real officer would be asked for his resignation. But Chaplin has not given up his mustache or shoes. Despite the costume, it is the same Chaplin, the same carriage, the same walk and the same queer antics.

Oddly, the same April 15, 1916, issue of *Motography* seemed blind to the extended version's flaws, and gave what can be considered a rave review by critic Genevieve Harris:

> With Charles Chaplin as Darn Hosiery (Don Jose), this version of *Carmen* furnishes four acts of fun, both because of Chaplin's clowning and because of the clever travesty of scenes from the opera. It is at once an elaborate parody and a slapstick comedy, and the blending is clever since neither is overdone. The main points of the story are suggested and the most important scenes are acted with a difference. The players act their parts with great seriousness throughout, which adds to the humor of the situations. At no time do they seem conscious of their own clowning. Much of the humor lies in unexpected twists given to scenes worked up in a most serious manner.
> Edna Purviance, as Carmen, is a pretty and effective foil for Chaplin. She and May White as Chiquita, stage a most furious fight. The band of smugglers in the mountains and along the rocky coast appear in melodramatic makeup. Darn Hosiery is sent to subdue them and before they can bribe him, he steals all their money. But he falls victim to Carmen's charm, and fights a duel with another officer. Then he is obliged to leave the country, and he goes to the mountains. But Carmen will have nothing to do with him since he is out of a job and she runs away with a toreador. Later they appear as the "idols of Saville" in a carriage drawn by a very large hose and a tiny donkey. Darn Hosiery sees them and follows them. He meets Carmen near the arena and stabs her then himself. But when the toreador falls over them they come back to life because the knife Darn Hosiery used was a stage dagger with a disappearing blade. The supporting cast includes John Rand as the toreador, Leo White as the officer, and Jack Henderson, Ben Turpin, and Wesley Ruggles. The play will delight both

those who like Chaplin and those who like a skillfully produced parody.

By this review, one would assume that Ms. Harris screened Chaplin's original two-reel cut, especially since her comments center upon Chaplin's footage and relegates Ben Turpin to the last sentence of supporting players, with no comment on the subplot in which he stars. However, it is certain that Essanay only released the four-reel version, and Turpin does not appear in Chaplin's two-reel cut, so it can therefore be determined that the critic carefully picked out the expert Chaplin footage and ignored the excess Turpin material in her review.

Chaplin, however, certainly did notice. In the April 29, 1916, issue of *Motography*, the comedian's ire was fully reported:

> Last week Charlie Chaplin made a request — or was it a demand? — of the Essanay company to the effect that his burlesque of *Carmen* should not be released in four reels, as it was, he claims,

Essanay's ad for Chaplin's *Burlesque on Carmen*.

originally intended for but two. Since that time he has brought suit against Essanay and VLSE (Vitagraph-Lubin-Selig-Essanay) for a permanent injunction against the distribution of the film. He charges that the four reel *Carmen* will injure his reputation. An order to show cause has been issued by Justice Nathan Bijur of the New York state supreme court. Nathan Burkan has been retained as Chaplin's attorney. The application for the injunction is accompanied by an affidavit by Sidney Chaplin, brother of Charlie, setting forth facts in regard to the making of the picture and citing the effect upon Charlie's reputation of adverse criticisms which are likely to appear in newspapers, trade, and dramatic journals. It is charged that the release of *Carmen* in four reels instead of two is a violation of Chaplin's contract with Essanay, and that Ben Turpin was employed in some scenes for the purpose of completing the four reels. At the time the news of the injunction was received the Essanay company had not been notified of Chaplin's act and therefore had no statement to offer.

Chaplin was so upset by Essanay's tampering with his work that it sent him to bed for two days. He filed a lawsuit against the company, with the May 6, 1916, issue of *Moving Picture World* reporting:

> Under the terms of his contract, Chaplin alleges that the Essanay company agreed that no pictures bearing his name should be released without his approval and final OK. He says that he made a two-reel *Carmen* and directly charges that the Essanay company, after he had completed the picture and left the employ of the company, employed one Ben Turpin and other actors to make additional pictures with which *Carmen* was padded. The application for injunction cites the fact that the distributing concern, the VLSE, has circulated advertising matter all over the country with the film, calculated to convey the impression to the public and falsely to lead the public to believe that the said film exhibited by the defendants is the film based on a scenario created by the plaintiff and that said photoplay was produced, directed, and made under the supervision of the plaintiff.

What was most frustrating was the reception the four-reel *Burlesque on Carmen* was receiving from audiences. One particularly successful screening was covered in the May 6, 1916, issue of *Motography*:

> When announcement was made of Charlie Chaplin's debut as star of a four reel burlesque of *Carmen*, under the Essanay VLSE

banner, it was generally felt and predicted that the feature would prove a tremendous success. Several months having elapsed since Chaplin had been seen in a new picture, his legion of admirers were naturally expected to gather in full force to welcome the eccentric comedian extraordinary of the screen world. Yet even the most optimistic believer in the drawing power of the Chaplin film would not have ventured to prophesy the utterly unprecedented reception which was given the *Carmen* fantasy at the Broadway theater last week. At the opening performance Sunday it was not merely a packed house that greeted the flitting form of the inimitable Charlie, it was a made mob of enthusiasts tightly jammed together, with lines extending out into the street and down Broadway for several blocks. And the same crowds continued night after night.

Spoor and Essanay filed a countersuit, as detailed in that same issue:

Newspapers state the Essanay Company has sued Charles Chaplin for a sum approximating $700, 000 or a little more than Chaplin expects to secure from the Mutual Film Corporation this year. This, of course, will not have the slightest effect on either the Lone Star Film Corporation or the amount of money the Mutual company will make as it is simply a personal issue between George K. Spoor and Charlie Chaplin. Any damages that may have resulted to the Essanay Company through Chaplin's failure to go through with a few of the weeks under his contract with them, could not possibly amount to more than a very small fraction of the amount of damages claimed, but then the film industry loves to expand figures and has ever been handicapped by over modesty in thinking in terms of six figures when four or five would more than suffice.

The same issue also indicated that bookings on the Chaplin Mutual series had gone over one million dollars, according to trustworthy New York sources. Meanwhile, the court case regarding *Burlesque on Carmen* continued, as reported in the May 27, 1916, issue of *Moving Picture World*:

Charlie Chaplin's much advertised motion for injunction to restrain Vitagraph-Lubin-Selig-Essanay's distribution of the Essanay four reel burlesque on *Carmen* was argued before Judge Hotchkiss of the Supreme Court, New York City, on Friday May 12. Chaplin's counsel argued that under the contract which he'd had with Essanay, he reserved the right to approve or disapprove pictures in which he personally appeared, and that because his

4. Chaplin Signs with Mutual

burlesque on *Carmen* had been distributed in four reels by VLSE instead of two as he had left it, the Essanay Company ought to be enjoined from representing it as his burlesque.

The Essanay Company was represented by William N. Seabury who showed that the contract upon which Chaplin relied had been entirely abandoned by both parties, and the picture made under a contract with contained no such restrictions.

According to Ted Okuda and Dave Maska in their book *Charlie Chaplin at Keystone and Essanay*, Spoor actually claimed in one court appearance that *Burlesque on Carmen* was the first film Chaplin edited himself, and the result was a picture unworthy of release. Spoor explained that the film was restructured to make it palatable for audiences, its success with moviegoers proving his point. Of course this is ridiculous. Chaplin had been editing his own films since first joining the Essanay company. His original edit was perfectly acceptable; in fact, it is one of the finest films of his career. The bloated release print prepared by Essanay is, as Okuda and Maska indicated, the reason why *Burlesque on Carmen* can be considered both his best and his worst film from this period.

Chaplin's creative freedom did not necessarily mean artistic control, however, and the following was reported in the June 10, 1916, issue of *Moving Picture World*:

> Judge Hotchkiss of the Supreme Court of the state of New York on Monday May 24 denied the application of Charlie Chaplin for an injunction to restrain the VLSE and the Essanay Company from distributing the four-reel Essanay-Chaplin comedy, *Charlie Chaplin's Burlesque on Carmen.*
>
> First — Plaintiff's right under paragraph three of the contract of December 1914 to enjoin the production because he had not approved of the play is doubtful.
>
> Second. The play itself is undoubtedly the property of the Essanay Film Manufacturing Company.
>
> Third. The facts do not justify the claim that the association of the plaintiff's name with the play, as produced, amounts to a fraud upon the public. A fair construction of the advertisements of the play is not that plaintiff is the author or producer but that he is the star or principal actor.
>
> Fourth. It's not claimed that so far as he is pictured in the play, his part is garbled or distorted. Whatever of him is shown is a truthful representation.

Fifth. Whether plaintiff will suffer any damage from the production is problematical while an injunction is certain to work loss for defendants.

Chaplin appealed the decision, carrying the case to the Appellate Division of the Supreme Court. It failed, but the suit against him by Essanay dragged on, even after the company closed. Spoor even attempted to gain distribution of *The Kid*, Chaplin's 1921 feature for First National.

The bottom line: Chaplin was defeated. Had it not been for David Shepard's hard work at reconstructing the original edit from Chaplin's existing papers, all we would have of *Burlesque on Carmen* is the awful four-reel edit. To add insult to injury, this four-reeler continued to garner good press. The July 8, 1916, issue of *Motography* reported:

> The Essanay-Chaplin *Burlesque on Carmen* was shown to the inmates of Sing Sing prison and the reports are they are laughing yet. Chaplin has the appreciation of every man in Sing Sing for making their lives so much brighter.

One fairly amusing event did occur regarding Chaplin's film. A comedy series in which youngsters remake current movies decided to take on *Burlesque on Carmen*. The Juvenile Film Corp. did a whole series of kids comedies that starred Joseph Monahan (born 1907) and Janethel Monahan (born 1908). These were put out by the Cosmofotofilm Co. and released on the states rights market. They were produced and directed by James Fitzpatrick. The plot of this movie has the kids attending a screening of Chaplin's *Burlesque on Carmen*, when Joseph falls asleep and dreams that he and his sister are in their own parody. Although *Chip's Carmen* is just a low-budget novelty, it did receive a review in the June 10, 1916, issue of *Motography*:

> Though appreciating full well its uncertainty, we doubt that the future holds concealed in its gray mist a day when we will not be filled with amused wonderment at the mimetic talent when possessed by beings of such tender years as the two Monahan children, Joseph and Janethel. *Chip's Carmen* burlesques a burlesque. Joseph Monahan, who is Chip, takes a nap after a visit to the picture show where he saw the *Carmen* of Chaplin, and then in a

4. Chaplin Signs with Mutual

dream he does a little *Carmen* himself. Joseph's Bon Doze is an excellent imitation of Chaplin's Darn Hosiery. Janethel as Carmen is, to be sure, very remarkable and scores a personal triumph. The director, James A. FitzPatrick, with the release of *Chip's Carmen*, adds another to the list of successful pictures credited to him. Now well under way, FitzPatrick is doubtless headed straight for a brilliant reputation in his chosen field. In producing such pictures as the Chip comedies, he is doing a great deal for the children's program. The most notable thing is that the guardian need have little fear of being bored should a visit to the theater showing Chip pictures be decided upon by the powers that be.

As we examine each version of *Burlesque on Carmen*, the differences are fascinating on several levels. As previously noted, this was Chaplin's most ambitious film to date. But what is immediately striking, at least to this writer, is how completely the four-reel edit was able to ruin the original two-reel concept. Now that we have the closest possible approximation to Chaplin's original vision, *Burlesque on Carmen* is a revelation — not so much that the two-reel edit is so much better (which is a logical conclusion), but the fact that the four-reel extension has turned an exceptionally great Chaplin film from this period into a fairly terrible one.

Chaplin's original two-reel edit opens with a brief shot of smugglers on the shore retrieving an arriving boat. They are immediately told of a new officer guarding the breach in the wall. It is Darn Hosiery (Charlie), who is introduced in the very next shot. This sequence lasts mere seconds. The four-reel version opens with a Foreword that runs longer than the opening sequence in the two-reel edit. Then we are given the same opening shot of the gypsies waiting on the shore. But the camera cuts to a boat in the water, then back to the same shot of the gypsies, then another shot of the boat, then again to the same shot of the gypsies. Then the boat arrives and this scene continues, with bumbling Ben Turpin among the gypsies trying to climb a mountain with the wares they have collected from the boat. A gypsy camp is then shown at the top of the mountain as Ben finally arrives, clearly smitten by Frasquita (May White). She ignores him, while he drops to his knees and proclaims his love with blatant histrionics that quite obviously could never have been directed by Chaplin. He is shoved away by a rival, and a comic battle ensues. Finally, this scene ends and the film cuts to Darn Hosiery's opening bit.

Chaplin at Essanay

Here, then, is a perfect example illustrating the difference between the two versions of Chaplin's *Burlesque on Carmen*. The two-reel edit has a brief establishing shot of the gypsies collecting wares from a boat on the shore. After only seconds, Charlie, as Don Hosiery, is onscreen doing his amusing opening bit and offering another great entrance (as with all of the Essanay productions). The four-reeler opens with seven minutes of Ben Turpin hijinks before we even see Chaplin, the star of the film. And the four-reeler even takes editing liberties with Darn Hosiery's introduction. Hosiery trips over a rock and orders it killed. The guards shoot at it, and Hosiery reacts. In the four-reeler, the ridiculous title card "kill that bug" is inserted, and Hosiery's reaction to the shooting is clumsily shown twice. The Chaplin bit in the four-reeler also cuts away to new footage of Pastia, then goes to Hosiery and Pastia's meeting. The two-reeler does not have the excess footage.

So the first ten minutes of either film offers conclusive evidence of how Essanay effectively ruined Chaplin's original two-reel burlesque. Chaplin carefully edited his films to a certain rhythm. Essanay's intrusive additions threw that rhythm off and therefore obliterated the comic possibilities. It is alternately fascinating and disgusting.

The next scene, Carmen's first meeting with Darn Hosiery, and her stirring up of the rivalry between him and the officer of the guard (Leo White), is presented the same in both versions. But the four-reeler then throws the rhythm off once again by following up with more footage of Ben Turpin as Remendado, which was shot for the expanded version and sorely lacks Chaplin's more subtle direction. Even when Hosiery meets Carmen in the grotto, the newer version inserts more distracting footage of Turpin pursuing hefty May White.

In calling attention to the obtrusive footage featuring Ben Turpin, it must be noted that this is not intended to undermine Mr. Turpin as a comedian. Turpin made some very funny movies with Sennett, and at the low-budget Weiss Brothers production company, during the 1920s. His footage in this film is unwelcome due to its ad hoc status ruining an already finished film, not because Turpin himself was an overall lesser talent. When actually directed by Chaplin, such as in *His New Job* or *A Night Out*, he does quite well indeed.

There is a great deal of drama in this burlesque, and both Chaplin and Edna Purviance rise to the occasion. Edna, especially, reveals her dramatic acting background here, but vamps it up in some scenes, making it evident that she truly enjoyed her role.

Ted Okuda and David Maska, in their book *Charlie Chaplin at Keystone and Essanay*, point out a couple of scenes shot by Chaplin that do appear in the four-reel version but not in the two-reel edit. Likely these are outtakes rejected by Chaplin in his final edit. But the highlight of either version is the superb death scene at the end, when Darn Hosiery kills Carmen and then stabs himself to death with the same knife. Chaplin waits for just the right number of beats before he and Edna get up and reveal to the audience that a rubber knife was used. Chaplin staged the sequence so beautifully that we forget we are watching a burlesque. The suddenness of the gag is startling — and hilarious.

Chaplin's continuous artistic progress throughout his year at Essanay is underlined by the original two-reel version of *Burlesque on Carmen*. His understanding of story structure, set design, costumes, and the expert blending of the original dramatic story with gentle, clever comic parody is outstanding. The idea that the four-reel debacle has been our only representation of the film from its release until the end of the 20th Century is especially galling in regard to any previous studies on Chaplin that had only this version to assess.

From his experience with *Burlesque on Carmen*, Chaplin learned to carefully place a no-tampering clause in all subsequent contracts. And although this period contained some of his most important films, Chaplin became disdainful of his Essanay output for the rest of his life, which is unfortunate because he says little about the films in his 1964 autobiography.

It is perhaps worth noting in conclusion that, while Chaplin felt bitter towards his Essanay period due to circumstances such as this, he did not appear to have held any grudge against the actors who participated. He continued to speak highly of Ben Turpin, used May White in a few of his Mutual films, and engaged Leo White's services as late as *The Great Dictator* in 1940. The fact that he continued to work with White periodically all the way up to his first talkie is interesting, especially when considering that White also was responsible for the added footage that resulted in *Triple Trouble*.

Of course, the fact that such a thing as *Triple Trouble* was produced is further proof that Spoor was going to profit somehow from every frame of Chaplin footage he had. There is some justification for this practice. Other studies discussing this period will admit that anyone who had unreleased Chaplin footage in their vault would be foolish not to cash in on the most popular star in films. But to take a finished short film and clumsily extend it to feature length by adding two reels of extra footage, or to gather random snippets and build a story around them purely for exploitation purposes, is hardly the sort of decision one can understand, even from a purely business perspective. The fact that Spoor claimed that *Burlesque on Carmen* was re-edited because Chaplin's edit was unsatisfactory due to it being the only film the actor edited himself, and that he also offered press releases to newspapers claiming that *Triple Trouble* was a bonafide Chaplin film prepared by the artist himself, makes his exploitative efforts truly unsavory.

While Chaplin himself was an artist ruled essentially by promises of creative freedom and an open schedule, he certainly was fully accepting of his astronomical salary. Spoor, then, was fully aware of how much money could be had by the extension of *Carmen* and the creation of *Triple Trouble*. So, pleased with the results of the protracted *Burlesque on Carmen*, Spoor then assigned Leo White to see what he could put together using the discarded, unreleased footage Chaplin had shot for his proposed Essanay feature *Life*. The result was a new two-reel subject from the world's most popular comedian.

Triple Trouble
Cast

Charles Chaplin	Charlie, the Janitor
Edna Purviance	Maid
Billy Armstrong	Cook and Pickpocket
Wesley Ruggles	Crook
Leo White	Diplomat/Spy and Flophouse Owner
James T. Kelley	Singing Drunk
Bud Jamison	Flophouse Patron

Credits

Charles Chaplin	Director, Screenwriter
Harry Ensign	Cinematographer

4. Chaplin Signs with Mutual

Ernest Van Pelt . . . . .Assistant Director
Jess Robbins . . . . .Producer
Leo White . . . . .Director of 1918 material

Released August 11, 1918. Two Reels.

Triple Trouble is one of the most fascinating films in the Chaplin filmography, as well as one of the most disturbing. Created by Essanay two years after Chaplin left the studio, using footage that still lurked in their vault, and some new footage helmed by actor Leo White, *Triple Trouble* is a crazy quilt that somehow holds together better than its history would suggest. But to assess it as a Chaplin film would be unfair, for while Chaplin did indeed direct each sequence in which he appears, he did not approve of their being taken out of context and placed haphazardly with new footage directed by someone else.

This was not the first time Essanay recycled their Chaplin films for extra profit. On October 21, 1916, they released *The Essanay-Chaplin Revue of 1916*, a collection of three Chaplin shorts, *The Tramp*, *His New Job*, and *A Night Out*. However, they strung them together and, with intertitles, tried to create a feature-length story out of the three separate shorts.

In a surprisingly positive review that appeared in the October 28, 1916, issue of *Motography*, reviewer G. Harris stated:

> This "revue," which is five reels, is a clever method of reissuing three of the two-reel Essanay Chaplin comedies. *The Tramp*, *His New Job* and *A Night Out* have been put together, cut to five reels and supplied with connecting subtitles to form a continuous narrative. For a Chaplin loving audience, this arrangement should prove a delight, providing them with five reels of mirth. The offering is packed with comedy business which Chaplin fans enjoy and, unless the viewers grow exhausted from laughing, we do not believe the five reel version can be called tiresome.

In the September 22, 1917, issue of *Motography* it was announced that Essanay was re-releasing all of their Chaplin films:

> Essanay is to put out new prints of all the Essanay-Chaplin productions. The first one will be offered on September 15, and one a month will be issued thereafter. *The Champion* will head the program. this will be followed by other equally humorous come-

dies, including *In the Park, Shanghaied, By the Sea, A Woman, Work, A Jitney Elopement, The Bank, A Night in the Show*, and others. They will be distributed through the General Film Company, Inc.

Then, in *Motography*'s November 3, 1917, issue, a statement from Harry Everhart of the National Theater in Greenville, Oregon, indicated that a screening of *The Champion* was a hit with his patrons, stating that it played to capacity business. Chaplin was such a beloved star that people apparently didn't care whether they were seeing first run material or not.

That same year, British director Langford Reed put together a collection of Essanay scenes in an attempt to create a continuous story, calling it *Chase Me Charlie*. According to Ted Okuda and Dave Maska, in their book *Chaplin at Keystone and Essanay*:

> Charlie falls in loved with Edna, a farmers daughter (in scenes from *The Tramp*). Seeking permission from Edna's father to win her hand, Charlie does the unthinkable: he goes to work. The narrative follows his adventures as a bank guard (from *The Bank*), prizefighter (from *The Champion*), paperhanger (*Work*), stagehand and actor (*His New Job*). Finally he disguises himself (*A Woman*) to influence Edna's father.

Essanay approved Reed's crazy quilt collection of Chaplin footage and released it in America in April of 1918. It was released again by an independent distributor in 1932, with narration by Teddy Bergman (who, as Alan Reed, later became the voice of Fred Flintstone until his death in 1977). It was released yet again by Citation Films, Inc., in February of 1960.

So, Essanay was hardly above exploitation; hence *Triple Trouble*.

Triple Trouble is not without interest. Since 1915, Chaplin had been dabbling with a proposed feature-length production for Essanay entitled *Life* and had shot some footage. His schedule to produce short films kept him from spending a great deal of time on this feature, and, of course, he had to abandon it altogether once he left the studio to work for Mutual. Perhaps we would never have seen what Chaplin shot for *Life* had Essanay not chosen to dust it off and use it as the basis for a new film, surrounded by new footage. However, George K. Spoor issued a statement to the press that misleadingly suggested this concoction had been fully supervised by Chaplin. In an August 1918 press release, Spoor stated:

> If you bought a piece of real estate and foresaw that its value would quadruple if you held it a certain length of time, what would you do? Certainly you would hold it. That's just what we did with *Triple Trouble*. Essanay made this picture with Charlie Chaplin when he was at the zenith of his laugh-making powers. We knew there would come a time when it would be worth many times its weight in gold. We held this negative in our vaults for the most opportune time of release, which we believe is now. There has been one new Chaplin film in several months. The public is eager for a new Chaplin comedy and will welcome *Triple Trouble*.

Of course, this was not a fully realized Chaplin production that had been sitting in the vaults. Along with the scenes shot for *Life* and the new footage helmed by White, *Triple Trouble* contained scenes from *Police* and the actual ending — literally the final shot — from *Work*.

One can understand Spoor's actions, to some extent. By 1918, Chaplin had completed his contract at Mutual and was now releasing through First National. He was at the height of his popularity. The important films he made for Essanay culminated in the brilliant work he did for Mutual, which was sustained at First National. Naturally, anyone who had Chaplin-shot footage would be foolish not to exploit it. Spoor owned the unseen material shot from *Life* and the right to release it. The controversy came from his addition of new footage directed by someone else, and his insistence that *Triple Trouble* was a complete, authentic Chaplin film.

Chaplin did not contest Spoor this time. He had learned his lesson from the debacle surrounding his *Burlesque on Carmen*. But this further cemented Chaplin's disdain for his work at Essanay, to the point where little was mentioned in his autobiography (curiously, though, *Triple Trouble* is included in that book's filmography).

Chaplin did, however, send a telegram, which was printed in *Moving Picture World*, August 10, 1918, under the headline "Charlie Chaplin Wires Vehement Denial," as follows:

HY LOSANGELES CALIF JUL 26
J D WILLIAMS FIRST NATIONAL EXHIBITORS CIRCUIT

Chaplin at Essanay

SIX AND EIGHT WEST FORTYEIGHT ST NEWYORK TRADE PAPERS ANNOUNCING ESSANAY ISSUE OF TRIPLE TROUBLE AS A NEW CHAPLIN PICTURE JUST ARRIVED ON THE COAST THIS IS NOT A NEW CHAPLIN BUT FROM THE ADVERTISING LAYOUT IN TRADE REVIEW MUST BE NOTHING BUT THE DISCARDED PORTIONS OF POLICE THE LAST PICTURE MADE BY CHARLIE CHAPLIN FOR ESSANAY FIRST NATIONAL SHOULD STOP THESE MISLEADING STATEMENTS AND ADVERTISING WHICH MUST BE STAMPED OUT CHAPLIN

There are some Chaplin experts who believe *Life* was never a project at all. They feel that announcements about this project was merely more bogus publicity from Essanay, no more believable than the press release labeling *Triple Trouble* a Chaplin project. These historians believe the new sequences used for *Triple Trouble* were actually discarded portions of *Police*. Chaplin shot them but decided not to use them, with the discarded footage remaining in the Essanay vaults.

There appears to be no mention of a Chaplin feature in any of the trade magazines from this period. There are no references to *Life* in any of Chaplin's interviews or his autobiography. It is only mentioned in an Essanay newsletter, without any further corroboration.

Of course, this is pure speculation on the part of these historians. That there is any mention at all of *Life* and its footage causes this writer to allow the benefit of the doubt and believe that a feature-length project was indeed considered by Chaplin for Essanay (shooting apparently occurred during the summer of 1915).

Triple Trouble is supposed to feature Chaplin as a janitor (or cook's assistant, depending on one's perspective) who is hired to work in the home of Colonel Nutt. The Colonel is experimenting with explosives, with the Pretzelstrassers, a foreign power, seeking information about the Colonel's inventions.

From this premise, Leo White tries to maintain the proper rhythm and match the Chaplin footage. He does a reasonable job, considering the difficult circumstances. Though far from seamless, the new footage and old blend together fairly well (well enough, anyway, to make it appear as a unified whole). But because White's capabilities as a director are average at best, he cannot match Chaplin's ability to present characters and situations in a funny and insightful manner. The White footage is bombastic, the Chaplin footage refined; and although they combine better than one would expect, any knowledgeable viewer will notice a difference, while the layperson will, at the very least, dismiss *Triple Trouble* as a weak Chaplin effort.

The Chaplin sequences that appear in *Triple Trouble* are a mixed bag. There is a flophouse sequence that was apparently originally filmed for *Police* but discarded and reshot (the copyright material for *Police* describes the flophouse scene that's in *Triple Trouble*, not the one appearing in *Police*). But footage of Edna Purviance as a maid is likely taken from the *Life* project (although some believe this may have been shot for *Police* as well, then discarded in order to feature Edna in another role entirely).

Triple Trouble opens with a close-up shot of Chaplin's face that fades in and fades out. This offers at least some minor interest. As previously stated, Chaplin's Essanay films liked to highlight Charlie's entrance. Because this film is a crazy quilt of patches and shreds, Charlie is introduced with a fade-in close-up. It fades out to reveal Colonel Nutt experimenting with his new wireless explosive, and then cuts to a shot of the Colonel's daughter.

The titles then read, "Charlie, the new janitor of the house," and the film cuts to a typically bombastic Billy Armstrong in a cook's uniform. Charlie makes his actual entrance a few seconds later. It is a rather clumsy introduction, but the Chaplin footage shows real finesse, with Charlie, while listening to Billy's instructions, casually leaning against tables covered with food plates, placing his hand into various sticky substances. Cut to Edna, a cleaning woman with her hair pulled back and her sleeves rolled up, vigorously scrubbing the floor. Meanwhile, Charlie gets ready to go to work assisting the cook. He takes off his coat and tosses it onto the plates of food. Billy returns and sees the coat covering the food, resulting in Charlie receiving a swift kick.

This footage from *Life* is a good example of what Chaplin wanted to do with a full-length feature. The longer running time would allow for greater character development, so Chaplin offers little exposition in the first few shots of himself and Edna. Of course, Charlie is himself; but Edna appears to be playing role with some depth, given the greater attention to minute details (such as the pulled-back hair and rolled-up sleeves). These careful externals define the character within the context of Chaplin's proposed feature examining the plight of the downtrodden moreso than a slapstick two-reeler might.

Two minutes into the film, with only this brief look at Charlie and Edna (and not together), we are taken back to the Leo White footage added for this release. First, the Colonel demonstrates his new wireless explosive. Then we see Pretzelstrasser diplomats at a board meeting, headed by White, being a read a telegram from the Colonel indicating his refusal to sell them his explosive formula. White announces, via title card, "I will go and tempt him with the Iron Double Cross," and hastily leaves the room.

Now the structure of *Triple Trouble* has been established. Colonel Nutt has perfected a wireless explosive. The Pretzelstrassers have been refused its formula, so their leader must find other means of acquiring it. However, this plot has not met up with the Chaplin story yet. And In the Chaplin scenes we have only been introduced to characters; there has been no exposition beyond that.

As the film cuts back to Chaplin, we see Charlie gathering the garbage from the kitchen. We next see Edna, still scrubbing the floor, then Charlie again, who has filled his garbage can. He walks in to where Edna is working, the full can flung over his shoulder. As Charlie walks past Edna, most of the can's contents spill over her hunched figure. He ventures outside and tosses the remainder of the garbage over the fence, spilling it over Leo White, who is standing on the other side.

Now the Chaplin footage and the White footage converge. Chaplin tossing garbage over the fence was shot in the summer 1915. Leo White being covered with garbage on the other side of the fence was shot in the winter of 1918. White links the Chaplin footage with his own appearance in order to blend the separate exploits of the characters — and the separate movies.

The difference in performance style seen in the Chaplin footage and that helmed by White is remarkable. The Colonel demonstrating his experiment to his daughter has him flailing his arms and wildly dancing her about. White's reaction to being covered with garbage also consists of blatant gestures. Charlie, however, is very casual and subtle, never realizing that some of his garbage can's contents spilled onto Edna. Edna's reaction to being covered with garbage while scrubbing the floor is one of shock and dismay, but it's a realistic (though comic) reaction, and one without the exaggerated grimacing found in the White footage.

Chaplin re-enters, sees Edna, notices the garbage on the floor, and realizes what he had done. He grins in embarrassment. He bends to pick up his mess and receives a kick from Edna, who cries over her hard work being ruined. Charlie, who meant no harm, eventually starts crying as well. It is a beautifully played scene, with Charlie sadly listening to Edna and then, very slowly, reacting in kind.

The very next sequence is among the film's most intriguing. Edna angrily tosses a wet rag at Charlie. It hits Leo White, who is standing outside in the hallway. He tosses it back, and it hits Billy Armstrong in the kitchen. Obviously, in the originally shot Chaplin footage the rag thrown by Edna hit Billy. But White edits himself into the skirmish to blend the padded footage. It seems that Billy Armstrong appears in both the Chaplin footage and the later White footage, serving as a bridge. Billy comes out into the hall, gets in an argument with White, shoves him down, and enters the room where Charlie and Edna are standing. Thus, the film shifts from White footage to Chaplin footage, and makes it appear the characters are all playing off each other. The sequence ends poorly, however. Billy acts rough with Edna, Charlie comes to her aid, then he and Billy tussle. Charlie is pushed back onto a table, lifts both feet, and kicks Billy. The scene then ends very abruptly, and quickly cuts to White, now in Colonel Nutt's study. Furthermore, this is all the footage of Edna that Chaplin had shot, so despite the film having just established the beginnings of a relationship between her and Charlie, it is her last appearance in the film.

Closer examination reveals that Billy does not actually appear in the new footage after all. It is actually another actor made up to look like him. Similarly, a double for actor Wesley Ruggles is employed in the new footage.

The rest of the film blends the various footage in much the same way. White is ordered out of Nutt's house, and is physically removed by a servant. Charlie, meanwhile, has finished work, so he goes to a flophouse to sleep. White and a henchman go after the Colonel's formula, while some cops chase after White and his accomplice. Charlie, in the flophouse, has to deal with an annoying drunk, a bullying patron who engages in throwing things, and a bothersome tramp who steals from the sleeping patrons and gets into a fight with Charlie. This escalates into a real donnybrook involving most of the bums in the flophouse, so Charlie escapes. He then runs into White's henchman, who, as it turns out, is an old friend. The henchman enlists Charlie in helping him rob Colonel Nutt. They approach the house, but Colonel Nutt hears them breaking in and alerts the cops, who are standing by in the living room. The henchman enters, is chased by the policemen, and is finally apprehended before an explosion goes off and the house is destroyed.

Whether intended for the *Life* project or originally shot for *Police* and then discarded, Chaplin's flophouse scenes remain noteworthy. He examines the characters more carefully than he might have for one of his two-reelers. The drunk is a pathetic sort, whom Charlie treats disdainfully, but whom Chaplin presents as more grotesque and disheveled than one might see in his other supporting characters. The same goes for the tramp who enters and steals from the others (causing Charlie to, in turn, steal from him). It is unknown whether Chaplin supervised the makeup on these characters, but their appearance is creepier than the usual comic villain. Perhaps this ugly imagery was Chaplin's way of presenting a grittier example of the characters for a more serious comic study of the downtrodden, as had been planned for *Life*.

The scene in which Charlie runs into the henchman, recognizing him as an old friend, is lifted directly from *Police*. In the earlier film, Charlie runs into an old cell mate who talks him into robbing a house. In *Triple Trouble* he is talked into helping rob Colonel Nutt. So we see Charlie and the henchman approach the door, but it is only the henchman running about the interior of the house, with the cops in pursuit. One brief cutaway to Charlie doing a pratfall in the kitchen, and rising from the debris after the explosion (both of these lifted from *Work*), is all we see of him.

White stages the police pursuit very much like they were the Keystone Cops, whose antics were already becoming clichéd by 1918. And the explosion sequence is especially outrageous. As Ted Okuda and Dave Maska point out in their book *Chaplin at Keystone and Essanay: Dawn of*

4. Chaplin Signs with Mutual

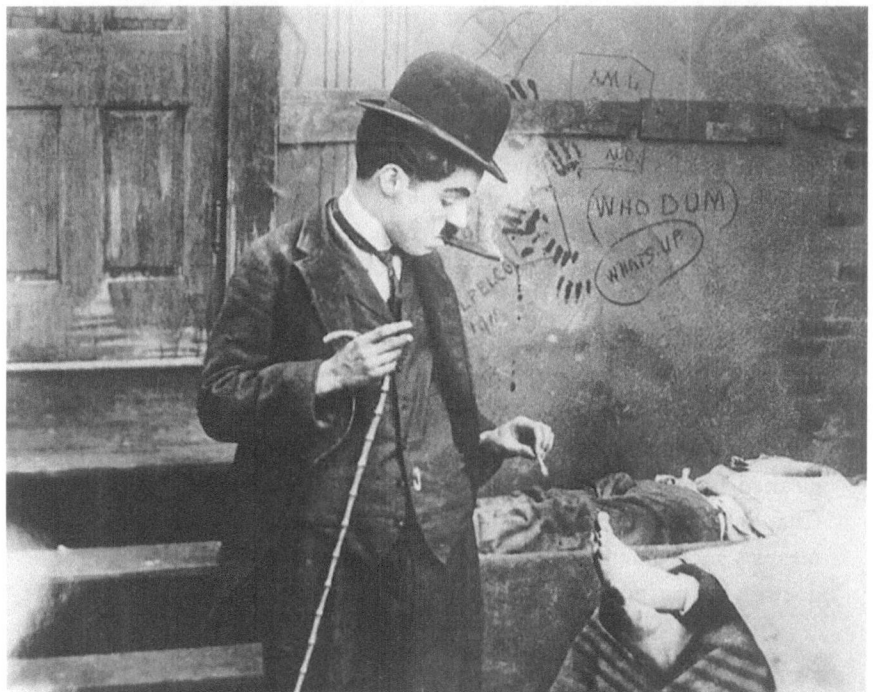

Charlie, in the flophouse, lights his match in this scene from the aborted feature *Life*, which was used in the Essanay pastiche *Triple Trouble*.

the Tramp, "the cops hurling through the air has to be seen to be believed." Okuda and Maska also indicate that *Triple Trouble* "has a certain archaeological value as an early example of creative film editing, juggling new and old footage."

Researching *Triple Trouble* presents serious stumbling blocks. While we have the film itself preserved, research has not disclosed the names of the actors playing Colonel Nutt, his daughter, their butler, the cops, or the Pretzelstrass agents. Even David Kiehn's exhaustive study *Broncho Billy and the Essanay Company* fails to provide such information. But by this time Essanay was having a great deal of trouble surviving, and released the pastiche that is *Triple Trouble* likely out of pure desperation.

The fact that *Triple Trouble* offers us sequences that Chaplin filmed and never used makes it worth seeing, if only for the sake of curiosity. If one wants to look past Essanay's shameless exploitation, one realizes that had the studio not decided to put this film together, the unseen Chaplin footage shot for *Life* would have remained in their vault and likely would have eventually been lost. In this respect Essanay should be commended (at least in a backhand fashion) for making the previously unseen Chaplin footage available. Anything Chaplin shot is important due to his significance in film history. And certainly the scenes shot for *Life* are the only truly interesting moments in this entire two-reeler. The rest might make a decent run-of-the-mill Essanay comedy, but these new sequences are far less interesting than what Chaplin could have done with them. Leo White, though quite good at blending his new material with the Chaplin footage, was clearly not at the same artistic level. White, like his performances, directs his actors to play it over-the-top. While there is some humor to be gleaned from blatant gestures, this style clashes with the more refined Chaplin approach. Though the pastiche that is *Triple Trouble* is by no means a good movie, the fact that it somehow hangs together as well as it does makes it truly remarkable.

5

Mutual and After

As Chaplin concluded his Essanay period, showing amazing growth as a comedian and filmmaker in the span of only a year, he had risen from comic favorite to serious artist. No less than the great American actress Minnie Maddern Fiske startled intellectual America in May 1916 when she wrote, "It will surprise numbers of well-meaning Americans to learn that a constantly increasing body of cultured, artistic people are beginning to regard the young English buffoon, Charles Chaplin, as an extraordinary artist, as well as a comic genius."

After Chaplin left Essanay and joined the Mutual corporation, most of the attendant press focused on his salary, which was enormous for the time. However, once he began making films for this company, his exacting methods of direction, multiple takes to get the scene right, and penchant for scrapping entire scenes after being filmed, rose to an even greater level. There is existing footage of Chaplin on the sets of various Mutual productions directing several takes of sequences that later do not appear in the finished film.

Perhaps Chaplin simply had to work his own way, for as much as the Essanay films were an improvement over Keystone, the Mutual series saw Chaplin at his best. His genius culminated in the twelve short films produced for this company. He would continue to make great movies, and his feature-length productions would add greater depth to his character portrayal and storytelling, but the best of these were only as good as his Mutuals.

Chaplin was later to call his Mutual period "the happiest days of my life." It was an extraordinarily creative period. As the Essanays were markedly superior in structure, style and content to any previous comedy films, the Mutuals surpassed even the Essanays. By the end of his Mutual

Edna is helped by Charlie in *The Rink* (Mutual, 1916).

contract, Chaplin was taking as long as three months to complete a two-reel comedy.

As this text is chiefly concerned with the importance of the Essanay period, a concluding chapter lauding what came next would perhaps seem disingenuous to some. Thus, it should be clarified that the twelve brilliant Mutual two-reelers that Chaplin produced upon completing his Essanay tenure are great only because of the growth Chaplin enjoyed at Essanay. As frequently pointed out in this text, Essanay was the bridge from the raucous Keystones to the refined, perfect Mutuals.

The Floorwalker was Chaplin's first Mutual picture, a two-reeler in which he finds himself working in a large department store, where he stumbles upon a couple of employees who are embezzling funds. Throughout the film we see the slapstick learned at Keystone and the character refinement developed at Essanay. But with more time to indulge in several takes and modified ideas, Chaplin's gags became even more creative. In *The Floorwalker* Chaplin uses an escalator for laughs, augmenting an old-fashioned chase scene with this fairly new piece of technology. Years later Mack Sennett would tell his biographer Gene Fowler how much he was impressed by this idea, adding, "Why didn't I think of that?"

The laughs and creativity in such brilliantly funny Mutual pictures as *Behind the Screen*, *The Fireman*, and *The Adventurer* were surpassed by Chaplin's more offbeat ventures whereby he challenged notion either by revisiting them or attempting that which had been heretofore unexplored. *The Vagabond* takes the pathos of *The Tramp* and adds a somewhat more dramatic story, with Edna once again appearing as a central character who is rescued by Charlie as the title character. Chaplin delves more deeply into character here, despite the same running time as the earlier film, exploring more straight acting opportunities for both him and Edna. The bombastic slapstick that *The Tramp* features is replaced by a lighter style in *The Vagabond*, making it even more effective.

One A.M. features Chaplin in a one-man show (save for a quick appearance by Albert Austin as the cab driver). This time Charlie is a society man coming home to his large house in an inebriated state, doing battle with a series of inanimate objects (from a stairway to a bed to a bearskin rug). Chaplin's comic creativity is at its zenith here, as he explores all the gag possibilities with the surrounding props, and allows a plotless two-reeler to build on the strength of its gags alone.

Easy Street could be considered Chaplin's greatest film, a fascinating look at Charlie's conflict between doing good and stealing to survive. Desperate for income, Charlie becomes a police officer in a rough neighborhood, being forced to maintain law and order among those with whom he could always relate, even if only on a socio-economic level. Chaplin explores the possibilities of this conflict on a David and Goliath level when the large and imposing Eric Campbell appears as the alpha bully of the neighborhood. Charlie's success in subduing him (with his wits) makes him the leader.

Once Chaplin had completed the brilliant Mutual shorts he ventured

Charlie appears with Jackie Coogan in his first starring feature, *The Kid* (First National, 1921).

to First National Pictures, where his output became more erratic. For every artistic triumph like the three-reelers *A Dog's Life* and *Shoulder Arms*, or the four-reeler *The Pilgrim*, there were comparative misfires like the two-reelers *Sunnyside* and *A Day's Pleasure*. Perhaps the most significant First National release was *The Kid*, a six-reel feature film, the first in which Chaplin had appeared since *Tillie's Punctured Romance* at Keystone. Drawing from his original ideas for *Life*, a planned feature at Essanay that was

5. Mutual and After

abandoned after a few scenes had been shot, Chaplin examined the impoverished from the eyes of the title character (Jackie Coogan), who Chaplin finds as an abandoned baby and raises as his own. Looking at *The Kid*, it becomes clear how much Chaplin's work had evolved since Keystone. His transition at Essanay and eventual perfection at Mutual are all evident, as he draws on ideas found in various films from both studios. While Chaplin's scenes with the youngster are moving as well as funny, the dramatic moments are emotionally draining. Chaplin maintains rhythm and pacing by presenting what can be called a relief gag within the framework of the most dramatic moments.

Chaplin's continued creative control allowed him to present some truly incredible cinema, but even greater opportunity — and responsibility — came along when he joined with Douglas Fairbanks and Mary Pickford to form United Artists, a studio for independent filmmakers to supervise productions in which they appear. Here Chaplin made his most famous features, including the consistently brilliant *The Gold Rush*, the experimental drama *A Woman of Paris*, and the unfairly neglected *The Circus*.

A Woman of Paris was Chaplin's attempt at a drama, in which he himself appears only in a brief cameo (and not as Charlie). It is an interesting failure. Featuring Adolphe Menjou and Edna Purviance in the lead roles, it was an attempt by Chaplin to present his longtime supporting player Edna in a role that would showcase her talents. However, her acting was indeed limited, and it was Menjou who was discovered and later achieved some measure of stardom.

The Gold Rush was Chaplin's most ambitious film up to that time. Often dismissed as an old-fashioned director who never really employed fancy camera angles or editing techniques, Chaplin's direction usually concentrated on character and narrative, as well as creative comedy situations. He was not one to enhance his cinema with technological wizardry (as would Buster Keaton). However, this was not necessarily a liability, for Chaplin had been making brilliant comedies that had evolved to an exceptional level and continued successfully and consistently.

The Circus, less ambitious than *The Gold Rush*, is likely overlooked because it is merely funny, with no further artistic pretense. Chaplin was, first and foremost, a comedian, and the funniest of his films would logically place them among his best. *The Circus* certainly qualifies.

Chaplin at Essanay

Chaplin balked at the talking picture revolution that had engulfed American cinema by the end of the 1920s. He had been working on another silent feature since 1928, so by the time it was ready for release in 1931, he refused to add dialog (as Harold Lloyd had done with his late silent, *Welcome Danger* [1929], with middling critical — but astounding box office — results).

The resulting film, *City Lights*, is generally considered Chaplin's feature-length masterpiece. Still, we see the genesis of this element of character in Essanay's *The Tramp*, with rudiments extending as far back as Keystone's *The New Janitor*. With our appreciation of Chaplin's feature productions, we can find an even greater respect for the earlier short films that provided their initial inspiration.

Theater critic Alexander Woolcott, in his review of *City Lights* in his book *While Rome Burns*, offered the usual reaction to talking pictures at this time:

> I suppose I should break down at this point and admit that if there is one thing I cannot abide in this raucous age it is the transitory monstrosity known as the talkie. This aversion is essentially undebatable, just as I could never explain to the manufacturer who put out a Venus de Milo with a clock in her stomach that he had, to my notion, got hold of a bad idea.
>
> The fact that the public has clasped to its multitudinous bosom this movie without a single spoken syllable in all its crowded length is no proof that the talkie is doomed or even on the wane, and no proof that any other player would be accepted at his face value.

This attitude towards talking pictures was quite common, even as late as 1931, when the screen offered such strong talking features as *Public Enemy* and *Monkey Business*. Film without spoken dialog had been perfected by the middle 1920s, and the latter part of that decade offered many outstanding movies, including *The General* (1926), *The Kid Brother* (1927), *Underworld* (1927), and *The Docks of New York* (1928). Cinema was tremendously popular and was having a great cultural impact. Some of the finest cinematic artists were offering their best work. Why change its entire concept and execution for the sake of a technological advancement such as sound on film?

Many believed sound pictures were a novelty, that silents would con-

5. Mutual and After

tinue to be made, with the occasional talkie coming out as an offbeat little curio. But at the dawn of the 1930s it was obvious that talking pictures had taken over. Still, there were many who continued to balk, like Alexander Woolcott. Silent films from any country could be shown anywhere else without a language barrier getting in the way. Actors and actresses with foreign accents or other vocal impediments would have their careers ruined. Some, such as Greta Garbo, survived despite her accent. Others, like silent movie comedian Raymond Griffith, had no voice and could find no place in talking pictures (although Griffith's moving performance in *All Quiet on the Western Front* [1930] should be mentioned).

By the time Chaplin made his next feature, *Modern Times* (1936), the talking picture had completely eclipsed silent movies. In fact, silents were now considered archaic and silly. Clips from some of the most brilliant

Man and Machine — Chaplin explores technology in *Modern Times* (United Artists, 1936).

and successful silent movies were being cut into one-reel shorts with silly sound effects and joking narration.

Chaplin maintained that Charlie should remain an international Everyman and not have a specific language. While there were some sound effects and brief dialog from other characters, *Modern Times* was largely silent. But we do get to hear Charlie's voice in the form of a song in gibberish. And, as per the effect of Chaplin's continued popularity, *Modern Times* was a tremendous success, despite it being an essentially silent movie released in an era that was comfortably equipped for sound.

Chaplin finally conceded his battle with talking pictures by 1940 with *The Great Dictator*. Playing a variation of Charlie, as well as Fascist dictator Adenoid Hynkel (a takeoff on Adolf Hitler), Chaplin's brilliantly creative ideas clashed with his indulgence. A very funny and interesting satire, but wildly uneven, *The Great Dictator* can be considered Chaplin's last truly

Jack Oakie and Chaplin take a break on the set of *The Great Dictator* (United Artists, 1940).

5. Mutual and After

great movie. His subsequent talkies maintained this flawed-but-interesting level, with large dollops of indulgence. There is still a great deal to recommend *Monsieur Verdoux*, *Limelight*, and *A King in New York*, but the general consensus among film buffs and scholars that Chaplin's talkies are, comparatively, the weakest films of his career is essentially true.

During this period Chaplin was also branded a communist by the House UnAmerican Activities Committee and denied re-entry into the United States after leaving for a vacation in 1952.

By the time he made *A Countess from Hong Kong* in 1967, with Marlon Brando and Sophia Loren in the leading roles (Chaplin appeared in a brief cameo role, as he did in *A Woman of Paris*), Chaplin's methods seemed quaint and out of date. The cinema of that period was offering films like *Bonnie and Clyde* and *The Graduate*, making Chaplin's old-fashioned style appear archaic.

For the final ten years of his life Chaplin re-released films from his private collection, (some with new music scores), accepted an honorary Oscar in 1972 (returning to the States after twenty years), and was knighted in 1975. The timeless artistry of his films remained popular and significant throughout this period. Television revivals, often with obtrusive music and sound effects, kept his work relevant to later generations. Distributors of 8mm and 16mm films aimed at collectors further preserved his legacy. Unfortunately, since his Keystone, Essanay, and Mutual productions had fallen out of copyright, the films were edited,

Chaplin directed Marlon Brando and Sophia Loren in *A Countess from Hong Kong* (Universal, 1967), but appeared only in a cameo.

retitled, and offered at varying levels of quality from a variety of distributors. The best prints were made available by Blackhawk Films, as they printed from the most complete masters available.

Charles Spencer Chaplin died on Christmas Day in 1977. In the wake of his passing, he remains among the most celebrated movie icons. People who have never seen a silent film, much less a Chaplin film, recognize his likeness, such is his enormous impact on popular culture. While this writer certainly admits that there were many, many greatly talented comedians during the silent era, it still remains an objective claim that none attained the level of Chaplin in terms of creative innovation, execution, and endurance. It is perhaps fitting to close the main portion of this text with the same sentence with which it began: Charles Spencer Chaplin is perhaps the single most important figure in the history of motion pictures.

Appendix A:
His Regeneration

Although it is not a Charlie Chaplin movie, it would be remiss to exclude *His Regeneration*, an Essanay production featuring G.M. "Broncho Billy" Anderson and an amusing, albeit terribly brief, cameo by Chaplin.

Chaplin did not make a lot of cameo appearances during this portion of his career. The only one of note is his turn as a comic referee in Roscoe Arbuckle's Keystone two-reeler *The Knockout* in 1914. But Chaplin did make a cameo appearance in *His Regeneration*, which was released May 7, 1915. The cast included, along with Gilbert M. "Broncho Billy" Anderson, Marguerite Clayton, Lee Willard, Hazel Applegate, Belle Mitchell, Lloyd Bacon, Robert McKenzie, Bill Cato, Darr Wittenmyer, Victor Potel, and the indefatigable Ben Turpin.

Anderson was among the first cowboy stars, and this one-reeler is a typically enjoyable western drama, enhanced by Chaplin's amusing cameo during a dance hall sequence. There is nothing terribly exceptional about his appearance, just some pleasantly funny hijinks involving Charlie's flirtation with a lady and some slapstick on the dance floor. And this is not a Broncho Billy film where Anderson plays the cowboy hero. Here he is a penniless drifter who resorts to crime out of desperation, but goes straight in the end.

Shortly after the opening scene of *His Regeneration*, in which Anderson's character is introduced, we are shown a restricted portion of a dance hall where the more elite patrons are served. It is interesting to note the waiter's reaction to the well-dressed couples that arrive, the attention allotted people in top hats and formal wear vs. the lowlifes in the visitors area.

Appendix A

This lower level area is where we find Charlie, whose entrance is quite noticeable, despite the crowd around him. Charlie immediately begins flirting with a woman in the crowd until her much larger boyfriend comes along and threatens him, causing Charlie to hurry away. A man and a woman are at a table in the foreground, and we see Charlie in the background. A dance number beings, during which Charlie is pushed around as he attempts to maneuver from place to place. Only minutes long, Charlie's appearance ends here.

Charlie's brief flirtation is something of a portent of Anderson doing the same with a woman whose boyfriend comes along and starts a brawl. The boyfriend is the man who was sitting in the foreground of the shot. When the boyfriend leaves the table, Anderson takes his place and buys a drink for his woman. When the man returns, he starts a fight. Anderson is shot during the fracas, and one of the women from the party of rich people (Marguerite Clayton) comes to his aid until police arrive and bring him to where he can obtain the necessary medical treatment.

Later, Anderson is shown, with an accomplice (Lee Willard), breaking into the home of some wealthy people, with the intention of robbing it. He discovers that it is the home of the society woman who helped him earlier, and decides not to rob her. His accomplice has other ideas, however, and a fight ensues, waking up the woman. The accomplice is shot and killed during the fracas. When the police arrive, the woman indicates that the intruder was shot in self defense, thus clearing Anderson of any crime. As a result, he vows to the woman that he will hereafter lead a life within the law, leaving a note that reads: "You saved me from a twenty year jolt. I'll try and make good." The film concludes with innocent citizen Anderson asking a passing cop for a match. The cop lights Anderson's cigarette, is thanked, and nods as the two part ways.

What is most interesting about *His Regeneration* is that it is essentially a blueprint for Chaplin's later two-reeler *Police*. In *Police*, Charlie, with an accomplice, returns to a life of crime out of desperation when he cannot find honest work after being released from prison. Edna is the homeowner who tries to get through to the thieves, causing Charlie to mend his ways and ultimately foil his accomplice's robbery attempt. In the end, Edna spares Charlie from intruding lawmen by claiming he is her husband.

His Regeneration

The other significant factor of *His Regeneration* is that it was shot by Rollie Totheroh, Anderson's usual cameraman, who would later become Chaplin's cinematographer at Mutual, remaining with him for the rest of his time in America. Even for a couple of years after Chaplin's exile, Totheroh acted as Chaplin's archivist. Totheroh provides some interesting work for *His Regeneration*, especially the scenes set in darkness. The shot of Anderson discovering the owner of the home by shining a flashlight on the sleeping woman is a nice bit of cinematography.

Chaplin would occasionally make cameos as favors to friends, and this was no exception. Anderson had appeared as an extra during the fight scene in Chaplin's *The Champion*, so Chaplin returned the favor here.

While it is a rather benign, ordinary one-reeler, *His Regeneration* holds some importance in its own historical and cultural context. First, it offers an example of what Essanay was doing outside of the Chaplin unit. Second, for those with any interest in the western genre, it offers Anderson a role other than his Broncho Billy cowboy persona (in fact, it puts him on the other side of the law). And third, it is significant as the only film in which Chaplin appeared outside of his own during this period of his career.

Despite Anderson's own popularity in 1915, period reviews of *His Regeneration* spent more time singling out Chaplin's unbilled appearance, which was quite brief and of no import to the plot. This further demonstrates the tremendous impact Chaplin had on popular culture in the midst of his Essanay tenure. Being unbilled, Chaplin naturally did not appear in any advertisements for the film. But word of mouth spread to the point where the picture's popularity benefited from Chaplin's cameo, which reportedly elicited roars of laughter and applause from moviegoers. *His Regeneration* became one of Broncho Billy Anderson's most popular films.

His Regeneration, while quite standard, is really not a bad little movie. It is a good, typical one-reel drama from the period. The fact that it stars Anderson, who himself is important to cinema's history, is a point in its favor. But Charlie Chaplin making a cameo appearance certainly bolsters its significance and makes it worth seeking out.

Note: *His Regeneration* was included on VHS and DVD in the restored Essanay series from David Shepard.

Appendix B: Edna Purviance

One of the key elements of Chaplin's success during his Essanay period was Edna Purviance, who started in small parts with him at Essanay, then became his leading lady for the next eight years. Chaplin worked with many women over the years, from Mabel Normand and Marie Dressler to Georgia Hale, Virginia Cherrill, Paulette Goddard, Martha Raye and Sophia Loren. Edna Purviance is the leading lady that appeared in the most Chaplin films, and her astuteness as an actress, her sense of fun, and her keen understanding of character provided perfect support for Charlie's downtrodden soul and heroic altruism.

Since she made only Chaplin films, and did almost nothing after her attempt at a star-making role in *A Woman of Paris* (1923), very little is known about Edna Purviance the person. Little was written about her while she was active, and almost nothing afterwards.

In an article entitled "The Star Soubrette" in the December 1915 issue of *Photoplay*, writer John H. Blackwood recounted a recent thirty-minute conversation he had had with the actress:

> The first thing that impressed me during a half hour talk with this Chaplin co-worker was that she is an unusually serious minded young woman. I had supposed that being a Chaplinette she must of course be one of those frolicsome creatures, fluffy-minded and blonde as to inclination as well as to hair. And then she completely upset all of my preconceived ideas of what a Star Soubrette ought to be by telling me she didn't care a tinker's cuss word for ragtime music; that she vastly preferred a Chopin nocturne or a Liszt rhapsody to an Irving Berlin rag number. Then, as if that wasn't good and sufficient enough, she went on and discussed

authors like a school ma'am from Boston — told me that her favorite writers were Shelley, Keats, Scott, and Burns — that she though *Vanity Fair* the greatest story she ever had read, and that she wondered who would be the Macaulay or Gibbon to record this War of the Worlds.

Edna as she appeared in *A Jitney Elopement*.

The article went on to state that Edna had thus far appeared in *A Night Out, In the Park, A Jitney Elopement, The Champion, The Tramp, By the Sea, Work, The Bank, A Woman,* and *Shanghaied.* Edna stated that she felt her best work still lay ahead of her. Of course, she was right. Even at Essanay she was able to exhibit a greater level of acting prowess in Chaplin's forthcoming *Burlesque on Carmen*, which showcased her talents even in the clumsy and padded four-reel edit.

The 1916 issue of *Reel Life* profiled Edna after she had moved with the Chaplin unit to Mutual. In this article she discussed her childhood interest in acting, her eventual acceptance of comedy performance, and her work with Chaplin:

> I always aspired to pay tragic and emotional roles when I was still in school, and I used to plan my dramatic career in detail. I had a private air-castle as a background and stage setting for most of my characters. I doted on Lady Macbeth, trailing down the grand staircase, bloody dagger in hand, hoarsely outing the damned spot.
> But art is long and time is fleeting — and I found comedy so much more remunerative for a beginner in pictures. So I decided to forget my dramatic ambitions and be content with hurling pies and undergoing abduction by a whiskered villain.
> ...After graduation, I returned to San Francisco, and went into charity and settlement work. I was asked to be the heroine in a playlet, given under the auspices of a charity organization with

which I was connected. Having a fondness for amateur theatricals, I went into the thing quite enthusiastically and worked up my part as well as possible, which was very fortunate for me as you will see.

The evening of the performance, while I was bowing after the second curtain call, a very dear friend of my father's and mine came to me and asked to present a Mr. Chaplin, who wished to congratulate me on my success with the part I had taken. I was naturally surprised to learn, later in the evening, that he was *the* Charlie Chaplin. Shortly after, when we had become better acquainted, he offered me a position with his company.

Then followed days of indecision. I wanted to be a legitimate actress and follow in the steps of the immortal Sarah [Bernhardt] of course, but leading lady to the world's most famous comedian was nothing to be lightly considered — so I accepted the offer, as you already know.

Mr. Chaplin asked me if I would like to act in pictures with him. I laughed at the idea, but agreed to try it. I guess he took me because I had nothing to unlearn and he could teach me in his own way.

I began work immediately at the Essanay studios in Niles, California. My training received at school came in well those days because the simplicity of motion picture acting is something we hear about but never experience. I want to tell you that I suffered untold agonies. Eyes seemed to be everywhere. I was simply frightened to death. But he had unlimited patience in directing me and teaching me.

When Mr. Chaplin signed his contract with the Mutual Film Corporation, he took most of his company with him, and in March 1916 we began work here at the Mutual studios in Los Angeles. Our first picture was *The Floorwalker*, followed by *The Fireman*. The one you saw us working on now is going to be released under the title of *The Vagabond*. I consider it the best we have done so far for Mutual.

This long series of quotes is what little we have on record of Edna Purviance's voice. Chaplin believed her to be the perfect leading lady, and she remained with his company from Essanay to Mutual and on through to First National.

It was at United Artists where Chaplin decided to make Edna a leading lady in her own right. Pairing her with newcomer Adolphe Menjou in his drama *A Woman of Paris*, Chaplin had high hopes for her eventual stardom. But it was not to be. The film was a commercial failure, and although it did launch Menjou's career, Edna's subsequent career went nowhere. She appeared in Josef Von Sternberg's Chaplin-produced ill-fated *The Sea Gull* in 1926, then retired. An older, portly Edna turned up as an extra in two later Chaplin films, *Monsieur Verdoux* (1947) and *Limelight* (1952). Chaplin had wanted to cast her in a larger role in *Monsieur Verdoux*, but had to admit to himself that the now overweight Edna was no longer right for the part. Her fleeting appearances in this and *Limelight* were certainly predicated on sheer sentiment.

A glamour shot of Edna from 1915.

Edna and Chaplin reportedly were romantically involved during the years 1915 through 1918. It was not exclusive, but it was consistent, and also said to be trouble-free. Those who knew Chaplin believed that had he maintained a romance with Edna, and eventually married her, he would have been spared the marital difficulties and scandals with which he was beset in later years. Many have surmised that had this happened, his head would have been clearer, and his life more relaxed and organized. Would that have affected his artistic accomplishment? Did the stress have anything to do with his being so creatively driven? One cannot say for sure. But it can be said that Chaplin and Edna truly got along as friends after their romance was destroyed when Chaplin was forced to marry the pregnant Mildred Harris. Edna, understanding and supportive, remained a trusted friend through all of Chaplin's troubled times.

Although she officially retired in 1926, Chaplin kept Edna on his payroll for the rest of her life. They maintained a correspondence, but in *My Autobiography* Chaplin admitted it was often one-sided, as he rarely wrote letters himself. He also recalled the last time he heard from her, which was after she had been diagnosed with the lung cancer that would eventually end her life. Chaplin stated in his autobiography:

Appendix B

Her last letter was an acknowledgment of the news that she was still on the payroll:

Dear Charlie,

Here I am again with a heart full of thanks, and back in the hospital taking cobalt X-ray treatment on my neck. It all comes while one can wriggle even a little finger. However, it is the best known treatment for what ails me. Hope to be home at the end of the week, then can be an outside patient (how wonderful!). Am thankful my innards are OK, this is purely and simply local, so they say — all of which reminds me of the fellow standing on the corner of Seventh and Broadway tearing up little bits of paper, throwing them to the four winds. A cop comes along and asks him, what was the big idea. He answers, "Just keeping the elephants away." The cop says: "There aren't any elephants around here." The fellow answers, "Well, it works, doesn't it?" This is my silly for the day, so forgive me. Hope you and the family are well and enjoying everything you have worked for.

Love always,
Edna

Shortly after I received this letter she died. And so the world grows young. And youth takes over. And we who have lived a little longer become a little more estranged as we journey on our way.

With beauty, charm, and a discernible charisma, Edna Purviance enhanced the Chaplin films at Essanay, Mutual, and First National — moreso than any of Chaplin's other supporting actresses in earlier or later films. Since she worked with Chaplin during a most significant period in his career — the transitional Essanays, the perfected Mutuals, and the continued level of perfection at First National — she is the woman with whom Chaplin is most identified on screen. Her contribution to these movies is one of the keys to their success. It has to be believed that her presence had some sort of inspirational impact on Chaplin's creative process, and since she worked with him during the period of his career when he was at his absolute most creative, it makes her an extremely important aspect of his success.

Was Edna Purviance Chaplin's muse during the most important years of his film career? Perhaps to some extent. For even without documented evidence of Chaplin ever referring to Edna as such, it is clear by screening the films in which she appears that her presence had an impact on several different levels. From the innocent ingenue to the amused observer, and from the supportive girlfriend to the overwrought bereaved mother, Edna Purviance was outstanding as an actress in the Chaplin canon.

Appendix C: Chaplin's Post-Essanay Film List

Mutual Studios Films

(all two reels in length, written and directed by Chaplin, and featuring Edna Purviance and Eric Campbell):

1916

The Floorwalker (Released May 15)
The Fireman (Released June 12)
The Vagabond (Released July 10)
One A.M. (Released August 7)
The Count (Released September 4)
The Pawnshop (Released October 2)
Behind the Screen (Released November 13)
The Rink (Released December 4)

1917

Easy Street (Released January 22)
The Cure (Released April 16)
The Immigrant (Released June 17)
The Adventurer (Released October 23)

First National Films

(all written and directed by Chaplin):

A Dog's Life (1918), three reels, released April 14
Shoulder Arms (1918), three reels, released October 20
Sunnyside (1919), two reels, released June 15
A Day's Pleasure (1919), two reels, released December 7
The Kid (1921), six reels, released February 6
The Idle Class (1921), two reels, released September 25
Pay Day (1922), two reels, released April 2
The Pilgrim (1923), four reels, released February 25

United Artists Films

(all written and directed by Chaplin)

A Woman of Paris (1923)
    Adolphe Menjou, Edna Purviance, 84 minutes, released October 1

The Gold Rush (1925)
    Georgia Hale, Mack Swain, 82 minutes, released August 16

The Circus (1928)
    Merna Kennedy, Allen Garcia, 71 minutes, released January 7

City Lights (1931)
    Virginia Cherrill, Harry Meyers, 87 minutes, released February 6

Modern Times (1936)
    Paulette Goddard, 87 minutes, released February 5

The Great Dictator (1940)
    Paulette Goddard, Reginald Gardner, 126 minutes, released October 15

Monsieur Verdoux (1947)
    Martha Raye, Marilyn Nash, 123 minutes, released April 11

Limelight (1952)
    Claire Bloom, Buster Keaton, 143 minutes, released October 23

Others

A King in New York (1957)

Appendix C

Dawn Addams, Michael Chaplin, 110 minutes, released September 12 by the Attica Film Company (not seen in the United States until 1973)

A Countess from Hong Kong (1967)

Marlon Brando, Sophia Loren, 108 minutes, released January 5 by Universal Studios

Chaplin also made guest appearances in the films *The Nut* (United Artists, 1921), *Hollywood* (Paramount, 1923), and *Show People* (MGM, 1928). He appeared in the half-reel subject *The Bond* for the Liberty Loan Committee in 1918, having also written and directed the film.

Appendix D: Supporting Players

While Edna Purviance really deserved an appendix of her own, there should be some mention of the supporting players in Chaplin's films from the Essanay period. One of the many things Chaplin perfected during his Essanay tenure was directing other characters in his pictures to respond to the rhythm and presentation of his style. Most of them were able to rise to the occasion. And while a great deal is said about the likes of Bud Jamison and Leo White in the body of the text, this section offers capsule biographical information on the supporting players in Chaplin's films, including some mention of what each actor accomplished after leaving the Chaplin unit. It should be noted that despite the use of many very good reference sources, as well as assistance by such showbiz necrologists as Billy Doyle and Bill Cappello, there are some lost players among these supporting actors for which we have a paucity of information, and no birth or death dates.

Gilbert M. Anderson

Early western film actor, billed as Broncho Billy Anderson in some of the first western movies. He and George K. Spoor were the founders of the Essanay company. He sold his share of the company to Spoor in January 1916. He later produced films with Lewis Selznick and Lawrence Weber, and by the beginning of the twenties he was producing short comedies starring Stan Laurel, including the milestone *Lucky Dog* (1921), in which Laurel appears for the first time with Oliver Hardy (who was a supporting player — they would not team for another six years). Anderson quit the film business in 1923. He returned for a brief cameo in *The Bounty*

Killer (1965). It was the only time his voice was heard onscreen. Anderson died in 1971 at the age of 90.

Leona Anderson

Sister of G.M. Anderson, she appeared in Chaplin's *In the Park*, as well as a handful of other Essanay productions between January and August 1915. She had been in several Broadway musicals, and did a few later films, from Stan Laurel's solo silent *Mud and Sand* (1922) to William Castle's *The House on Haunted Hill* (1958). She returned to vocal music in the mid-1950s, singing on television variety programs hosted by the likes of Jack Paar and Steve Allen. She died on Christmas Day 1973 at the age of 88.

Billy Armstrong

Worked in England with Chaplin in Fred Karno's troop from 1910 to 1914. His first film with Chaplin was *The Tramp*, and he continued with the unit until Chaplin left the studio for Mutual. Armstrong also worked briefly at Keystone. He died of tuberculosis in 1924 at the age of 33.

Lloyd Bacon

This vaudeville actor joined Essanay in 1915 and worked with the Chaplin unit until January 1916. He left with Chaplin for Mutual, appearing with him in *The Vagabond* and *Easy Street*. He later became a director at Warner Brothers, helming such films as *Marked Woman* (1938) and *The Oklahoma Kid* (1939). He died in 1955 at the age of 65.

Bill Cato

Essanay stunt double for Broncho Billy and others, he appeared with Chaplin in *The Champion* in a small role. Cato died in 1965 at the age of 77.

Frank Coleman

An actor in several Essanay Chaplins, he left with Chaplin to join Mutual. His birth and death dates are not known.

Thomas J. Crizer

Helped edit the Chaplin films at Niles and Los Angeles. Crizer later worked as an editor at the Hal Roach studios, and still later became a writer, co-writing Harold Loyd's *The Kid Brother* (1927), among others. He died in 1963 at the age of 74.

Harry Ensign

Ensign was first a cameraman for Essanay's Snakeville comedies in 1913, then left the company before returning in late 1914. He worked on Chaplin's first four Essanay films, and later joined Chaplin's unit in Los Angeles. He remained with Essanay until the company disbanded in 1916. He later became the head of the film lab at Paramount Pictures. Ensign died in 1943 at the age of 60.

Marta Golden

Stage actress who appeared with Chaplin in *A Woman* and *Work*. She also worked for a short time at Keystone. Her birth and death dates are not known.

Fred Goodwins

Veteran stage actor who began with Chaplin as a thief in *The Bank* and continued to work for him, including acting as his press agent at Mutual. Goodwins directed several films in England during the late teens. He died in 1923.

Al Herman

Former prizefighter who worked as both a prop man and actor at Essanay. He worked with the Chaplin unit in Los Angeles, and later became a director. He is among the comparative few whose career began during the early days of silent pictures and persevered through the many changes over the decades, lasting into the early days of television production. He died in 1958.

Charles Inslee

Veteran actor whose career can be traced back to 1908. He began in the Chaplin unit with *Work*, and stayed until October 1915. Birth and death dates are not known.

Bud Jamison (né Jamieson)

A popular, well-liked supporting player, especially in short films, Jamison was a big, imposing man who was not above playing a sissy when called upon to do so; but he also felt comfortable in roles as a tough guy or person of authority (such as a policeman). Bud appeared in several Chaplin Essanays, beginning with *A Night Out*, and later appeared with Stan Laurel in *Just Ramblin Along*, Harry Langdon in *The Chaser*, W.C. Fields in *The Dentist*, and in several films at Columbia with the Three Stooges and others until his death in 1944 at the age of 60. His last appearance was a small role in the feature *Nob Hill*, released in 1945.

James T. Kelly

Veteran stage actor, he joined the Chaplin unit in September 1915, remaining with Chaplin after he left for Mutual. Kelly later spent time at the Hal Roach studios and at Universal. He died in 1933 at the age of 79.

Dee Lampton

Heavyset actor Dee Lampton joined the Chaplin unit at Essanay in 1915, appearing most prominently in *A Night in the Show*. Lampton had previously worked at Keystone, and later had his own series at Rolin. He died in 1919 at the age of 28.

Emil T. Mazy

Scenic painter who worked with Chaplin at both Essanay and Mutual. He died in 1943 at the age of 77.

Paddy McGuire

Appeared in many of the Chaplin Essanays from February 1915. He worked for Vogue Films with Ben Turpin in 1916, and Fox in 1917. He also worked for Sennett. McGuire suffered from emotional troubles and ended up in a mental institution in Norwalk, California, where he was confined for a couple of years. The reported cause of his death at age 39 in 1923 was insanity. Since one cannot die of insanity, it is assumed other, unreported factors were involved.

Charlotte Mineau

Began with Selig in the summer of 1914. She appeared with Chaplin in his first Essanay production (*His New Job*, shot in Chicago), and later acted with him at Mutual. Mineau acted throughout the twenties in films with such stars as Mary Pickford and Mabel Normand, and was active into the early talkie era, appearing with the Marx Brothers in *Monkey Business*. She died in 1979 at the age of 92.

Harry "Snub" Pollard

Pollard appeared in small parts in a few Chaplin Essanays, then later supported Harold Lloyd in the Lonesome Luke comedies at Rolin. He went with Lloyd to the Roach studios, where he eventually starred in his own series. His one-reeler *It's a Gift* is considered a minor classic. Pollard later appeared opposite rotund comic Marvin Lobeck for Weiss Brothers in a series of comedies attempting to rival the popular Laurel and Hardy. Never a top ranking star, Pollard's steady career lasted well into the talking picture era, when he played supporting roles and bits in films featuring everyone from the Three Stooges to Jerry Lewis. Lewis even amusingly addresses him by his noted nickname during the closing scene of *The Errand Boy* (1963). Pollard's sister was actress Daphne Pollard. He died in 1962 at the age of 68.

Edna Purviance

Beginning with *A Night Out*, Ms. Purviance eventually became Chaplin's leading lady at Essanay, exhibiting an inimitable charm that enhanced each film in which she appeared. She continued in this role with Chaplin at Mutual, and then First National. She also starred, with Adolphe Menjou, in Chaplin's later feature *A Woman of Paris*. She never made a non–Chaplin film. (See Appendix B.)

John F. Rand

Joined the Chaplin unit in July 1915. Rand later appeared with Chaplin at Mutual, and also in later films such as *The Circus* (1928), *City Lights* (1931), and *Modern Times* (1936). His background was as an acrobatic vaudeville performer. Rand died in 1940 at age 68.

Hal Roach

Producer Hal Roach began in films in 1914 with partner Dan Linthicum after inheriting $3000. After his company, Rolin, folded in one year, Roach found work at Essanay directing films at Chaplin's Los Angeles studio and the Bradbury mansion, using the Chaplin stock company that was not being used for the Chaplin film currently in production. After doing this for a month, Roach and Linthicum's company received a distribution deal with Pathe, and began producing Lonesome Luke comedies with newcomer Harold Lloyd. Linthicum was eventually bought out and Rolin became the Hal Roach Studios, home to Laurel and Hardy, Charley Chase, and Our Gang. Roach lived to be 100 years old, dying in November 1992.

Jess Robbins

Became a cameraman with Essanay in 1908. He produced Chaplin's first Essanays, and later worked at G.M. Anderson's Amalgamated studios, including directing *The Lucky Dog* (1921), which was the first time Stan Laurel and Oliver Hardy appeared onscreen together (they would not team for another six years). Robbins' later career is interesting in that it reveals him as a tireless jack of all trades who pursued a variety of different occupations. While he left films in 1929, he worked continually to the end of his life, doing many different things, from running a taxi service to acting as a machinist, even when past his 80th birthday.

Wesley Ruggles

Ruggles started his career at Keystone, later joining the Chaplin Essanay unit in July of 1915, and remaining with it until Chaplin left for Mutual. He worked as an actor at Vitagraph during the later teens, and eventually became a director during the 1920s. Working at several major studios, including Paramount, Universal, RKO, Columbia, and MGM, among his directorial efforts was the Oscar winner *Cimarron* (Paramount, 1931). He was the brother of noted actor Charlie Ruggles. Wesley died in 1969 at age 82.

Carl Stockdale

While Stockdale was a notable actor in silent pictures, and appeared in many westerns with Broncho Billy at Essanay, he appeared only once with Chaplin, in *The Bank*. Stockdale is best known today for having appeared in D.W. Griffith's mammoth *Intolerance* (1916), although he remained active into the talking picture era. Stockdale died in 1953 at age 79.

Rollie Totheroh

Totheroh was a noted Essanay cameraman who worked with Chaplin from the Mutual period until his retirement in 1954. While Totheroh is frequently credited in several sources as being Chaplin's cameraman at Essanay, he, in fact, never shot a Chaplin picture while both were with the company. The only Essanay production Totheroh filmed in which Chaplin appeared (and then only as a cameo) was G.M. Anderson's *His Regeneration* (released in May of 1915). Totheroh died in 1967 at age 76.

Ben Turpin

Legendary cross-eyed comic whose affliction was his fortune (so much so that he allegedly had his eyes insured with Lloyds of London against ever uncrossing). He was in the very first Essanay comedies in 1907, sometimes appearing with his wife Carrie (1878–1925). He left to return to vaudeville in a Happy Hooligan act, then returned to Essanay in 1913. Turpin worked as a veritable co-star with Chaplin in *His New Job* and *A Night Out*, but was relegated to a cameo in *The Champion*. He later appeared in the new footage allegedly directed by Leo White and tacked onto *Burlesque on Carmen*. Turpin became quite popular upon joining Sennett's Keystone studio, appearing in such films as *A Clever Dummy*, *The Daredevil*, *Yukon Jake*, and *The Prodigal Bridegroom*. Turpin then later headlined a successful series for the Weiss Brothers, starring in such titles as *Idle Eyes, The Eyes Have It,* and *The Cockeyed Family.* A wealthy man who made shrewd real estate investments early on, Turpin eventually acted only when he wanted to, but did appear in films to the end of his life, including such talkies as *Million Dollar Legs* (1932) with W.C. Fields, the silent comedy homage *Keystone Hotel* (1935), with Ford Sterling, Chester Conklin, and Hank Mann, and the Laurel and Hardy feature *Saps at Sea* (1940), which was Ben Turpin's final film appearance. Died in 1940 at the age of 70.

Ernest Van Pelt

Veteran theater actor, Van Pelt also appeared in vaudeville (in a double act with his wife Ella called the Chattering Chums). He began with Essanay in July 1914 as Hiram Clutts in the Snakeville comedies. Van Pelt appeared with Chaplin in several comedies at Niles. Many sources that include Chaplin Essanay filmographies often misidentify Van Pelt as another actor, Fred Goodwins (qv), who did appear in Chaplin films but does not look like Van Pelt and did not start appearing with Chaplin until *The Bank.* Van Pelt also served as assistant director for Chaplin during this period. He left Essanay in 1915, eventually becoming a public relations man, but continued to act occasionally into the talking picture era. He died in 1961 at age 78.

Leo White

Stage actor Leo White joined Essanay's Chicago studio in July 1912. He appeared in Chaplin's first Essanay production, *His New Job,* and appeared in many subsequent Chaplin films at Niles and Los Angeles. When Chaplin left for Mutual, White directed additional scenes tacked onto *Burlesque on Carmen*; while Chaplin was furious about this tampering with his film, he never held White accountable, later hiring him to appear in Mutual films and using him even as late as *The Great Dictator* (1940). White was said to be of German descent, but other sources insist he was English born. He died in 1948.

May White

May White appeared with Chaplin at Niles and Los Angeles, was in the original and newly shot footage for *Burlesque on Carmen*, and also appeared with Chaplin at Mutual. Birth and death dates are not known. There are birth and death dates for a "May White" in the late Eugene Vazzanna's reference book *Silent Film Necrology* (McFarland, 2003), but the birth date does not logically match up with this actress.

Appendix E: Compilation Films and Anthologies Featuring Chaplin Essanay Footage

There have been a number of anthology films saluting silent screen comedy, beginning in the late 1950s when producer Robert Youngson put together *The Golden Age of Comedy*, a compilation of silent comedy scenes that generated a renewed interest in the era. Youngson featured no Chaplin footage in *The Golden Age of Comedy*, perhaps due to it being produced during a period when Chaplin was still looked upon by some as a Communist sympathizer. However, Youngson did include some Chaplin Keystone footage in his next anthology, *When Comedy Was King* (1960), and some Mutual footage a few years later in *30 Years of Fun* (1963).

Since the Keystone, Essanay, and Mutual footage was readily available (due to it having fallen into the public domain), many anthologies that sprang up after Youngson's first efforts would include representative Chaplin footage from this period in his career. Essanay films also were spotlighted on television's *Charlie Chaplin Comedy Theater*, which was run pretty extensively in syndication throughout the 1960s.

While Chaplin's later features were not in regular distribution during this period, it is these earlier films, especially their appearance in compilations, that helped keep Chaplin's name alive for future generations. Some, including this writer, enjoyed their first Chaplin viewing experience through these presentations.

The following is a list of compilations and anthologies that feature

Compilation Films and Anthologies Featuring Chaplin Essanay Footage

Chaplin Essanay footage, and the material that each contains (not including *The Chaplin Essanay Review of 1916* and *Chase Me Charlie*, Essanay releases already covered in the text). The films are listed chronologically.

Merry Go Round (1962)

Compilation film made in Europe that contains scenes from *The Champion*, *By the Sea*, *The Tramp*, and *Triple Trouble*.

Chaplin's Art of Comedy (1966)

Chaplin tribute complied by Sam Sherman and including material from the Essanay films *A Night in the Show*, *The Champion*, *The Tramp*, and *A Woman*.

The Funniest Man in the World (1967)

Douglas Fairbanks Jr. narrates this compilation written and directed by Vernon P. Becker, who was behind television's syndicated *Charlie Chaplin Comedy Theater*. It contains footage from Keystone, Essanay, and Mutual films. The Essanay material including scenes from *His New Job*, *A Night Out*, *A Jitney Elopement*, *The Tramp*, *A Woman*, *A Night in the Show*, *Police*, and *Triple Trouble*.

The Chaplin Puzzle (1992)

A two-part documentary written by Joe Adamson, directed by Don McGlynn, and narrated by Burgess Meredith. The first part *Chaplin Invents Himself*, deals with his Keystone and Essanay films; while the second, *A Classic Restored*, tries to make the claim that the Essanay film *Police* is actually a three-reeler inserting the flophouse scenes from *Triple Trouble* that had actually been shot for the aborted feature *Life*.

Charlie: The Life and Art of Charlie Chaplin (2003)

Richard Schickel's excellent documentary examining Chaplin's life and career, with narration by Sydney Pollack and comments by various actors and film scholars. The Essanay section is perhaps the best anthological piece on this period, with scenes from *His New Job*, *A Night Out*,

Appendix E

The Champion, In the Park, By the Sea, The Tramp, Work, A Woman, The Bank, Shanghaied, A Night in the Show, and *Triple Trouble.*

SlapHappy the Movie (2004)

Great compilation of silent comedy footage, some of it quite rare. This is a feature film composite of a ten-part TV series, shown on PBS, spotlighting the silent screen comedians, and focusing as much on the lesser known and forgotten stars as on the legendary figures. The movie includes a scene from *The Champion*. The Chaplin footage in the series appears in Volume 8.

Appendix F: Chaplin Cartoons

Charlie Chaplin's enormous level of stardom spread his image across a variety of mediums. His name or image was tied to songs, dances, comic books, and animated cartoons. It is worth adding information about a couple of popular Charlie Chaplin cartoon series, which were produced around the time Chaplin was ending his Essanay tenure.

The first series was produced by S.J. Sangretti and animated by John C. Terry, G. A. Bronstrup, and Hugh Shields, circa 1916:

1. *Charlie in Carmen*
2. *Charlie Across the Rio Grande*
3. *Charlie Has Some Wonderful Adventures in India*
4. *Charlie in Cuckoo Land*
5. *Charlie's Barnyard Pets*
6. *Charlie's Busted Romance*
7. *Charlie's White Elephant*
8. *Charlie the Blacksmith*
9. *Charlie Throws the Bull*
10. *The Rooster's Nightmare*

The second group of Chaplin-related cartoons was produced by Pat Sullivan of Felix the Cat fame, in 1918 and 1919. The character was originally called Charlie, but the spelling was changed to Charley to avoid copyright problems after Chaplin allegedly complained about the unapproved use of his likeness. Some of these cartoons survive in private collections, others in the Nederlands Filmmuseum. A handful appeared as special features on a low budget DVD collection of Chaplin films that had fallen into the public domain. It has been stated that animation veteran Otto Messmer got his start on these cartoons. What meager information we have about the animated shorts is not always accurate. The cartoons demonstrated Chaplin's massive popularity during and around the time of his Essanay period; that level of popularity led others to trade off his likeness.

The synopses are based upon cartoon historian and expert David A. Gerstein's listing of pre–Felix the Cat cartoons produced by Pat Sullivan, available at http://felix.goldenagecartoons.com/prefelixfilms.html. Release dates are given when known.

1918

How Charlie Captured the Kaiser (Sep. 10): Charlie (Chaplin, though not explicitly identified) attempts to cross the ocean in a tub, where he does battle with a German submarine, then hangs onto a stork's feet and is flown to the German front. When he arrives, he engages in a successful battle with the enemy.

Over the Rhine with Charlie (Dec. 18): Charlie engages in further adventures in Berlin.

1919

Charlie in Turkey (Jan. 25): According to the original copyright synopsis, Charlie "embarks upon the Bagdad [sic] Express for Turkey."

Charlie Treats 'Em Rough (Mar. 26): Charlie puts limburger in trenches to drive out the enemy, then pelts them with rotten eggs.

Charley at the Circus—"Charley" sneaks into the circus and disrupts several acts.

Charley on the Farm: "Charley" gets a job on a farm, milking cows and other such activities.

Charley at the Beach: "Charley" frolics at the beach, peeking into girls' dressing rooms until being chased away by a police officer. (According to Gerstein, the synopsis is taken from existing fragments).

Charley Out West: "Charley" rescues a girl from Indians.

Bibliography

The research sources utilized on this project range from general silent film era studies to those that deal with Chaplin's life and career. The general studies help the writer better understand the period in which the Essanay productions were made, and the state of cinema in comparison to the innovations that Chaplin was discovering with each production. The career overviews and biographies represent hard work accomplished by pioneering writers on cinema's history who have laid the groundwork for those of us who came along later on. Those that deal specifically with this period in Chaplin's career have been good starter studies, allowing for this text to examine the same period in greater detail and with more depth.
The articles cited are from the period during which Chaplin was active with Essanay, from news stories to features to reviews of the films. What was said about Chaplin in the press and the trade magazines adds a stronger historical context to the impact and significance of each production during this most important period.

In this day and age, internet sources are as much a part of any research as the print material that has sustained us for the years prior to the technology of the information age. They are included at the end of this bibliography.

It should be noted that, along with the written sources included in this bibliography, several historians volunteered their assistance and provided a great deal of important material. These helpful people are mentioned in the acknowledgments.

Finally, and quite obviously, it is the films themselves that provide the basis of information on, and appreciation for, the Essanay period. Even such travesties as the extended *Burlesque on Carmen* and the crazy quilt that became *Triple Trouble* are important for study. We are fortunate that none of the films Chaplin made for Essanay are lost. They are here for future generations to study, appreciate, and enjoy.

Books

Agee, James. *Agee on Film: Reviews and Comments*. Boston: Beacon Press, 1964.
Asplund, Uno. *Chaplin's Films*. South Brunswick and New York: A.S. Barnes, 1976.
Brownlow, Kevin. *Hollywood: The Pioneers* New York: Knopf, 1979.
____. *The Parade's Gone By...*. New York: Knopf, 1968.
Chaplin, Charles. *My Autobiography*. London: The Bodley Head, 1964.
____. *My Life in Pictures*. London: The Bodley Head, 1974.
Doyle, Billy. *The Ultimate Directory of Silent and Sound Era Performers*. Metuchen, NJ: Scarecrow Press, 1999.
Durgnat, Raymond. *The Crazy Mirror: Hollywood Comedy and the American Image*. New York: Horizon Press, 1969.
Fowler, Gene. *Father Goose: The Story of Mack Sennett*. New York: Covici, Friede Publishers, 1934.
Fussell, Betty Harper. *Mabel*. New York: Ticknor & Fields, 1982.
Geduld, Harry M. *Chapliniana Vol. 1: The Keystone Films*. Bloomington: Indiana University Press, 1987.
Gifford, Denis. *Chaplin*. London: Macmillan, 1974.
Huff, Theodore. *Charlie Chaplin*. New York: Henry Shuman, 1951.
Jacobs, Lewis. *The Rise of the American Film*. New York: Harcourt, Brace, 1939.
Kerr, Walter. *The Silent Clowns*. New York: Alfred A. Knopf, 1975.
Kiehn, David. *Broncho Billy and the Essanay Company*. Berkeley: Farwell Books, 2003.
Lahue, Karlton. *Mack Sennett's Keystone*. South Brunswick, NJ: A.S. Barnes, 1971.
____, and Samuel Gill. *Clown Princes and Court Jesters*. South Brunswick, NJ: A.S. Barnes, 1970.
____, and Terry Brewer. *Kops and Custards: The Legend of the Keystone Films*. Norman: University of Oklahoma Press, 1968.
Louvish, Simon. *Keystone: The Life and Clowns of Mack Sennett*. London: Faber and Faber, 2004.
Maltin, Leonard. *The Great Movie Comedians*. New York: Harmony Books, 1978.
Manvell, Roger. *Chaplin*. Boston: Little, Brown, 1974.
Mast, Gerald. *The Comic Mind: Comedy and the Movies*. Indianapolis: Bobbs-Merrill, 1973.
____. *A Short History of the Movies*. New York: Bobbs-Merrill, 1971.
McCabe, John. *Charlie Chaplin*. Garden City, NY: Doubleday, 1978.
McCaffrey, Donald. *Four Great Comedians: Chaplin, Lloyd, Keaton, Langdon*. New York: A.S. Barnes, 1968.
McDonald, Gerald D., Michael Conaway, and Mark Ricci. *The Films of Charlie Chaplin*. New York: Citadel Press, 1965.

Bibliography

Mitchell, Glenn. *The Chaplin Encyclopedia*. London: B.T. Batsford, 1997.
Neibaur, James L. *Movie Comedians: The Complete Guide*. Jefferson, NC: McFarland, 1986.
Okuda, Ted, and David Maska. *Charlie Chaplin at Keystone and Essanay*. Lincoln, NE: iUniverse, 2005.
Quigley, Isabel. *Charlie Chaplin: Early Comedies*. London: Studio Vista, 1968.
Reeves, May, and Claire Goll, translation, editing, and introduction by Constance Brown Kuriyama. *The Intimate Charlie Chaplin*. Jefferson, NC: McFarland, 2001.
Robinson, David. *Chaplin: His Life and Art*. New York: McGraw-Hill, 1985.
Sennett, Mack. *King of Comedy*. Garden City, NY: Doubleday, 1954.
Slide, Anthony. *The American Film Industry*. Westport, CT: Greenwood Press, 1986.
Tyler, Parker. *Chaplin: Last of the Clowns*. New York: Vanguard Press, 1947.
Vance, Jeffrey. *Chaplin: Genius of the Cinema*. New York: Harry N. Abrams, 2003.
Vazzana, Eugene. *The Silent Film Necrology*. Jefferson, NC: McFarland, 2001.

Articles

"Actor More to Some People Than God," *Washington Post*, 2/13/16.
As a Dramatic Critic Sees Us," *Moving Picture World*, 11/13/15.
"Ben Turpin interview," *American Magazine*, 1924.
"Chaplin Asks Injunction," *Motography*, 4/29/16.
"Chaplin in Third Suit," *Motography*, 5/13/16.
"Chaplin Leaves Keystone," *New York Daily Mirror*, 12/23/14.
"Chaplin Loses Carmen Suit," *Moving Picture World*, 7/8/16.
"Chaplin Seeks to Enjoin Carmen," *Moving Picture World*, 5/16/16.
"Chaplin Versus V-L-S-E," *Moving Picture World*, 5/27/16.
"Chaplin's Burlesque of Carmen," *Motography*, 12/25/15.
"Chaplin's Carmen Ready," *Motography*, 4/15/16.
"Chaplin's Unique Career," *The Washington Post*, 10/3/15.
"Charlie Chaplin in a Serious Mood," *Motography*, 1/16/15.
"Charlie Chaplin's Carmen," *Motography*, 4/15/16.
"Charlie Chaplin's Story," *Photoplay Magazine*, July, 1915.
"*Chip's Carmen* Review," *Motography*, 6/10/16.
"Essanay-Chaplin Carmen Breaks Records," *Motography*, 5/6/16.
"*The Essanay-Chaplin Revue of 1916* Review," *Motography*, 10/28/16.
"Essanay Re-Issues Chaplins," *Motography*, 9/22/17.
"Essanay Sues Chaplin," *Motography*, 5/6/16.
"Essanay vs. Chaplin," *Moving Picture World*, 6/3/16.
"First Mutual Chaplin Nears Completion," *Reel Life*, 4/22/16.
"Fred Goodwins," *Pearson's Weekly*, 1916.
"*His New Job* Review," *Moving Picture World*, 2/20/15.

Bibliography

"An Hour with Chaplin's Leading Lady," *Reel Life*, 4/22/16.
"Husband Madly Jealous of Chaplin Films," *Washington Post*, 2/27/16.
"Looking Into July with V-L-S-E," *Motography*, 7/8/16.
"No Injunction for Chaplin," *Moving Picture World*, 6/10/16.
"Review of Feature Films, *The Tramp*," *New York Dramatic Mirror*, Vol. 73, NO1 1897, 4/28/15.
"Rollie Totheroh Interview," *Film Culture*, 1967.
"Star Soubrette," *Photoplay Magazine*, December 1915.
"*Work* Review," *Motography*, 6/26/15.

Internet Sources

Internet Movie Database (www.imdb.com)
www.animationshow.com
www.silentcomedians.com
www.tv.com

NOTE: Because at the time of this writing the internet sources for this early period in film history are incomplete or otherwise flawed, the online research in this case was merely an addendum to that which could be found in print media.

Index

The Adventurer 6, 171
All Quiet on the Western Front 175
American Magazine 55
Anderson, G.M. (Broncho Billy) 2, 23, 25–31, 59, 67, 106, 179–181
Anderson, Leona 70–74
Applegate, Hazel 179
Arbuckle, Roscoe 3, 4, 13, 17, 20, 21, 23, 24, 126, 179
Armstrong, Billy 95–97, 163, 164
As You Like It 107
An Awful Skate 27

Bacon, Lloyd 179
The Bandit King 26
The Bank 6, 7, 9, 85, 113–122, 123, 143, 160, 183
The Beatles 121
Beery, Wallace 28
Behind the Screen 124, 171
The Better Ole 132
Beverly Hillbillies 39
Bioscope 43
Birth of a Nation 100
Blackhawk Films 135, 178
Blackton, J. Stuart 25
Bloom, Claire 54
The Bond 94
Bonnie and Clyde 177
Brando, Marlon 182
Broncho Billy's Redemption 27
Burlesque on Carmen 7, 9, 133, 142, 144–158
Bushman, Francis X. 28, 29
A Busy Day 17, 107
By the Sea 93, 94–99, 105, 160, 183

Caine, Clarence J. 29–30

Campbell, Eric 171
Carlson, Wallace 84
Carney, Augustus 27–28
Cato, Bill 179
Caught in a Cabaret 16
Caught in the Rain 17, 52, 75–76
The Champion 7, 9, 57–67, 70, 78, 90, 92, 94, 98, 160, 181, 183
Chaplin, Sydney 126, 131–132
Chase, Charley 23
Chase Me Charlie 135, 160
Cherrill, Virginia 54, 182
Chicago Tribune 44, 133–134
Chip's Carmen 154–155
The Circus 6, 148, 173
Citation Films 160
City Lights 6, 174
Clayton, Marguerite 179, 180
The Cockeyed Family 55
Conklin, Chester 13, 97
Conway, Michael 93
Coogan, Jackie 173
Cosmofotofilm Company 154
A Countess from Hong Kong 177
Crash Goes the Hash 72

The Daredevil 55
Davenport, Alice 13
A Day's Pleasure 172
DeMille, Cecil 146
The Docks of New York 174
A Dog's Life 67, 107, 172
Dough and Dynamite 4
Dressler, Marie 20, 182
Drew, Sidney 120
Durfee, Minta 13

Eastwood, Clint 27

Index

Easy Street 171
The Essanay-Chaplin Review of 1916 135, 159
The Eyes Have It 55

Fairbanks, Douglas 173
Fatty and Mabel Adrift 21
Fatty's Tintype Tangle 21
Film Culture 53
The Fireman 171
First National Pictures 67, 107, 172, 186
Fitzpatrick, James 154–155
The Floorwalker 170–171, 184

Garbo, Greta 175
The General 174
General Film Company 160
Gentlemen of Nerve 17
Girl from Montana 26
Goddard, Paulette 54, 182
The Gold Rush 2, 6, 18, 148, 173
Golden, Marta 101
Goodwins, Fred 120
The Graduate 177
The Great Dictator 2, 176
The Great Train Robbery 25
Griffith, D.W. 1, 13, 62, 100
Griffith, Raymond 175

Hale, Georgia 182
Harris, Mildred 185
Hart, William S. 27
His New Job 4, 31, 33–46, 56, 85, 142, 159
His Prehistoric Past 43
His Regeneration 179–181
His Trysting Place 4

Idle Eyes 55
The Immigrant 9, 125
In the Park 68–76, 92, 94, 99, 160, 183
Inslee, Charles 102, 123
Introducing Charlie Chaplin 83
It's a Gift 69

Jamison, Bud 49–54, 61–64, 71–74, 96
A Jitney Elopement 5–6, 9, 74, 76–83, 92, 100, 116, 160, 183
Juvenile Film Corporation 154

Karno, Fred 11–12, 127
Keaton, Buster 3, 4, 24, 91

Kerr, Walter 141–142
Keystone 2–4, 6, 11–24, 28, 35–36, 57, 70, 80, 87, 109, 114, 125, 133, 136, 172, 179
Keystone Cops 13
The Kid 2, 6, 67, 154, 172, 173
Kid Auto Races 4, 14
The Kid Brother 174
Kiehn, David 54, 112
A King in New York 2, 177
The Knockout 179

Langdon, Harry 23
Laughing Gas 17, 21
Laurel, Stan 91
Laurel and Hardy 55, 112, 122
Lehrman, Henry 8, 15
Lewis, Jerry 148
Life 134, 160–162, 163, 166, 167, 168, 172
Limelight 110, 177, 185
The Live Ghost 122
Lloyd, Harold 3, 23
Lloyds of London 55
Loren, Sophia 177, 182
Lucas, Wilfred 17
Lundgren, Dolph 62
Lyons, Timothy 53

Mabel's Busy Day 21
Mabel's Married Life 4, 21
MacDonald, Margaret 44
Mace, Fred 13, 23
Mack Sennett Bathing Beauties 15
Maddern, Joseph 17
Majestic Studios 112
Making a Living 6, 14
Manvell, Roger 30, 35
Maska, David 45, 92, 105, 107, 133, 142, 153, 157, 166–167
The Masquerader 17, 107
Mast, Gerald 103
McCabe, John 88, 91, 103
McDonald, Gerald D. 93
McGuire, Paddy 97
McKenzie, Robert 179
Méliès, Georges 1
Mineau, Charlotte 40
Mitchell, Belle 179
Modern Times 6, 18, 175, 176
Monkey Business 174
Monohan, Janethel 154–155
Monohan, Joseph 154–155

210

Index

Monsieur Verdoux 7, 177, 185
Motion Picture Classic 42
Motography 29, 120–121, 145–146, 147, 148–152, 159, 160
Moving Picture World 23, 44, 113, 119, 125, 151, 152–153, 161
Mumming Birds 127
Murray, Charley 13
Mutual 2–7, 67, 124, 125, 131–132, 133–135, 136, 152, 169–171, 184, 186

The New Janitor 18, 114, 174
New York Dramatic Mirror 23, 27, 34, 59, 90, 111, 133
Nichols, George 8, 15, 17
A Night in the Show 47, 126–132, 160
A Night Out 4, 18, 46–56, 70, 85, 142, 148, 159, 183
Normand, Mabel 8, 13, 15–17, 19–21, 182

Official Films 60
Okuda, Ted 45, 92, 105, 107, 133, 142, 153, 157, 166–167
One A.M. 4, 19

Pearson's Weekly 120
Photoplay 11, 18, 182–183
Pickford, Mary 173
Picture Play 65
The Pilgrim 172
Playing Dead 120
Police 7, 85, 133, 135–144, 146, 147, 161, 163, 166, 180
Pollard, Harry "Snub" 69
Porter, Edwin S. 1, 25, 62
Potel, Victor 179
Presley, Elvis 121
The Property Man 4, 129
The Public Enemy 174
Purviance, Edna 51–54, 62–64, 70–74, 76–83, 86–90, 96–97, 101–108, 110–111, 114–119, 124–125, 140–141, 148–149, 157–158, 163, 164, 170, 182–187

Raffles 25
Reed, Alan 160
Reel Life 134, 183–184
Ricci, Mark 93
Rieger, Margie 70, 95
The Road Agents 27
Robbins, Jess 28, 53

Robinson, David 31, 91
Rock, William T. 25
Rocky 62
Rocky IV 62
The Rounders 4, 17, 47, 52
Ruggles, Wesley 165

St. John, Al 13, 23
San Francisco Chronicle 27
Saps at Sea 55
Schickel, Richard 43
The Sea Gull 185
Seabury, William N. 153
Sennett, Mack 2–3, 11–24, 80
Shakespeare, William 2, 107
Shanghaied 9, 119, 121–126, 160, 183
Shepard, David 5, 33, 45, 135, 147, 181
Shoulder Arms 172
Show Business 110
Smith, Alfred E. 25
Some Like It Hot 112
Sparring Partner 60
Spoor, George K. 2, 23, 25–31, 67, 106, 125–126, 152, 154, 160–161
Stallone, Sylvester 62
Sterling, Ford 13, 17, 23
A Submarine Pirate 132
Sunnyside 172
Sunset Boulevard 39
Swain, Mack 19, 61
Swanson, Gloria 38–39

Thornby, Robert 17
Three Sappy People 72
Three Stooges 72, 97–98
Tillie's Punctured Romance 19–20, 172
Totheroh, Roland 53, 181
The Tramp 5, 7, 9, 67, 84–94, 95, 98, 100, 116, 143, 160, 171, 174, 183
Triple Trouble 6, 142, 157, 158–168
Turpin, Ben 4, 23, 28, 37–38, 41–42, 47–56, 149–150, 151, 155, 156–157, 179
Twenty Minutes of Love 70
Twice Two 112

Underworld 174
United Artists 173

The Vagabond 67, 107, 171, 184
Vitagraph 25
VLSE (Vitagraph-Lubin-Selig-Essanay) 151, 152–153

211

Index

Walker, Brent 16–18
Walsh, Raoul 146
Washington Post 14, 64, 121
Wayne, John 27
Welcome Danger 174
While Rome Burns 174
White, Leo 42, 47–49, 63–64, 70–74, 76–83, 91, 101, 122, 148, 149, 158–166
White, May 149, 155, 156–157, 162–163
Wilder, Billy 39
Willard, Lee 179, 180

Williams, Frank D. 15
Wittenmyer, Darr 179
A Woman 107–113, 160
A Woman of Paris 173, 182, 184
Woolcott, Alexander 174
Work 9, 85, 99–107, 160, 161, 183

Yukon Jake 55

Ziegfeld, Florenz 66

www.ingramcontent.com/pod-product-compliance
Lightning Source LLC
Chambersburg PA
CBHW032055300426
44116CB00007B/746